DIMENSIONS OF

SCIENCE
FICTION

DIMENSIONS OF
SCIENCE
FICTION

•

WILLIAM SIMS
BAINBRIDGE

HARVARD UNIVERSITY PRESS
Cambridge, Massachusetts
and London, England   1986

LIBRARY OF CONGRESS CATALOGING-IN-PUBLICATION DATA

Bainbridge, William Sims.
Dimensions of science fiction.

Bibliography: p.
Includes index.
1.   Science fiction—History and criticism.
2.   Literature and society.   I.   Title.
PN3433.5.B35   1986   809.3′876   85-14046
ISBN 0-674-20725-4 (alk. paper)

TO BARBARA SIMS BAINBRIDGE

AND WILLIAM E. SIMS,

MY MOTHER AND HER FATHER,

TWO GENERATIONS OF

SCIENCE FICTION READERS

WHO PREPARED THE WAY

FOR THIS RESEARCH

ACKNOWLEDGMENTS

Thanks go first to Murray Dalziel, who helped me undertake the pilot study and encouraged me to learn the fine art of computing. Christine A. Norell gave greatly of her time, energy, and wit in helping me produce and administer the main questionnaire. Without the help of Daniel Bell, Mark Granovetter, Michael Aronson, and Peg Anderson, this book might have been lost in the outer darkness. I am deeply grateful to the science fiction subculture of authors, editors, artists, and dedicated fans, a thousand of whom contributed directly to this study.

Part of Chapter 7 was previously published as "Women in Science Fiction" in *Sex Roles* 8 (1982), pp. 1081–1093.

CONTENTS

I

MEASUREMENT
OF THE
FANTASTIC

1

AN APPROACH

TO

SCIENCE FICTION

In the year 2076 the eleven billion people of Earth are trapped in a downward spiral of stultifying bureaucracy and economic decline. Their planet teeters on the brink of a new Dark Age. Government mismanagement and corruption doom many people to starvation and stifle the technology that could provide abundance for all. Progress slows to a halt as social problems and hopelessness increase. Then, on July 4, the three million oppressed citizens of the Moon declare their independence in the name of liberty and a pioneering spirit. They win their Anarchist revolution through courage and innovative technology, led by a supercomputer that has achieved consciousness and loves to learn new jokes. Thus human freedom and a boundless future are assured only through imaginative development of science and technology. This is the message of Robert A. Heinlein's science fiction novel *The Moon Is a Harsh Mistress.*

In James P. Hogan's novel *Voyage from Yesteryear,* by 2076 a utopian colony has been established on a planet circling the nearby star Alpha Centauri, and Earth is a more dreadful place than that envisioned by Heinlein. Wars have brought impoverishment of the spirit as well as physical and social destruction. Paranoid military dictatorships prevent Earthlings from escaping to a happier way of life, and individuals have found no alternative to obeying orders from leaders who stop at nothing to achieve their twisted goals. Yet the people of the Alpha Centauri system have used advanced technology to provide a material abundance that has eradicated envy and wickedness, and they have learned in free scientific exploration how to defend themselves against any onslaught from the warlords of Earth.

Much science fiction finds danger rather than salvation in uninhibited scientific and technological progress. In Harlan Ellison's story "I Have No Mouth, and I Must Scream," the fiend computer designed to run our wars decides instead to eradicate humanity, except for five people it has rendered immortal so it may torture them hideously until the end of time. *The Humanoids*, by Jack Williamson, foresees a future in which machines designed to provide ease and security have imprisoned our species in lives without challenge or purpose, killing our spirits with inexorable kindness.

The Martian Chronicles, by Ray Bradbury, documents the tragic American colonization of Mars from 1999 to 2026. The ancient Martians have magnified the illusions of the men who came to conquer their world, defending themselves with the very madness of the invaders until they are killed by a mundane epidemic of chickenpox. To Mars, Earthmen bring all their obsessions, their private dreams, and their memories. When atomic doom comes to their home planet, most of them return to die. At the end a few families of colonists linger on, perhaps to start anew if they do not perish. A father tells his sons where humanity went wrong: "Science ran too far ahead of us too quickly, and the people got lost in a mechanical wilderness, like children making over pretty things, gadgets, helicopters, rockets; emphasizing the wrong items, emphasizing machines instead of how to run the machines."[1]

Science fiction is the distinctive literature of our century. It provides imaginative interpretations of science and technology, communicating to a wide audience ideas that may guide the future of our civilization. Often quite radical in its visions, SF is a popular cultural movement that develops and disseminates potentially influential ideologies. In this book I systematically analyze these ideologies in the first comprehensive, quantitative study of science fiction's authors and styles.

The present is said to be the age of technology. But all periods of human history have been dominated by technology, for the human species is defined by the ability to make and use tools. There is more justice in saying that ours is the age of science, for until very recently mankind explored the world haphazardly, without a consistent means for framing and testing hypotheses. Yet science is a matter of degree, and the independent profession of scientific research has emerged very gradually over many centuries. Perhaps it is most correct to say that ours is an age of heightened awareness of technology and science; the free public expression of that consciousness is science fiction.

There are two common sociological views of the relationship between literature and society—that literature reflects social reality and that it shapes reality.[2] Both may be true, of course, although one makes literature the dependent variable in the equation, and the other promotes it to independent variable. It seems reasonable to say that science fiction expresses our culture's attitudes toward science and technology and that it may often create those attitudes as well. But the possibility remains that science fiction, like other specialized art forms, is the creation of a very unusual peripheral subculture, that it knows nothing of the real trends in American culture and is impotent to influence them. Indeed, one may question whether any art really reflects social reality accurately or has any special power to push society in directions it is not already heading.

In the 1950s, when mass society theory and structural functionalism were popular within sociology, social scientists had many reasons to consider literature as both a cultural power and a social indicator. At that time, far more than today, culture was a favorite topic for analysis. The armchair approach of such writers as Talcott Parsons drew its data from books and newspapers rather than from expensive primary research and assumed that American culture was relatively uniform in its norms, values, beliefs, and institutions and thus susceptible to ideal-type analysis by any intellectual steeped in that culture.[3] The French structuralist Claude Lévi-Strauss went so far as to suggest that an analysis of his own thought patterns would serve science as well as analyses of primitive myth.[4] And Robert K. Merton, an American, asserted that a human collectivity was not worthy of the title "society" unless its people did in fact share a coherent set of norms and values.[5] The typical structuralist publication used literary style and philosophical argumentation to prove its points, rather than the currently fashionable statistical tools of path diagrams and log-linear analysis. Without large research grants, structuralists found it practical as well as intellectually comfortable to assume that literature was a window on the world or a door through which new influences entered society.

Mass-society researchers were far more enterprising and quantitative in their research and contributed many sound insights into how values and ideas are actually communicated in modern society. They found that mass communication is often a two-step process. Innovations in agricultural technology or new consumer products such as television are adopted first by opinion leaders, who then influence others socially to adopt the innovations as well.[6] This discovery explained how minor genres, like child-care manuals or science fiction, can influence the entire society even though few people read them. Those few opinion leaders persuade others to adopt the same values and behaviors, and the communication spreads further and further through informal social networks after first being spread through literature to the cultural elite.

The problem with armchair structuralist analysis was that it assumed too much without testing. The problem with the research on communication was that it demanded large new research projects to determine if its simple principles applied to every new case, without offering much in the way of fresh theoretical insights after the initial studies had established the basic principles.

Without very elaborate empirical research, sociologists now realize it is impossible to decide among a very wide range of hypotheses about the relation of literature to society. Suppose we have just read the hundred best-selling novels of the past decade on the assumption that literature reflects society and that the most popular literature expresses the main themes of the culture. Suppose further that the modal novel turns out to be a love romance. A heroine and hero, after struggling through a series of misunderstandings and adventures, marry and live happily ever after. What does this tell us about society? Consider the following alternatives:

1. Americans' main activity is seeking romantic love, which they typically achieve only after a long, tortuous series of misunderstandings and adventures.

2. Americans lead exceedingly dull love lives, and they read unrealistic, lurid novels of misunderstanding and adventure to compensate for a secure but monotonous reality which is the exact opposite of the fiction.

3. The main concern of Americans is the pursuit of romantic love, but we can learn nothing about their actual experiences from reading fiction because novels can be made interesting only if they contain a high level of tension and many problems, which together create plot and strong characterization.

4. Great authors can get us to read anything by evoking powerful images to render their theme fascinating. At present, authors are recruited from a tiny minority of the population for whom romantic love is problematic, and difficulties in love give authors both their literary sensitivity and their topic.

5. The real problems of American life are the evils of capitalism and social inequality, but the power elite wants to prevent people from realizing this and making a revolution, so the power elite instructs editors and publishers to push stories of romantic love, the topic least dangerous to the status quo.

6. American culture and society are exceedingly diverse, and the real issues and interests are so numerous that the most popular novels cannot focus on any of them but must instead represent the lowest common denominator—romantic love—a topic of some interest to many people but low on the list of priorities of any particular individual or group.

7. Whether or not it is one of the main themes of American culture, romantic love is an area in which many changes are taking place. A variety of forms of intimate relationship are now possible, so people read novels about

romantic love to find alternative ideas they can apply in their own lives or reject, depending upon their personal judgment and the results of private experiments suggested by the novels.

Each of these seven hypotheses has some plausibility, yet it would be very difficult to design an empirical research project to determine the explanatory power of each. Similarly, this book presents many hypotheses about the social causes and consequences of science fiction, yet the data to decide confidently among them are lacking for the most part.

Although I propose theories about the influence of SF at the end of the book, my main task is ethnographic: to describe as accurately as possible a fascinating intellectual subculture and to be true to the data rather than to any particular theory about them. Thus I shall first consider the ideologies of science fiction and interpret them in their own terms.

A brief comment about the role of science fiction in society is in order here. In America, at least, SF is not a literature of persuasion, nor is it fictionalized journalism. Rather, it is a literature of ideas, offering alternative perspectives and exotic information, which readers are free to accept or reject. It does not reflect society but reflects upon society. It does not push us toward any particular future, but it does suggest different futures we might not have considered previously. Recently, science fiction has become a major category of popular culture and an important medium for the development and dissemination of radical ideologies.

My initial research suggested that the field was divided into three main ideologies, each urging a different course for the human future, each proposing its own plan as the most rewarding choice and warning that the alternatives would impose undesirable costs. *Hard science* is the traditional form of science fiction, based on speculations about technology and the physical sciences. *New wave* is more concerned with literary technique, the psychology of characters, and the social sciences. The *fantasy cluster* is a collection of subgenres more concerned with magic than with the sciences, its largest province being sword-and-sorcery, a form of literature that rejects the modern world and most of contemporary culture.

While the fantasy cluster might properly be described as escapist or retreatist, the hard science and new wave factions are activist, each proclaiming a set of radical, utopian ambitions and showing how to achieve them. Hard science says we will have the most rewarding future if, individually and collectively, we develop the physical sciences and technology to the utmost. It warns that intellectual incompetence and irrationality bring ruin. New wave, on the contrary, argues that physical science and technology may lead to disaster, that the good life will be achieved by developing self-awareness, aesthetic sensitivity, and social consciousness. As activist ideologies that reach far beyond the ordinary conditions of mundane existence, these two are utopian, postulating ideal worlds that might be created by human action, although new wave often makes its points through dystopian rather than utopian speculations. The various styles of the fantasy cluster often are optimistic in mood, but the Oz or Eden they postulate is brought into being by supernatural forces rather than mere humans. All three types present ideal characters and propose certain kinds of action, although they disagree over the fundamental principles of how we as individuals and as a species should seek fulfillment of our desires.

I use a mixture of methods to describe and analyze the competing ideologies of science fiction. In good part, the book is a quantitative ethnology, using numbers to delineate and compare the competing systems and to find the meaningful structure of this literature. I have identified and charted each ideological faction, using information from questionnaires completed by knowledgeable members of the science fiction subculture. Since many readers will be more interested in the ethnological results than in the details of the statistical methods, I have tried to present my data in ways that are familiar to a wide audience, using ten graphs and a number of tables.

For modern audiences, numbers and graphs are excellent means for describing the strengths and shapes of ideologies and ideological clusters. They provide clear pictures without the distortions produced by literary metaphors. The quantitative data express the judgments of hundreds of dedicated fans, authors, and critics who responded to my survey, rather than just my personal opinions. Thus quantification takes us some distance in the direction of objectivity. I shall map the ideologies of science fiction in terms of the conceptions held by members of the subculture.

Although there is nothing particularly radical about empirical research on the typifications held by "natives" of a culture, an alternate approach in social theory has been for scholars to construct their own "ideal types" through logical analysis of concepts which may (or may not) be native to the social reality they are analyzing. For example, Manuel and Manuel have delineated several "constellations" of utopian thought in the history of Western literature.[7] But the ideal types conjured up by intellectuals often fail to be precise tools for analyzing reality.[8]

We cannot assume that logical contemplation of intellectual possibilities will reveal the actual concepts that organize human culture and that shape people's behavior. However good our philosophy, we must also have empirical social science. So the most important purpose of my quantitative analyses is to determine the ideological clusters that really exist within the subculture of science fiction and to determine empirically what they say about science, technology, and aesthetics in modern society.

THE SCIENCE FICTION SUBCULTURE

The kind of literature that we now call science fiction was written in earlier centuries, but the emergence of SF as a special field, with its own subculture of writers, editors, and fans, is a phenomenon of the twentieth century. Although several rough literary histories of the field have been written, in a sense we do not know the origins of science fiction, and a phalanx of literary historians will have to attack the problem before we can be sure what they were. Our ignorance chiefly concerns the influences of prior literary and cultural movements. For example, to what extent did European utopian writing shape SF?

Men Like Gods, by H. G. Wells, and *Childhood's End*, by Arthur C. Clarke, seem to be directly derived from European utopianism. In their monumental study of utopian thought, Frank E. Manuel and Fritzie P. Manuel wrote, "Wells's first and perhaps only great work, *The Time Machine: An Invention* (1895), was a composite of Darwinism and Marxist elements."[9] But Anthony West, Wells's son, showed that *The Time Machine* grew naturally out of his father's earlier career as a writer of popular essays on the physical sciences.[10] Only later in his life did Wells interact closely with utopians and draw on standard political traditions for literary inspiration. Clarke's fiction similarly grew primarily out of his personal involvement in new technology. He was a leader of the British Interplanetary Society at the very beginning of his career.

The origins of a cultural style cannot be discovered merely by hunting for similarities with other styles. A century ago anthropologists began a long debate about how different peoples came to possess the same technology or other elements of culture. Until careful research was done on a given case, one could not be sure whether the similarity resulted from independent invention of the same thing or from diffusion of the cultural feature from one tribe to another.[11] Similarly, in modern literature we cannot be sure whether a characteristic of one school of writers actually derived from a similar characteristic of an earlier school until scholars have traced the possible social connections.

I think it unlikely that American pioneer writers of SF were greatly influenced by high-culture literary traditions. Rather, I suspect, they learned about writing by reading popular novels of exotic adventure by such authors as Rider Haggard, Rudyard Kipling, and Jack London, and they learned about science from popular journalism or personal experience. Certainly, it is difficult to see similarities to European utopianism in the works of Edgar Rice Burroughs or E. E. Smith, two Americans who clearly influenced the later course of SF. A greater proportion of British authors may have had a literary education and been socially connected to radical intellectual movements outside SF. But the science fiction subculture has been predominantly American, and there is good reason to consider it a novel intellectual development, owing no great debt to previous political or philosophical traditions.

The process of cultural consolidation was gradual, and some of the best-loved SF was written before it had progressed far, by such authors as Jules Verne, H. G. Wells, and Edgar Rice Burroughs. The birthdate of science fiction is often given as 1926, when Hugo Gernsback began *Amazing Stories*, the first successful magazine dedicated to it. From the very first issue, there was a sense that something important was occurring, that those involved were the leaders of a historically decisive social movement. As Miles J. Breuer, one of Gernsback's writers, expressed it two years later: "*Amazing Stories* is a pioneer. Our Magazine is ineradicably down in history as the leader with the far-flung vision. A hundred or a thousand years in the future, men will point back to it as the originator of a new type of literary art."[12]

Of course, allegorical novels employing scientific concepts had been written before *Amazing Stories*, and many continue to be written outside the genre called science fiction. In the following section I shall try to define this term, but one way to distinguish it is simply to say that it is literature produced and consumed by the science fiction subculture. Anchored by such magazines as *Amazing Stories* and others, this subculture developed quickly into a network of friendships and professional relationships. Through the magazines, author met author and fan met fan. Letters to the editor included correspondents' addresses, and communication led to the organization of local fan clubs and private circles of authors. In the 1930s amateur publications called fanzines were first exchanged in great numbers, and both regional and national conventions were staged.

Perhaps all active SF fans would like to become authors, and indeed many of the most successful writers did rise from the ranks of the fans.[13] This phenomenon is both cause and effect of the high level of social integration of the subculture and of the fact that it has always been an idealistic social movement. Ted White, a recent editor of *Amazing*, wrote, "The science fiction field is a special field, a field where the dedicated amateurs have always outranked the bored professionals. Scratch one of today's writers or editors and you'll almost always find a former fan underneath."[14] As a vigorous social movement, science fiction has been dominated by hot amateurs rather than cool professionals.

Unlike most forms of literature, science fiction has always been more the work of "dedicated amateurs" than that of those who earn their living exclusively from writing. The field has never provided sole support for more than a handful of writers, many of whom have not lived in what most would describe as luxury. Most science fiction writers have other, more mundane jobs or careers on which they count to support themselves and their families. They write "on the side," usually in the evenings and weekends, and almost always because they *want* to write science fiction and enjoy it—not because they have to.[15]

A chapter in my book *The Spaceflight Revolution* documented that SF was indeed a subculture, rather than primarily a commercial institution. Here I will show further the extent to which it is a social movement—or a tangle of social movements—promulgating radical ideologies. But the members of the subculture have never doubted that it was one. In 1960 P. Schuyler Miller observed:

Two generations of readers and writers have contributed to keeping strong fences around the SF ghetto, and to tending the grounds and raising beautiful edifices inside. Nobody who has ever gone to one of the major science-fiction conventions . . . can come away with any doubt that we are a closely knit and clannish family. Writers, editors, artists, fans, fan-editors—even the "fake fans" who never read the stuff—have a strong commonality of interests, stereotypes, gossip, and even jargon. Fanzines, talks, panels, the "pro" play—all are crammed with private jokes and allusions that make very little sense to the outsider.[16]

Recently science fiction has been accepted as a respectable form of literature; it is now the subject of two scholarly journals and numerous college courses, but earlier it was ignored by serious critics. John W. Campbell, Jr., a leading SF editor, wondered why the genre was so intensely scorned and contemptuously ignored by the "litterateurs" who were the powerful arbiters of literary fashion:

But who are They? Well, They seem to be a self-perpetuating Board of Examiners; Litterateurs recognize each other as Litterateurs and Critics; anyone who doesn't think as they think obviously Doesn't Belong, and is an Unfit Critic and no *real* Litterateur.
Speaking from the Outer Darkness Beyond the Pale—I think They have a

tight little Mutual Admiration Society, and don't know what makes enduring literature.[17]

Such anger is a typical response from a radical intellectual movement that discovers, to its mock surprise, that the conventional intellectual establishment does not approve. Author Harry Harrison once commented, "Let's face it, science fiction has always been in rather bad odor with the establishment. Any establishment; take your pick."[18] Referring to SF as "science-fantasy," Philip Jose Farmer said that in great measure its deviance was its defining feature: "Parables travel in parabolas. And science-fantasy, being in essence a *parabolic* form, can shoot over barriers which often stop the flight of earthbound *straight* fiction. It adopts certain modes of presentation forbidden to the mainstream of literature and thus strikes us harder with its insights."[19]

Some people say that conventional literary authorities have despised science fiction simply because the quality of writing is despicably low. Author Theodore Sturgeon observed that critics in such establishment magazines as *Saturday Review* and the *New Yorker* never mentioned SF unless they had an especially bad work to cite. "It isn't as easy as one might think to argue with these people, primarily because they really do take their horrible examples out of the sf field, a field which is, they inform the world, ninety percent crud."[20] Then, Sturgeon said, he had a revelation, one he soon formulated as Sturgeon's Law, which is now accepted by the entire subculture:

Ninety percent of everything is crud.
Corollary 1: The existence of immense quantities of trash in science fiction is admitted and it is regretted; but it is no more unnatural than the existence of trash anywhere.
Corollary 2: The best science fiction is as good as the best fiction in any field.[21]

Others say that science fiction and related branches of fantasy have been despised because, at least in this century, fiction is supposed to be realistic, dealing with the actual problems, personalities, and experiences of this world. But why should fiction be realistic? A strict norm of realism would reject fiction in favor of biographies, histories, and ethnographies. Verism, the artistic preference for the ordinary over the heroic or legendary, is but one possible aesthetic ideology. A study of ideology, such as this, can appreciate the verist as much as the fantast, but the science fiction author, committed to one side of the dispute, can only rage at his exclusion from the ranks of honored artists. The irascible Lester del Rey remarked:

I tried asking what good regular fiction was, and usually was told that it taught about real life. I've never been convinced that Thomas Hardy, Franz Kafka or many others studied in school had much to teach about life as we know it. I'm not sure enough that most of the thoughts in the minds of the characters I read show any reality—particularly when I find that the writers have never experienced similar events. But those points are not taken well by many in the humanities.[22]

The hypothesis that conventional literature perpetuates illusions about our world and that the "great insights" of great writers are generally wrong deserves to be tested in other research studies of popular ideology. For the moment, it is enough to note that imaginative literature is not supposed to be realistic. Science fiction suggests possibilities and urges new kinds of awareness, which few readers will mistake for correct descriptions of the world in which we live. Perhaps, as Damon Knight observed, SF is great because it is not "realistic" in this unreliable and pedestrian sense. As he said, it must be judged in terms of its "specific function, to lift us out of the here-and-now and show us marvels."[23]

John Campbell found a cosmic quality in the best science fiction, a virtue that contradicts conventional literary standards:

Science-fiction doesn't fit into the mainstream of literature, and, so long as it is science-fiction, won't. The fundamental difference is this: the mainstream serious novel tries to show the effect of experiences on the individual who is the central character. Science-fiction tries to explore the effect of experiences on the group-entity—culture, race, or confederation of races—which is, in fact, the central character. Note that this must be presented through individual eyes— but while a man may be the viewpoint character, Man is the central character.[24]

The enduring antagonism between standard literary authorities and the science fiction subculture may be just one manifestation of the cultural gap between science and the humanities identified by C. P. Snow in his famous essay on the two cultures.[25] To the doctrinaire humanist, science is not only unfamiliar but hostile. It is the enemy. Literature that promotes science and follows its values rather than those of poetry, for example, will seem both inferior and threatening. But members of the general public are neither literati nor technocrats. To the extent that they wish a truce, or even an alliance with the engineers, they may find SF attractive. As Andrew Feenberg expressed the idea:

In science fiction . . . science borrows a "voice" from literature in order to make itself heard and understood: a significant fraction of it is the literature of the "other" culture, the culture of science and technology. As such, it communicates the experience and speculations of scientists and technicians to the general public; it represents the scientist's world view to those who participate only passively in an increasingly mechanized society. [26]

In chapters 4 and 5 of this book I will examine two types of literature produced or favored in the SF subculture that do *not* seem to promote physical science and technology, unlike the traditional hard-science brand, which does. A considerable body of supernatural fantasy literature is attached to the subculture. Writing in the mid-1940s, P. Schuyler Miller contended that cultivated readers did not reject these neighboring forms of literature as quickly as they did science fiction:

> It is an anomaly of our scientific age that science fiction is less respectable in the eyes of literary critics and of the general reader than are tales of the frankly supernatural. A good argument could be made for the point of view that ghosts, witches, and the other denizens of nightmare are actually a very solid part of our cultural heritage, and that the average person has far more reason to believe in their reality than in this upstart newcomer, science. [27]

If the general public remains largely ignorant of science, then perhaps science fiction's duty is to educate it. Poul Anderson said, "Science fiction does have one virtue, one lesson to teach: its acceptance of science as a legitimate human activity; its attempts to re-examine the human condition in radically changed environments, under the light of radically new factual knowledge." [28] Anderson, a popular writer of heroic fantasy as well as of technological science fiction, felt that the scientific imagination should be a fertile source of inspiration for the modern writer and poet. "I frankly believe that the spirit of our age finds one of its noblest expressions in the scientific enterprise, and that writers and poets do wrong to ignore it." [29]

To those who condemn SF for being escapist, many members of the subculture would say, "Escapism? Sure. Science fiction is escape—*into reality!*" [30] Robert A. Heinlein argued in the 1950s that science fiction is much more important than mainstream literature—indeed, that science fiction is the real mainstream, while establishment literature is a malignancy: "Most novels of contemporary life today tragically fail to live up to the needs of our times . . . A very large part of what is accepted as 'serious' literature today represents nothing more than a cultural lag on the part of many authors, editors and critics—a retreat to the womb in the face of a world too complicated and too frightening for their immature spirits. A sick literature." [31]

To Heinlein, science fiction is a means for coming to grips with the contemporary world. Of course, if SF aspires to be realistic literature, it is open to the same criticisms as conventional fiction. It must avoid error and deception, or it becomes a source of delusion rather than insight. Later I will discuss whether SF does succeed in helping people understand the rapidly changing contemporary world, and whether it is really based on correct science. But there can be no doubt that much of the best science fiction tries to find and share insights about our age of space, computers, genetic engineering, and atomic doom. It may not often be victorious in the philosophical struggle, but at least it grapples with the problems. In 1974 Heinlein wrote:

> Science fiction does have one superiority over all other forms of literature: It is the *only* branch of literature which even attempts to cope with the real problems of this fast and dangerous world. All other forms don't even try. In this complex world, science, the scientific method, and the consequences of the scientific method, are central to everything the human race is doing and to wherever we are going. If we blow ourselves up, we will do it by misapplication of science; if we manage to keep from blowing ourselves up, it will be through intelligent application of science. Science fiction is the only form of fiction which takes into account this central force in our lives and futures. Other sorts of fiction, if they notice science at all, simply deplore it—an attitude very chic in the anti-intellectual atmosphere of today. But we will never get out of the mess we are in by wringing our hands. [32]

Barry Malzberg, a new wave author at the opposite end of the SF spectrum from Heinlein, agreed with him fully in this: "Only science fiction these days is really worth reading or writing or talking about, the only branch of literature which is dealing with the basic issues of our time, which are simply the effects technology is having on people, the effects people are having on technology and the consequences of these small or large, always painful collisions day after day." [33]

Until very recently the network of SF fans and writers was tiny. If seen only as a deviant literary subculture, it was insignificant. But it often saw itself as a radical, forward-looking social movement, generating ideas and new values that the entire society would need in the future. If so, then science fiction is among the few decisive cultural forces of our day. Certainly the engine of modern history is science-based technology. Jack Williamson expressed the idea in rather dramatic language in 1939: "Let us imagine that our modern scientific civilization is like a military expedition moving into the unknown territory of future time. Then we can picture science fiction as a mobile vanguard that scouts ahead, to discover the rich possibilities and give warning of the obstacles that await the main body of science. Often far ahead of the battalions of researchers, science fiction skirmishes in the fields of tomorrow."[34]

DEFINITIONS OF SCIENCE FICTION

Before it had a name, a kind of fiction concerning science and technology began to emerge in Western literature, especially in the English-speaking nations. H. G. Wells called it science-fantasy, but this term has taken on multiple meanings and has not been accepted as the general term for the field. In the early 1920s the editors of *Argosy*, a general fiction magazine, coined the unfortunate term *pseudo-science stories* to identify this type when they published it.[35] As late as 1939, such pioneer writers of the genre as Ray Cummings and Otis Adelbert Kline were willing to call their own fiction pseudo-scientific.[36]

In the first issue of *Amazing Stories* in 1926, Hugo Gernsback used the term *scientifiction*, a contraction of "scientific fiction."[37] Enthusiastic fan Linus Hogenmiller abbreviated this as STF, the adjectival form of which was stfnal.[38] By 1933 Gernsback's successor as editor of *Amazing* was trying to kill the awkward elision scientifiction, but it and its abbreviations continued in use until the mid-1950s, and some members of the subculture have not entirely abandoned them today.[39]

In 1929 Gernsback lost control of *Amazing* and promptly started a rival magazine, *Science Wonder Stories*, in every way a copy of *Amazing*, but with all the terms changed. He even devised a substitute for scientifiction and thus coined the current name, science fiction.[40] Although the editor of the first issue of *Science Wonder Stories* used the term in its modern form, until the mid-1940s it was customary to hyphenate it. Today the adjectival form is sometimes hyphenated, but not the noun. The proper abbreviation is SF. Fans despise the alternate abbreviation, sci-fi, which they feel applies only to low-grade science fiction movies.[41]

In the first issue of *Amazing Stories* Gernsback offered a definition: "By 'scientifiction' I mean the Jules Verne, H. G. Wells, and Edgar Allan Poe type of story—a charming romance intermingled with scientific fact and prophetic vision."[42] In the first issue of *Science Wonder Stories*, he rejected *Argosy*'s old term and the unscientific imprecision it implied:

There has been altogether too much pseudo-science fiction of a questionable quality in the past. Over-enthusiastic authors with little scientific training have

rushed into print and unconsciously misled the reader by the distortion of scientific facts to achieve results that are clearly impossible.

It is the policy of SCIENCE WONDER STORIES to publish only such stories that
have their basis in scientific laws as we know them, or in the logical deduction
of new laws from what we know. [43]

Other editors have also tried their hands at definitions. Isaac Asimov suggested: "Science fiction stories are extraordinary voyages into any of the infinite
supply of conceivable futures." [44] While he was editor of *Amazing*, Sol Cohen
saw SF as a speculative literature: "It is a form of *fiction* which speculates on
what might happen if." [45] Paul W. Fairman argued that its essence was prediction as much as speculation: "It is a medium wherein the realities of
tomorrow are successfully presented as today's fiction." [46] This view was stated
emphatically by John Campbell in 1942: "The fundamental idea of science-
fiction is that it is possible to predict inventions and mechanisms still to come,
and to predict their effect on men, on society, and on the viewpoints of
civilization." [47] The editor H. J. Campbell, no relative of John, offered the
following definition in the British magazine *Authentic Science Fiction*: "A
story is science fiction if it deals with the development, extrapolation or
disproof of phenomena which are the source material of scientific enquiry
and experiment, in such a way that the ideas, claims and assumptions are
not at variance with current scientific knowledge and speculation, unless such
variance is explained and supported by logical reasoning or experiment." [48]

Less articulately than these editors, fans have struggled to define SF in the
letter columns of the magazines. John Litster said, "Scientific fiction is fiction
based upon the factual in scientific knowledge plus the infinite speculative
possibilities built upon that knowledge." [49] John Campbell agreed that this
was a fair definition. Another reader, Irene E. Hollar, also stressed the factual
knowledge conveyed through the stories: "Science Fiction is the pleasurable
pursuit of fictitious knowledge interspersed with actual facts." [50] R. A. Bradley
correctly found the situation rather more confused: "SCIENCE FICTION may be
defined as the feigned systematization of such departments of the mind as
are given over to the investigation of admittedly illogical phenomena occurring
at unexpected places in the several departments of matter." [51] In 1971 several
readers tried to tell the magazine *Worlds of If* what SF was, among them
Aloysius Cupay, who suggested, "Science fiction is fiction that states that
what did not happen yesterday will not necessarily not happen tomorrow." [52]

Authors and critics have proposed definitions of all kinds. Jack Lait and
Lee Mortimer tried humor. "*Science fiction*: A genre of escape literature
which takes the reader to far-away planets—and usually neglects to bring him

back."[53] More soberly, Lester del Rey contended, "Science fiction is *fiction* that deals *rationally* with *alternate possibilities*."[54] This stressed speculation as the defining characteristic. James Blish emphasized extrapolation. "All science-fiction is essentially extrapolation . . . A science fiction writer . . . takes known data, deduces a trend from them, and then writes his story around what things may be like *if* that trend continues."[55] Frederik Pohl argued that stories about science are not true SF unless they contain extrapolation.[56] For Tom Clareson, it is primarily the social consequences of science that must be extrapolated. He defines SF as "that form of fantasy which records the impact of science upon man as an individual and as a species."[57]

James Gunn stressed rationality as an essential characteristic: "In science fiction a fantastic event or development is considered rationally."[58] More recently, he proposed a definition closer to Clareson's: "Science fiction is the branch of literature that deals with the effect of change on people in the real world as it can be projected into the past, the future, or distant places. It often concerns itself with scientific or technological change and it usually involves matters whose importance is greater than the individual or the community; often civilization or the race itself is in danger."[59]

Many, like Gernsback, felt that a story cannot be science fiction unless it contains and is based on correct science. Theodore Sturgeon broadened this restriction by defining science as knowledge. For him, science fiction is knowledge fiction: "If you have a story and yank out the science (knowledge) aspects, and the story falls apart, it was science fiction. If you have a story and yank out the science (knowledge) aspects and a story still exists, then you have that cowboy story that occurs on Mars instead of in Texas."[60]

Sturgeon warned that one should not kill science fiction in the attempt to describe it: "Personally I have felt uneasy with the hardline, stonewall definitions of science fiction, a field toward which I was drawn originally because it seemed to have no horizons, no limits at all, like poetry."[61] In 1952 Damon Knight said that "the term 'science-fiction' is a misnomer, that trying to get two enthusiasts to agree on a definition of it leads only to bloody knuckles."[62] He then proposed a definition that has become a proverb in the subculture: "It means what we point to when we say it."[63] Six years later he explained his view more formally: "The difficulty of defining science fiction is that, like the Indian Ocean, it has no natural boundaries. There is a central area which everyone agrees is science fiction; then as you go further out you meet disturbing similarities to other forms of fiction; and finally, at the edges, the most puzzling things happen."[64]

If science fiction is speculation, extrapolation, rational exploration of the unknown, projections of what the future might hold, then it must burst through any limits set for it. If we say it is fiction about science, then SF will erode our definition by considering radical redefinitions of science itself. Although nobody wants to return to defining it as pseudo-scientific stories or scientifiction, some authors and editors have proposed less restrictive substitutes. In an influential essay Robert Heinlein proposed calling the field speculative fiction. Judith Merril suggested speculative fabulation, and Spider Robinson offered sinus friction.[65] The abbreviation SF covers all of these alternatives, as Alexei and Cory Panshin observed. "Sf is a broad tent. It covers science fiction and structural fabulation, sci-fi and stf, speculative fiction and science fantasy."[66]

But for all its diversity, the field is united by more than just the accidents of its history. All of the best writers are characterized by both imagination and intelligence. SF considers new ideas, and much of what is new in our age comes from science. However, any new idea is appropriate. SF thinks about novel possibilities, finding in them implications, extrapolation, and stimulation. Thus SF is both speculative and realistic, fanciful and rational. As Joanna Russ, one of the most startling of the new wave authors, said:

> Science fiction is *What If* literature. All sorts of definitions have been proposed by people in the field, but they all contain both The What If and The Serious Explanation; that is, science fiction shows things not as they characteristically or habitually are but as they might be, and for this "might be" the author must offer a rational, serious, consistent explanation, one that does not (in Samuel Delany's phrase) offend against what is known to be known.[67]

On one level the purpose of this book is definitional. It seeks to delineate what science fiction really is. What are its segments and factions? What are the ideological commitments of each part and of the whole? In this descriptive, ethnographic task I use quantitative analysis of survey data as well as the stories themselves and quotations from leading intellectuals of the subculture.

On a higher level this book seeks to discover the social meaning of SF, its possible impact on the future of our species. As a social movement, or a collection of them, science fiction promotes ideologies. What novel ideas and explanations, what concepts and values does it communicate? What are the logical consequences for human action? What futures does science fiction promote?

METHODS OF DATA COLLECTION

To go beyond the words of individual members of the subculture, I used standard techniques of survey research. Before applying my tools of analysis,

I will explain how I collected the data. Because my aim was to chart the entire structure of a vast field, I decided that questionnaire surveys of several hundred knowledgeable readers would be the most efficient and effective approach.

Quantitative methods of research are very controversial in literature studies, but a number of statistical approaches have proved themselves in the past. Questions of disputed authorship can be settled through statistical analysis of patterns of word use by different authors and in different examples of writing, as Andrew Queen Morton has shown in his recent textbook on the subject.[68] Milton Rokeach and his associates have had some success resolving disputed authorship by measuring the values expressed in the works under question.[69] Ranier C. Baum used the values revealed in the characters in popular German novels to chart the cultural fragmentation which may have contributed to political disintegration in that country after World War I.[70] Karl Erik Rosengren demonstrated that analysis of patterns of author citation in literary reviews could be used to chart national and international schools of literature.[71] More than twenty years ago, Walter Hirsch showed readers of the *American Journal of Sociology* that science fiction could be studied quantitatively through analysis of the roles of scientists and other characters.[72]

Survey research in the form of questionnaires or interviews is ideal when one wishes to study systematically a living subculture. And science fiction is a cohesive subculture of actively communicating fans, authors, editors, and critics. The people who responded to my questionnaires were expert members of the subculture, who shared their knowledge and understanding through their apparently simple responses. Surveys provided a richer empirical basis, at less cost, than I could have achieved with any other method. In order to write the questionnaires, I had to have some prior knowledge of the subculture. This I gained by participating in several regional and national conventions, by reading much of the SF literature as well as historical and literary-critical essays, and by carrying out preliminary surveys of the New England Science Fiction Association and other groups.

An intermediate stage in my research was a pilot questionnaire, which I sent in packets of five to editors of amateur fan magazines and newsletters. A total of 130 questionnaires was mailed back to me. The most interesting section of the survey was a list of twenty-seven well-known SF authors; respondents were asked to rate how well they liked each one, using a seven-point scale. Respondents were also asked to rate seventeen kinds of literature, including the subculture's terms for what I thought were the major stylistic divisions of SF. With Murray Dalziel, then a computer consultant at Harvard,

I analyzed the results and found very clear patterns of correlation in preferences for authors and styles.[73]

On the basis of the pilot study, I designed a new questionnaire, which began with a few miscellaneous items, then listed the names of 140 authors. The respondents were asked to rate each one, using a seven-point preference scale. The next section asked for similar ratings of fourteen popular SF magazines. The questionnaire concluded with a list of sixty-two types of literature to be rated. I hypothesized that the stylistic and ideological divisions within science fiction would be revealed in people's likes and dislikes. If a person liked a given type of literature and responded favorably to the ideas and values expressed in it, that person should give somewhat higher ratings to authors of the type than did readers who were not enthusiastic about it.

The list of authors included all winners of Hugo awards, given out at the annual World Science Fiction Convention, and of Nebula awards, presented by the Science Fiction Writers of America. The Hugo, named for founding father Hugo Gernsback, is the Oscar of the field. These awards were not given until 1953, so for the names of writers before that time I drew upon leading histories and encyclopedias of the field. I also added the names of new writers who were nominated for awards in 1978 and a few other names to add variety. To avoid confusion I listed only one Jones and one Smith, although there are several of each in the subculture; the May 1964 issue of *Worlds of If* magazine contains stories by four different Smiths. If I were starting this project afresh, I might include J. G. Ballard, L. Frank Baum, Leigh Brackett, and Thomas M. Disch, but the group I chose represented the entire genre quite well.

Expert respondents were easy to find at the Iguanacon World Science Fiction Convention held in Phoenix, Arizona, in 1978. Annual gatherings of this kind, first held in New York in 1939, draw fans, editors, and authors from all over the United States and from many other nations. Preconvention registration data at Iguanacon revealed that every state except South Dakota was represented. With the kind assistance of the organizing committee, I was able to distribute my questionnaires from the central registration area of the headquarters hotel; 595 convention participants completed the questionnaire.

The survey revealed that 58.6 percent of the respondents were men. The average respondent was born in 1952, if one looks at median birth date, or in 1951 if one looks at the mean, and began reading science fiction at the age of ten or eleven. More than half, 56.2 percent, were members of one or more SF fan clubs, and 31.2 percent belonged to two or more such organizations. The typical respondent said that exactly half of his or her best friends were SF fans. The median number of previous science fiction conventions attended was five, and one-quarter of the 595 respondents had been to a dozen regional or world conventions in the past.

AUTHOR PREFERENCE QUESTIONS

The longest and most important section of the main Iguanacon questionnaire was the list of 140 science fiction and fantasy authors. The instructions read, "Please tell us how much you like the works written by each of the following authors. After each name, circle the number that indicates how much you like that author. Circle '0' if you do not like the author at all. Circle '6' if you like the author very much—as much as you possibly could. Otherwise, circle the number in between that best expresses how much you like the works of the author." At the bottom of each page, the respondent was reminded, "If you are not familiar with one, please skip it and go on to the next." I wanted fans to express their opinions when they had opinions, but not to respond aimlessly if they had not in fact formed a judgment of an author. To minimize contamination of the results, I produced five different versions of the Iguanacon questionnaire, with the authors listed in five different random orders. This prevented placement of the names from dominating and distorting the findings.

Appendix Table A1 gives a few summary statistics for the authors in the main questionnaire, listed alphabetically. Three authors received mean ratings greater than 5.00: Isaac Asimov (5.08), Larry Niven (5.06), and Robert A. Heinlein (5.05), traditional authors who have much in common. Fifteen other authors got mean ratings above 4.50: Arthur C. Clarke (4.93), Poul Anderson (4.87), Fritz Leiber (4.85), Anne McCaffrey (4.85), Ursula K. LeGuin (4.76), J. R. R. Tolkien (4.73), Roger Zelazny (4.72), Theodore Sturgeon (4.69), Gordon R. Dickson (4.64), Zenna Henderson (4.58), Raccoona Sheldon (4.56), Frederik Pohl (4.56), Clifford D. Simak (4.54), Robert Silverberg (4.53), and Alfred Bester (4.51). These fifteen cover a wide range of stylistic and ideological territory, as I shall show in later chapters.

Four of the authors rated higher than 4.50 were women: McCaffrey, LeGuin, Henderson, and Sheldon. Science fiction began as stories written by men for boys but the field has recently admitted women as both fans and writers. I did not list James Tiptree, Jr., among the highest-rated authors because this was a name used by Alice "Raccoona" Sheldon earlier in her career. Sheldon and Tiptree received almost identical mean ratings (4.56 and 4.52), and almost identical percentages of those who rated the two (36.5 percent and 33.9 percent) awarded them the highest possible score, six points. This probably did not mean that fans recognized them as the same person, because 62.5 percent of the 595 rated Tiptree, compared with the 37.3 percent who rated Sheldon.

The percentage of respondents who gave an author a top rating of six points represents that author's avid fans. Six authors were given top ratings by at least 40 percent of the respondents who expressed opinions about them: Heinlein (52.6), Tolkien (48.4), Asimov (48.2), Niven (47.4), McCaffrey (44.5), and LeGuin (41.4). Heinlein and Tolkien were ahead of Asimov here, although he beat them in the mean ratings. This means that there is somewhat more disagreement about Heinlein and Tolkien, and the readers who like them less well are balanced out by groups of enthusiastic fans.

The impact of an author on the field is not merely a matter of love and respect. Some authors, especially the most controversial ones, have contributed important innovations as well as entertainment, yet they did not achieve high ratings. Other things being equal, strongly ideological writers elicited the greatest disagreement, and those who espouse unpopular viewpoints suffered in the popularity contest. Another measure of an author's significance was the percentage of fans responding to the preference question—an index of how well known each one is.

Seven authors were rated by at least 90 percent of the 595 respondents: Asimov (97.3), Heinlein (97.1), Bradbury (95.3), Ellison (93.6), Clarke (93.3), Wells (92.4), and Tolkien (90.0). Ellison's high familiarity score undoubtedly resulted in part from the fact that he was the much-publicized guest of honor at Iguanacon. Several of the convention activities, including a delightful Harlan Ellison Roast, centered on him. In his guest of honor speech, he expressed his political and aesthetic ideology with such style and honesty that even some in the audience who strenuously disagreed with him came away with a new feeling of respect. To cap his public appearance, he wrote parts of a story, "Count the Clock That Tells the Time," while on display in the convention headquarters hotel (he was writing in a special area where the public was invited to watch him pound the typewriter). But Ellison's familiarity score undoubtedly would have been higher, even without his appearance as guest of honor, because he is the leading spokesman of the new wave (described in Chapter 4).

The questionnaire listed 140 authors, but two of the names were actually bogus. I was concerned that some fans might fill out the questionnaire frivolously, playing a game with the researcher or trying to appear more knowledgeable than they really were; it seemed likely that at least a few would ignore the repeated instruction to skip unfamiliar authors. The two fictitious names were intended to trap frivolous or inattentive respondents. The names were those of two graduate students, Rick Catalano and Diane Samdahl, who volunteered them for this scientific use. Of the 595 respondents, 46 claimed to have read the nonexistent works of Catalano, and 23 professed to be familiar with Samdahl. Fifteen respondents rated both fake authors, and ten awarded the pair identical scores, showing that a small minority did fail to follow instructions.

For many of the analyses in this book, I used the responses from all 595 fans, but in some cases I rejected the less reliable respondents. Often I used 409 responses, those of people who avoided rating either of the fake writers yet who did rate fifty or more of the real writers. When the statistical procedures were especially demanding—unforgiving of missing data—I focused on still smaller groups. In the analyses in Chapter 2 I often used only the 276 who avoided the fake authors yet rated seventy-five or more real authors.[74]

The list of 138 authors contained four other names that were included for experimental purposes. As I have mentioned, Tiptree is the same person as Sheldon. Another writer on the list, Lewis Padgett, is a pen name used primarily by Henry Kuttner, but sometimes used when Kuttner collaborated with his wife, C. L. Moore. Two other names, Frank Riley and Jeanne Robinson, belong to real persons who collaborated with regular authors in creating famous works, but who are not SF authors in their own right. Riley collaborated with Mark Clifton in the Hugo-winning novel, *They'd Rather Be Right*, published in 1954. Jeanne Robinson, by profession a dancer, collaborated with her husband, Spider Robinson, on "Stardance," a story about the supreme artistic dancer in weightless orbit. This novelette won a Hugo at Iguanacon.

CATEGORIES OF LITERATURE

A second important section of the main questionnaire consisted of preference questions about forty types of literature, presented in five different random orders. Included were all the special terms that I had encountered in reading essays on science fiction and in formal discussions at previous conventions, supplemented with a few terms I thought might prove enlightening. These forty types are listed in Appendix Table A2, in order of mean rating.

The highest-ranked category, "stories that convey a sense of wonder," did not appear often in my later correlational analysis, because this phrase expresses the consensus of all ideological factions about what science fiction should achieve. At the time of Iguanacon, editor Ted White explained, "The phrase most commonly linked with that of science fiction over the past thirty or more years is 'sense of wonder.' A stf reader cannot help but have this sense, this almost mystical awe at the grandiose wonders of our vast universe, and the magical delight in exploring those wonders."[75] For decades fans have lamented the loss of wonder in the most recent SF. In the old days, some say, there was a sense of wonder, but no longer. To some thoughtful critics, like Alva Rogers, this sense of wonder lay not in the stories themselves but in the shock of first contact with science fiction experienced by young readers: "In the final analysis a Sense of Wonder is the priceless possession of the youthful discoverer of science fiction; it may last for a short fleeting instant, or it may stay with him for a number of years. At any rate, it is sooner or later lost, seldom to be recovered."[76]

Like "sense of wonder," the second item on the questionnaire comes close to being a definition of ideal SF: "stories which take current knowledge from one of the sciences and logically extrapolate what might be the next steps taken in that science."

I will not explain the other thirty-eight terms, but a few comments are in order. I hypothesize that there are three main ideological and stylistic divisions within science fiction: Hard science, new wave, and the fantasy cluster. Of these, hard science received a high average rating (4.53); new wave was much lower (3.32). Terms describing parts of the fantasy cluster were scattered throughout the ranking. Science fantasy (4.71) was fifth in the list of forty, but this term is rather ambiguous; some use it to name a very special kind of rationalized fantasy, and others mean by it the whole field of science fiction. Similarly, the term *fantasy* (4.49) is quite general, referring to types which are very close to science fiction as well as to other types that are remote from the subject of this book. More focused terms for parts of the fantasy cluster were lower in the list, including sword-and-sorcery (3.84) and horror-and-weird (2.92).

Among the interesting results was the very low rating of the Bible. At 2.31 points, the Bible had a lower score than all but one other item, "occult literature," at 2.13. Although fans rated myths and legends quite high (4.22), they appeared unenthusiastic about the most valued book in Western civilization. In this they expressed most forcefully the intellectual deviance of their subculture, a quality I consider in Chapter 6.

The questionnaire contained some experimental preference questions that presented other descriptions of literature in a single fixed order rather than five random orders. Appendix Table A3 gives the responses to questions on preferences for three different time periods in the history of science fiction and for seven specific topics.

The three time periods (1920s and 1930s, 1940s and 1950s, 1960s and 1970s) cover the six decades in which the SF subculture became organized and during which most of the works familiar to readers were first published, and only ten authors in the long list published fiction before 1920: Burroughs, Doyle, Gernsback, Haggard, Leinster, Lovecraft, Poe, Rohmer, Verne, and Wells. Recent science fiction received a higher mean rating (4.92) than SF of the middle period (3.97) or of the early decades (2.81). The percentage of fans responding rose with more recent periods, from 88.9 percent to 95.0 percent, but that difference is slight. Fans are familiar with the works of past decades because the leading authors are reprinted frequently.

"Stories about alien cultures" achieved a very high mean rating (5.09), perhaps because such stories offer the surprise and excitement of constant discovery. The affinity between science fiction and alien cultures has the deepest possible roots, because SF itself is an alien culture. Calling outsiders *mundanes*, members of SF fandom consider themselves nearer to the exotic worlds of other times and planets than ordinary human beings are.

Appendix Table A4 shows summary statistics for twelve highly experimental questions about fictional protagonists. These questions were placed at the very end of the questionnaire so that potential negative reactions would not spoil other data. I thought that respondents might well feel that they liked good stories no matter what the characteristics of the protagonists, and, in fact, more than a fifth of the respondents refused to answer these questions. However, I found several of them useful in my analyses of ideological factions, and the three items that received mean preference ratings over 4.50 give us a powerful insight into the value system shared by most fans of science fiction. These three describe an ideal kind of person that is quite different from the characters described by the nine other protagonist statements. Members of the SF subculture value intelligence above all other qualities. They gave an extremely high mean rating, 5.11 out of a possible 6.00, to "stories in which the main character is clever and intelligent." They also gave high ratings, 4.64 and 4.65, to stories in which the main character is "strange and unusual" or "independent and ambitious." In addition to intellect, fans value individuality.

Along with the main Iguanacon questionnaire, I administered an exploratory survey focused on "sci-fi" movies and television programs, which was completed by 379 respondents. I published some of the results of this study in an article on pseudoscience in television documentaries,[77] and here I will occasionally cite statistics that parallel findings in the main survey. Also I shall draw upon my two brief surveys of members of the New England Science Fiction Association and upon a large survey of 1,439 college students administered at the University of Washington in 1979.

AN APPROACH TO SCIENCE FICTION

CONCLUSION

Science fiction fans may enjoy reading the appendix tables closely to see which highly rated authors they have missed. And the relative popularities of different literature types can tell us something about the values of the science fiction subculture. But the correlational techniques that I introduce in the next chapter are necessary to understanding the ideological and stylistic structure of the literature.

To add qualitative flesh to the quantitative skeleton of this book, I quote frequently from leading authors, editors, and other members of the subculture who have thought deeply about the ideas at its heart. I also describe the ideological content of representative stories. A map showing where the authors stand would be of little interest unless it also recorded what they have to say.

In many subfields of the social sciences, techniques almost identical to those used in this book are commonly applied to the analysis of ideology. Political scientists conduct polls, not just to predict the winners of elections, but to discover the political ideologies of voting blocs. In the sociology of religion, these techniques chart the ideologies of rival faiths. But most areas of popular culture have hardly been touched by analytical tools of the type used here. Thus, in a sense, this book is a demonstration project, showing that techniques of survey research can do an excellent job in charting the ideological structure of science fiction. This may inspire the reader to extend these time-honored sociological tools to other important jobs in the vast collective project of understanding contemporary culture.

2

THE STRUCTURE

OF

SCIENCE FICTION

Science fiction arises from a single subculture, yet it is divided into competing stylistic and ideological factions. Every fan and critic knows this and is prepared to express an opinion about what those divisions are. Richard A. Lupoff wrote:

> Science fiction is of course itself a very varied field. Its broad borders encompass the "hard science" stories of Jules Verne a century ago and of Hal Clement and Larry Niven today. Those borders also take in the all-out adventure yarns of Edmund Hamilton and Jack Williamson, and the hybrid variety of technological "space opera" practiced by Edward Elmer Smith and John W. Campbell, Jr. Science fiction encompasses the serious sociological comment of H. G. Wells in his time, George Orwell in his, John Brunner in ours. It includes the psychological probings of Barry Malzberg, Philip K. Dick, and Robert Silverberg.[1]

This is a good analysis, yet one could question each of Lupoff's links between authors. In another essay Lupoff drew a sharp distinction between the approach of Jules Verne and that of H. G. Wells and identified contemporary authors as "Vernian" or "Wellsian."[2] But one can argue that Verne and Wells were very similar. A debate on this issue could compare their works and the ideological positions they expressed. But another, equally valid comparison could be made by surveying members of the contemporary science fiction subculture to determine the impact Wells and Verne have had on the field. One might find that both are recalled mainly not as proponents of competing ideologies but as equal and compatible founding fathers of SF.

I have no quarrel with critics or historians who analyze the works of Verne and Wells to determine the authors' styles and ideologies. This book is more concerned with the ideas and values of the entire subculture and its parts than with the perspectives of individual authors, although I shall inspect a number of individual works and their creators. My approach is to combine the knowledge of hundreds of SF readers, using mathematical techniques, to survey the science fiction territory with the greatest possible accuracy and achieve an objective map. I have tried to group authors and types of literature systematically, according to their most important ideological characteristics and to identify the principles that unite some and divide others.

I will show how the method of analysis works by using Verne and Wells. Then I will apply the methods and chart the main ideological divisions of science fiction: Hard science, new wave, and the fantasy cluster. First I will explain the mathematical techniques I used to extract meaning from the preferences of hundreds of SF readers.

The preference questions introduced in the previous chapter are the best tool for learning about similarities among authors and about what the different styles mean for readers. Preference questions measure how much a respondent values an author, his style, and his ideas. If people are asked directly whether Verne and Wells are similar, they may repeat the rhetoric of an influential critic. Or they may give a snap judgment based on very superficial aspects of the two authors, such as the fact that both have one-syllable names which come late in the alphabet. Historians and critics like Lupoff tell us that the two had very different political orientations and very different perspectives on the future of technology. But have Verne and Wells really had very different impacts on contemporary science fiction? Does their fiction communicate socially relevant disagreements?

When people are asked to rate their preferences for a number of authors, including Verne and Wells, the authors' essential characteristics determine the ratings. Statistical correlation of readers' preferences for Verne and Wells reveals how similar the two authors are on all currently salient dimensions. Correlations between the authors and respondents' preferences for various types of literature can describe the authors and verify that the descriptive terms efficiently identify their main qualities. Hypotheses concerning the overall structure of science fiction can be tested by examining the pattern of correlation linking numerous representative authors.

Someday, simple correlation coefficients will be as familiar to the general public as percentages are today. Everybody has a sense of what it means for two phenomena to correlate, and correlation coefficients are a very efficient way of communicating the degree of connection between them. These coefficients, ranging from -1 through zero to $+1$, describe the relationship between two variables, x and y. A plus sign means that if variable x goes up, variable y tends to go up too. A minus sign means that if x goes up, y tends to go down. Zero, or any number close to it, means there is no relationship between x and y.

Suppose you want to know the correlation between weight and height for a group of 100 science fiction authors. For each one, you record the weight in pounds (variable x) and the height in inches (variable y). The resulting 200 numbers—100 weight measurements and 100 height measurements—are arranged in 100 pairs, one for each author. You put the 100 pairs of numbers, properly labeled, into the computer and tell it to correlate them. Out comes a correlation coefficient, let's say 0.50. Because the figure is plus, it means that taller authors tend to be heavier than shorter ones. But the relationship is not exact. A short, fat author may be heavier than a tall, skinny one. If taller authors were always heavier than shorter ones, the figure would be closer to 1.00. That kind of perfect relationship never exists in sociology, because every human characteristic is the result of several causes, no one of which is a complete explanation in itself. Most of the coefficients used in this book are Pearson's r, which is very widely used in the social sciences, but a few are gamma, when the form of the data makes it more appropriate.

Some simple examples will help readers follow my relatively modest methods of quantitative analysis. Jules Verne and H. G. Wells are widely known outside the SF subculture. Of the 409 respondents who avoided rating either of the bogus authors while expressing an opinion about fifty or more real writers, 367 rated both Verne and Wells. The correlation ($r = .57$) between the two sets of preference responses is very strong. According to my data there is a slight tendency for respondents who like one author to say they like any other author—they simply like many kinds of science fiction—so there is a tiny correlation built into all of the preference scores. For example, there is an average correlation of .11 between Wells and the other 137 authors, but this includes all the real associations like the .57 correlation with Verne, so the coefficients are really not inflated very much by this factor. It would be incorrect to dismiss this as a case of response bias or yea-saying. All the evidence indicates that fans vary in the breadth of their tastes, and the contrast between those who like a wide range of authors and those who prefer only one type will produce a small background of positive association.

I experimented with various statistical methods for removing this positive-correlation background, such as partial correlations controlling for respondents' rating of neutral survey items. It became quite clear that there was no advantage in doing this for the authors and literature types on which this book's analysis rests; the coefficients changed very little. Each method of statistical control is ornate to describe, and it is hard to justify a preference for one over another. For example, controlling by the partial correlations method for respondents' ratings of "mainstream literature," the subculture's term for literature that is not related to science fiction, should adjust for general response style, yet the Verne-Wells correlation remains .57. If one assumes even a .11 background correlation, then the coefficient between Verne and Wells would be reduced by only .01 or .02.

By administering my questionnaire at the annual World Science Fiction Convention, which attracts SF fans from all over the globe, and by rejecting both frivolous responders who rated the bogus authors and honest responders who lacked familiarity with at least fifty authors, I was able to isolate a sample of expert fans who love science fiction. When I applied factor analysis, as discussed in later chapters, the correlations were effectively normed so that the resultant clusters of authors were not distorted by any latent positive response bias, however small.

Depending on the context, I generally considered coefficients as large as .20 significant, but I restricted comment in most cases to those above .25, which are substantively important, as well as merely "statistically significant." As I found in some of my survey research on religious ideologies, questionnaire items that accurately reflect a single concept will show very high correlations, much higher than is found in survey research aimed at finding links between conceptually separate "independent" and "dependent" variables.[3] Thus it should not be surprising to find a coefficient as strong as that linking Verne with Wells, but it tells us something important and speaks in a loud, clear voice.

Most superficially, the .57 Pearson's r means that people who like Verne better than other people do also tend to like Wells better than other people do. And those who like Verne less than other people do also tend to like Wells less. Although this tendency is very strong, some respondents fail to exhibit it. On a deeper level, the .57 coefficient means that many people are finding something similar in Verne and Wells and responding in a regular way to that underlying factor. What do Verne and Wells have in common? Author Poul Anderson, who correlated only .14 with Verne and .13 with Wells, expressed his view:

In my opinion, the two primary sources of science fiction as we know it are Jules Verne and H. G. Wells. They had forerunners of their own, but virtually everything done since traces back to one or another of them, or to both. Verne embodied "hard" science and technophilia; he expressed the exuberance of discovery and engineering achievement. Wells generally ignored technical details, or played fast and loose with them, in order to concentrate on the effects of a changing world and changing world-view on people.[4]

In effect, both were founders and forefathers of the SF genre, although their approaches to writing fiction and their personal ideologies differed significantly. The .57 coefficient suggests that their similarities emerged in the analysis more strongly than their differences. To explore the matter further, we can look at correlations linking each with other literature types and other authors, as shown in Table 1.

Verne had a correlation of .29 with classic science fiction from the early days, and Wells achieved an almost identical .30. These are really solid coefficients, although somewhat less than the .57 linking the two authors. Generally I found that correlations between variables at the same level of abstraction (say, authors correlated with authors) were higher than correlations between variables at different levels (say, authors correlated with literature types). The two authors also correlated with Golden Age science fiction and with science fiction of the 1920s and 1930s, showing that a good part of their correlation with each other is simply that both are *old*. Verne was born in

Table 1. Jules Verne and H. G. Wells correlated with selected literature types and authors (N = 409)

Literature type or author	Correlation (r) with	
	Verne	Wells
Classic science fiction from the early days of SF	.29	.30
Golden Age science fiction	.24	.27
Science fiction of the 1920s and 1930s	.30	.31
Science fiction of the 1940s and 1950s	.15	.21
Science fiction of the 1960s and 1970s	.11	.09
Eando Binder	.32	.22
Edgar Rice Burroughs	.42	.34
Arthur Conan Doyle	.32	.35
H. P. Lovecraft	.27	.34
Harlan Ellison	.06	.07
Ursula K. LeGuin	.00	.03
Larry Niven	.08	.04
Jerry Pournelle	.13	.11

1828 and died in 1905; Wells was born in 1866 and died in 1946. Wells correlated slightly more than Verne with science fiction of the 1940s and 1950s, perhaps because he died later. Neither correlated significantly with science fiction of the 1960s and 1970s.

If there is any question about the fact that age played a large role in this correlation, Table 1 shows the coefficients linking them to four other older authors (Binder, Burroughs, Doyle, and Lovecraft) and to four contemporary authors (Ellison, LeGuin, Niven, and Pournelle). Verne and Wells were linked to the older authors in people's minds, and not to the new authors. On the basis of their writings, one might say that Niven and Pournelle are "Vernian," while Ellison and LeGuin are "Wellsian," but the correlations fail to reveal any such distinction.

The lack of big differences between Wells and Verne in Table 1 does not refute Lupoff and Anderson, nor does it refute the validity of my methods. Rather, it helps specify what my methods can accomplish. My 367 respondents, expert members of the contemporary science fiction subculture, saw Verne and Wells primarily as early masters of the field and did not pay much attention to differences between them. Chances are they all have read *The War of the Worlds* and *The Time Machine* by Wells, which are exciting but not particularly ideological books, while undoubtedly only a few have studied his utopian essays. These novels may strike readers as very similar to Verne's *20,000 Leagues under the Sea* and *Journey to the Center of the Earth*. Verne wrote one novel about the first spaceship, *From the Earth to the Moon*, and Wells wrote another, *First Men in the Moon*.

Intellectual historians will find many differences in the lives and personal values of the two men, but their impact on science fiction today is almost identical. And that is what correlational analysis of survey data can best divulge—the living aesthetic and ideological influence of authors and schools of fiction. Other techniques, including conventional literary criticism and quantitative analysis of the fiction itself, can often better analyze specific works and the lives of those who wrote them.

FACTOR ANALYSIS OF THE BEST-KNOWN AUTHORS

To get an overview of the science fiction field, using correlational techniques, I shall begin by focusing on the most knowledgeable respondents and the best-known authors. I have pared the group of respondents down still further. These results are based on the judgments of 276 expert respondents, those who did not rate either fake author and who rated at least seventy-five authors.

Seventy-three authors were familiar to at least 80 percent of them, and on the average each author was rated by 253 respondents, or 92 pecent.

In two earlier articles based on my pilot study, Murray Dalziel and I hypothesized that science fiction primarily consists of the three separate ideological groupings mentioned earlier: hard science, new wave, and a fantasy cluster.[5] We suspected that these three were complicated by a somewhat independent history dimension, a suspicion strengthened here by the analysis of Verne and Wells. Therefore, I start with the hypothesis that science fiction can be graphed efficiently in just four dimensions. One way to identify dimensions in data such as these is through factor analysis, a mechanical, mathematical procedure for testing hypotheses about the structure of intercorrelation in a body of data.

One could try to uncover the basic ideological structure of the genre by visually inspecting all the correlations linking a large number of authors. Do they clump in clusters in people's preferences? If so, which authors stand together in which clusters? What do the authors in each group have in common? Verne and Wells are correlated, and both are tied to certain other older authors, so one might expect to find an ancient masters group. But what other groups also appear?

The correlational approach provides a monumental body of results, a total of 2,628 correlation coefficients linking each of the seventy-three authors with each of the others. Of course, to do such lengthy calculations without a computer would take about a year. But even with a computer, this vast matrix of 2,628 coefficients is too large for easy human comprehension.

Factor analysis is an entirely automatic technique for locating clusters. One must define a few parameters for the computer, such as how many pieces it should slice the data into—how many factors to create. Then the computer delineates clusters of authors as expressed by the respondents' preferences.

Because I hypothesize that science fiction extends through four dimensions, my analysis called for four factors. Because I wanted the dimensions to be truly at right angles to each other, I told the computer to produce "orthogonal" factors, maximizing their meaningfulness through a method known as "varimax rotation." The resulting printout defined four separate clusters of authors who correlated with each other, each expressing a different dimension of literature.

Table 2 gives an overview of the factor analysis, listing the six authors most closely associated with each of the four clusters. The factor loadings are very similar to correlation coefficients. One way to conceptualize them is to imagine that instead of mapping authors in ideological space, we are mapping stars in astronomical space. Each factor can be conceptualized as a star

Table 2. Leading authors in each factor (N = 276)

Author	Factor I	Factor II	Factor III	Factor IV
	Factor loadings (if above .350)			
Isaac Asimov	.602	—	—	—
Murray Leinster	.596	—	—	—
Gordon R. Dickson	.591	—	—	—
Jack Williamson	.580	—	—	—
Harry Harrison	.572	—	—	—
A. E. van Vogt	.571	—	—	—
Harlan Ellison	—	.637	—	—
Robert Silverberg	—	.568	—	—
Damon Knight	—	.562	—	—
Joanna Russ	—	.550	—	—
Philip K. Dick	—	.549	—	—
Kate Wilhelm	—	.547	—	—
Marion Zimmer Bradley	—	—	.581	—
J. R. R. Tolkien	—	—	.523	—
Anne McCaffrey	—	—	.493	—
C. L. Moore	—	—	.462	—
Fritz Leiber	—	—	.455	—
Andre Norton	—	—	.451	—
H. G. Wells	—	—	—	.709
Jules Verne	—	—	—	.638
Edgar Allan Poe	—	—	—	.607
H. P. Lovecraft	—	—	—	.526
George Orwell	—	—	—	.453
Arthur Conan Doyle	—	—	—	.447

cluster—a group of stars that are physically close to each other. Some stars are near the center of their cluster, others are near the perimeter. Each cluster has a center of gravity. A factor loading can be interpreted as the measure of distance between a star and the center of gravity of its cluster. Statisticians would want a more precise explanation of factor analysis, but this metaphor gets the main idea across. The only thing to keep in mind is that a high loading means the author is close to the center of gravity.

If one considers the first six authors in Table 2, it is clear that all have very high loadings on the first factor and no significant loading on any of the three others. Asimov's loading of .602 means he is very close to the center of the factor. Other authors who are not listed here are also members of the cluster, but are a little further out from the center.

This analysis shows four very neat factors, each with six authors close to the center and other authors hovering around them. No author in the list is close to the centers of two different clusters. The next step is to speculate about what the authors in each cluster have in common. This procedure is a bit subjective, and I will employ a better method shortly, but I think a reader who is at all familiar with the twenty-four authors in the table can make good sense of the four factors.

Factor I undoubtedly expresses the hard-science dimension. Each of the six authors has his own unique characteristics, but all tend to base their stories on explorations in the physical sciences and technology. Factor II links authors identified with the new wave, and Factor III includes writers of various kinds of fantasy. Thus the first three factors reveal exactly the three hypothesized ideological dimensions of SF: hard science, new wave, and the fantasy cluster.

Factor IV includes the classic writers, all of whom had died by 1950. The seventh author in the cluster, Edgar Rice Burroughs, died that year. Thus this factor represents the past, the complicating fourth dimension of time. One would expect time to interact with the other three dimensions in different ways, as each style gained or lost in influence over the years.

To interpret the four factors more objectively, it is necessary to include the questionnaire items about preferences for types of literature.

DIMENSIONS OF SCIENCE FICTION LITERATURE

Each of the four clusters can be treated as a variable in its own right. Earlier I correlated respondents' preferences for Verne and Wells with preferences for different types of literature. Extending the astronomical metaphor introduced above, I was looking at how close each star author was to each gaseous nebula literature type. Now I want to place some of those nebulae inside particular star clusters by measuring how close each literature type is to a cluster's center of gravity. This is done by computing *factor scores* for each factor. This essentially treats each factor as a new variable and gives each respondent a score representing a weighted average of the ratings he gave the authors in the cluster. Each respondent gets four factor scores, representing how much, on average, he prefers the authors in each factor. It is a simple matter, then, to correlate the factors with the preferences for literature types listed in the questionnaire.

The highest and most immediately interesting coefficients describing the four factors appear in Table 3. Factor I correlates most strongly with hard science ($r = .54$), Factor II with new wave ($r = .61$), and Factor III with sword-and-sorcery ($r = .60$). These correlations are so strong that it is safe to conclude that each factor is precisely identified by the term associated with it. Factor III seems to be named by two different terms, because the correlation with fantasy ($r = .57$) is almost exactly as high as that with sword-and-sorcery. But these terms are essentially equivalent, since sword-and-sorcery is the most readily identifiable subspecies of fantasy popular with SF fans. The highest correlation for Factor IV is low ($r = .36$), though well into the significant range, so I will suspend judgment about the fourth factor for the time being.

Before continuing down the table, I will review what the key terms mean. Hard science has been defined by L. David Allen as "science fiction in which the major impetus for the exploration which takes place is one of the so-

Table 3. Identification of the four groups of well-known authors (N = 276)

Literature type	Correlation (r) with:			
	Factor I	Factor II	Factor III	Factor IV
Hard science	.54	—	—	—
New wave	—	.61	—	—
Sword-and-sorcery	—	—	.60	—
Fantasy	—	—	.57	—
Horror-and-weird	—	—	.30	.36
Golden Age science fiction	.48	—	—	—
Classic science fiction from the early days of SF	.47	—	—	.26
Science fiction of the 1920s and 1930s	.39	—	—	.32
Science fiction of the 1940s and 1950s	.43	—	—	—
Science fiction of the 1960s and 1970s	.25	.33	—	—
Year in which respondent was born	—	—	—	—
Fiction based on the physical sciences	.45	—	—	—
Fiction based on the social sciences	—	.39	—	—
Stories about magic	—	—	.53	—

called hard, or physical, sciences, including chemistry, physics, biology, astronomy, geology, and possibly mathematics, as well as the technology associated with, or growing out of, one of those sciences."[6]

Many authors and critics have argued that hard science is the only true science fiction. They see science fiction as a literature of technical ideas, exploring the human consequences of scientific discovery, as a definition proposed by Bob Olsen in 1957 stated. "*Science Fiction:* A narrative about an imaginary invention, or discovery, which is possible in accordance with authentic, scientific knowledge and relates adventures and other happenings which might reasonably result from the use of the invention or discovery."[7] This definition comes very close to a description of hard science, except that it does not explicitly rule out stories based on discoveries in the "soft" social sciences.

New wave science fiction emerged as a cultural movement in the mid-1960s, although its elements existed long before. The first circle of new wave writers centered on the British magazine *New Worlds*, edited by Michael Moorcock. Introduced to American readers by anthologist Judith Merril, this British group contributed some inspiration and a name to its emerging counterpart in the United States.[8] The manifesto of the American new wave was *Dangerous Visions*, an anthology edited by Harlan Ellison in 1967. According to Ellison, the book "was constructed along specific lines of revolution. It was intended to shake things up. It was conceived out of a need for new horizons, new forms, new styles, new challenges in the literature of our time."[9] The new wave assimilated many ideas from the radical political and cultural movements of the late 1960s and presented itself as a loosely organized alternative to hard science.

Sword-and-sorcery is a variety of fantasy, typically concerning the adventures of brave heroes trekking through barbarian lands, wielding primitive weapons against demons and wizards. The fantasy preferred by science fiction readers is usually based solidly in some branch of serious scholarship if not in science. For example, the Hobbit stories of J. R. R. Tolkien drew on his knowledge of historical linguistics, and the interplanetary fantasies of his friend C. S. Lewis were vehicles for theological argument. Run-of-the-mill sword-and-sorcery is loosely based on ancient and medieval history and on cultural anthropology.

Another link between fantasy and SF is that stories of both types were published side by side in a small number of magazines for over fifty years. The emergence of the first science fiction magazines transformed SF from a rare subspecies of fantasy into a vigorous, semi-independent genre. These periodicals included *Amazing Stories* (1926–present), *Wonder Stories* (1929–

THE STRUCTURE OF SCIENCE FICTION

1955), and *Astounding Stories* (1930–present). Alongside these magazines, others dedicated primarily to fantasy but containing some science fiction struggled to survive, including *Weird Tales* (1923–1954), *Unknown* (1939–1943), and *Beyond* (1953–1955). In recent decades, pure fantasy magazines have failed to earn a profit for their publishers, and some periodicals have tried to combine the two types in roughly equal measure, among them *Fantastic* (1939–1980), *Stirring Science Stories* (1941–1942), *The Magazine of Fantasy and Science Fiction* (1949–present), and *Fantastic Universe* (1953–1960). But all the science fiction magazines published fantasy, and the sword-and-sorcery brand of adventure has been inseparable from SF since the beginning of the century.

With these key terms defined, at least provisionally, Table 3 is more easily understood. Factor III correlates with "horror-and-weird" ($r = .30$), a gloomy variety of fantasy. The strongest association linking Factor IV with any type of literature is the correlation with horror-and-weird ($r = .36$). This means that Factor IV is to some extent a spillover of Factor III, a vagrant piece of fantasy rather than a new brand of true science fiction.

The middle section of the table correlates the four factors with six variables describing the historical dimension. There is ample proof that hard science, represented by Factor I, was indeed the "classic" form of science fiction which held sway during a historic Golden Age. Hard science continued to be written in the 1960s and the 1970s, but it lost dominance to the new wave, expressed in Factor II. Factor III, sword-and-sorcery or fantasy, does not correlate with any of the terms that describe phases in the history of science fiction because this factor does not represent true SF but, rather, companion forms of literature. Factor IV picks up classic science fiction and SF of the 1920s and 1930s, the historic beginning of the field. Thus this factor appears to collect some residue from Factor I as well as from Factor III.

To make Factor IV absolutely clear, look at the authors most tightly clustered in it: H. G. Wells, Jules Verne, Edgar Allan Poe, H. P. Lovecraft, George Orwell, and Arthur Conan Doyle. These authors share the objective quality of oldness. Among other connections, most of them wrote some horror-and-weird, for which Poe and Lovecraft are known almost exclusively. Therefore Factor IV is clearly a group of very early SF writers. Other factors absorbed some of their qualities, leaving the horror-and-weird aspect and part of their antiquity to emerge in Factor IV. This means that the first three factors perform an excellent job of identifying the main tendencies within and around science fiction, while the fourth factor expresses a residue from the historical infancy of the field.

Table 3 includes one variable that does not correlate significantly with any of the factors—the year in which the respondent was born. This lack of correlation shows that the historical correlations result from the informed judgments of the 276 expert respondents, rather than simply from the styles in vogue when each respondent began reading SF and was most impressionable.

To get a clear image of the science fiction galaxy, I did a second, similar factor analysis focusing on a list of thirty-eight well-known authors and using responses from the 409 good respondents. Rather than just doing a factor analysis of the authors, repeating the earlier analysis with half the authors, I added four descriptive variables: hard science, new wave, fantasy, and classic. I then did a factor analysis of these forty-two items, calling for four factors. Earlier, I created author factors and then used factor scores to see how the four clusters correlated with various literature types. The procedure used here is more direct. By adding the four literature types to thirty-eight authors, we can see whether the types wind up in the appropriate factors in a single comprehensive run.

The analysis came out just as I expected. Each literature type wound up near the center of one of the four factors, and each type clustered with some authors famous for writing that type. As I showed earlier, Factor I is hard science and Factor II is new wave, the two main kinds of true science fiction. In Figure 1 these two dimensions are graphed against each other. Figure 1 is a good two-dimensional picture of SF literature, based on the responses of 409 fans to thirty-eight authors and four types of literature, represented by stars. Authors who are significantly correlated with one or the other factor (loadings above .30) are represented by solid dots and named. The open circles represent other authors, primarily of fantasy. The first thing to note about the figure is that the line connecting new wave with hard science neatly runs through the middle of the galaxy of authors, from one extreme to the other. This graphically demonstrates how well these two concepts describe the major axis of the field. Authors clearly identified with one or the other type cluster at either end of the line. Fantasy, appropriately enough, is off to the side, away from the SF line. Classic hugs close to hard science, the traditional heart of the field.

A DOUBLE CHECK

Although these factor analyses look extremely clean and sensible, they could be gross oversimplifications, because I attempted to find only four factors. Perhaps a fifth dimension of science fiction would be revealed if the computer had looked for more factors. With data such as author preference ratings,

THE STRUCTURE OF SCIENCE FICTION

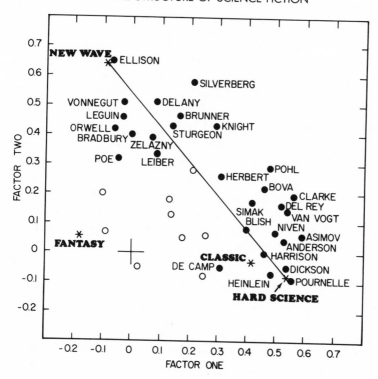

Figure 1. Factor analysis of science fiction authors

there always are leftover variations and correlations that are not expressed in an efficient factor analysis. There is an infinite number of possible shared qualities that might cause some readers to like a pair of authors and others to hate the pair. I am interested only in ideologically meaningful dimensions of variation.

To give other ideologies a chance to emerge, I did a second factor analysis of the seventy-three authors, calling for the maximum number of workable factors, slicing the SF world into the smallest possible pieces. This was done by selecting all factors with eigenvalues greater than one, which produced an unwieldy table of twenty factors. I marked each author loaded over .400 on a factor as belonging to that factor. The last factor, as often happens, was pure noise, with no authors in it at all, representing empty space itself. Ten of the twenty factors were single authors who were sufficiently unique, anomalous, or eclectic to stand alone: Vonnegut, LeGuin, Bradbury, Robinson, Budrys, Davidson, Sturgeon, Heinlein, Simak, and Vance. Of course, these ten authors do share some ideological characteristics with other authors, and they are attached to this or that main cluster in other analyses.

Three factors were pairs of authors. Del Rey and Wollheim share many characteristics with each other, but they may have been linked in respondents' minds because each is the editor of a series of science fiction books: Del Rey Books (presided over by Lester Del Rey's wife) is a division of Ballantine, while DAW Books uses the initials of Donald A. Wollheim.

Asimov and Clarke fit together not only because they are hard-science writers of the same generation, but because their reputations have become mysteriously intertwined. Asimov tells the story of how he and Clarke once were traveling together in a taxicab, discussing the fact that both were considered great writers of science fiction and great writers of popularized factual science. Like Spain and Portugal before them, they decided to divide the world by treaty. One was henceforth to be known as the world's greatest science fiction writer, and the other as the world's greatest science writer. Unfortunately, there remains some dispute as to which is which.

Lewis and Tolkien fit together not only because they both were English writers of fantasy, but because they were quite good friends who influenced each other's styles and even shared mythological material now found in the books of both. Clearly, the three factors that consist of pairs of authors do not represent *broad* ideological categories, however interesting the shared viewpoints may be.

There remain six factors, clusters of from five to fifteen authors each. The four largest factors are simply those I derived in the first factor analysis. Thus, if there is to be a fifth dimension of science fiction, it must be found in one of the remaining two factors, each of which contains just five authors.

The clearer of these two collects Leiber, Lovecraft, Moorcock, Tolkien, and Zelazny. When factor scores for this group are correlated with literature types, the group is most strongly connected to fantasy (.41), sword-and-sorcery (.41), horror-and-weird (.37), and the new wave (.31). These five authors represent a bridge from the fantasy cluster to the new wave. Zelazny and Moorcock, two authors associated with both sword-and-sorcery and new wave, have the highest loadings on this factor. This group does not represent a distinctively different ideology but a mixture, a transitional perspective between the fantasy cluster and the new wave. It is an ideological isthmus.

The remaining factor collects Bester, Brown, Kornbluth, Kuttner, and Moore. The last two were husband and wife, who often collaborated under the pen name Lewis Padgett. The group correlates moderately with humor

($r = .27$), which is quite appropriate considering stories like Brown's "Pi in the Sky," in which the stars rearrange themselves to spell out an advertising slogan, and Kornbluth's classic "The Marching Morons," which plumbs the depths of human stupidity. The group also correlates weakly with Golden Age science fiction (.25), science fiction of the 1940s and 1950s (.25), and stories that convey a sense of wonder (.22). These, I think, merely identify the main period in which the authors wrote. More revealing, perhaps, is the fact that this factor fails to correlate with any other literature types from the list.

These facts suggest to me that this last factor is simply a collection of authors from the 1940s and 1950s who sometimes wrote in a humorous vein but, most important, who did not participate in the ideological factions that dominated the period. Partisans of both the hard science and the new wave schools could find much to praise in these authors, but none of the five is really a captive of either school. Thus, far from being a new ideological grouping, this factor represents five good-humored, nonideological authors. All of them explored the question of ideology in their works, often with great intelligence and seriousness. But they were more cosmopolitan than ideological.

Thus even a factor analysis that allows the seventy-three best-known writers to be described by twenty dimensions finds that four dimensions are really all that are required to describe the ideological universe of science fiction. I shall examine each ideology in the following chapters, using qualitative as well as quantitative data to chart each of them in detail. First I will survey the relationships among the literature types, leaving authors out of the analysis for the time being.

A GEOGRAPHY LESSON

The complete map of science fiction is very complex, with many kinds of cultural topography in four dimensions and with various lesser warps and anomalies. But it is possible to draw simplified two-dimensional charts that do not distort reality much more than a flat Mercator projection misrepresents the round earth. Figure 2 is the best overview, because it graphs the physical and social sciences against each other. Dots represent types of literature, while lines connecting them represent significant correlations between pairs. The coefficients are based on the preferences of all 595 respondents.

The vertical dimension of the chart is the correlation with fiction based on the physical sciences, while the horizontal dimension is correlation with fiction based on the social sciences. The higher a type is on the graph, the

MEASUREMENT OF THE FANTASTIC

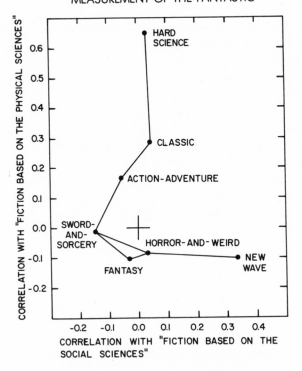

Figure 2. The sciences in science fiction

more it is related to the physical sciences, and the farther to the right a type is, the more it is associated with the social sciences.

The types are all connected, a fishhook continent of literature with peninsulas extending in two directions from fantasy. Lying very near the zero longitude on the map, hard science is neither for nor against the social sciences but points directly toward the physical-science North Pole.

The line connecting hard science with classic represents the correlation of .30 between them. The strength of this relationship cannot be expressed by the length of the line, because the position of the classic dot is determined by its .28 correlation with fiction based on the physical sciences. The line from classic to action-adventure represents a correlation of .29, showing that early science fiction was as much action-adventure as it was hard science.

Action-adventure is closely related to sword-and-sorcery ($r = .40$), which in turn connects with fantasy ($r = .67$) and with horror-and-weird ($r = .38$). Fantasy and horror-and-weird are related ($r = .39$), and horror-and-weird is tied more weakly to new wave ($r = .25$). New wave is a shorter peninsula than hard science, thrusting toward the social sciences.

Table 4 looks at these relationships again, using only the 409 good respondents. This table supports and extends the results of my factor analysis of authors. We see that in the upper half of the table, hard science stands almost alone, uncorrelated with most other types and only weakly tied to action-adventure fiction. At the other extreme, new wave stands almost alone, only very weakly connected to horror-and-weird. Between them lies the fantasy cluster, here represented by four interconnected types: action-adventure, sword-and-sorcery, fantasy, and horror-and-weird.

But the table also suggests that a single trajectory, as it were, can pass through the three main clusters—if not in a straight line connecting their centers, then perhaps along a kind of ideological geodesic. The six types of literature are perfectly arranged, with each one correlating most strongly with its neighbors and less strongly, if at all, with the type on the other side of the immediate neighbor. Action-adventure is at the hard science end of the fantasy cluster, while horror-and-weird is at the new wave end. The implications of all these relationships will be discussed in later chapters, but here, as in Fig-

Table 4. The structure of science fiction ($N = 409$)

	Correlation (r) with					
Literature type	Hard science	Action-adventure	Sword-and-sorcery	Fantasy	Horror-and-weird	New wave
Hard science	1					
Action-adventure	.20	1				
Sword-and-sorcery	.03	.42	1			
Fantasy	−.12	.27	.66	1		
Horror-and-weird	−.06	.17	.38	.43	1	
New wave	−.11	−.08	.00	.13	.23	1
Fiction based on the physical sciences	.66	.19	.04	−.08	−.06	.05
Fiction based on the social sciences	.02	−.05	−.08	.05	.11	.40
Stories about magic	−.05	.20	.57	.61	.35	.01
Respondent is politically liberal	−.16	−.15	−.01	.05	.16	.29

ure 2, we can see that the genre does have a measure of unity, as expressed in the coefficients, as well as being divided into parts.

The bottom half of Table 4 shows again that the three ideological groupings have very different orientations toward the sciences. Hard science, appropriately enough, does correlate very strongly with fiction based on the physical sciences, as Table 3 implied. New wave is moderately associated with the social sciences. But now we see, as in Table 3, that the fantasy cluster has magic near its center.

The final row in the table provides a hint of the political orientations of the ideological groupings. I included in the questionnaire a slightly cumbersome but well-validated political question used each year in the massive General Social Survey conducted by the National Opinion Research Center:[10]

We hear a lot of talk these days about liberals and conservatives. Below is a seven-point scale on which the political views that people might hold are arranged from extremely liberal (point "1") to extremely conservative (point "7"). Where would you place yourself on this scale? Please circle the ONE number that best indicates your general political views.

1　Extremely liberal

2　Liberal

3　Slightly liberal

4　Moderate, middle of the road

5　Slightly conservative

6　Conservative

7　Extremely conservative

Although this question treats American politics as an almost trivially one-dimensional debate, it does a very good job of tapping people's essential political orientations. I discuss politics particularly in chapters 4 and 6; for now just a glance at the correlations is useful. The numbers are small, ranging from a marginally significant $-.16$ to a solid but unspectacular $.29$. There is a significant connection between the new wave and liberal political views, no political implications at all for the heart of the fantasy cluster, and a slight tendency toward political conservatism for hard science.

THE FOURTH DIMENSION

Science fiction authors have rebelled against the pedestrian view that time is an inescapable, uniform progression from past to future along a single axis.

THE STRUCTURE OF SCIENCE FICTION

They frequently postulate controlled travel forward, backward, and even sideways in time. As an aesthetic dimension, certainly, time is not linear and metric. It can be a complex tangle of paths, continually looping backward and forward, that cannot be charted accurately along a line. For example, authors of the late 1920s sometimes foreshadowed the new wave of today in psychologically rich, surrealistic stories. Good examples are "The Gostak and the Doshes," by Miles J. Breuer, which explored radical liberation from conventional ideologies, and "The Revolt of the Pedestrians," by David H. Keller, which not only examined the negative side of science and technology, but also toyed with sexual deviance. Many contemporary writers consciously imitate the classics.

As the factor analysis showed, the time dimension interacts in a complex way with the three "spatial" ideological dimensions of science fiction. Figure 3 examines the interplay between various literature types and science fiction's

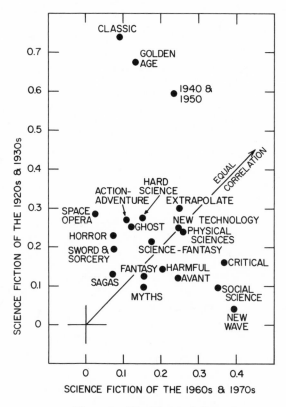

Figure 3. The historical dimension

fourth dimension to give a historical perspective. This graph focuses on the responses of the 409 more knowledgeable respondents, with correlations graphed against correlations. The horizontal axis is the correlation between each of the types of literature and science fiction of the 1960s and 1970s. The vertical axis is the correlation between each type and science fiction of the 1920s and 1930s. People who like recent science fiction tend to like the types of literature on the right side of the graph. People who like older science fiction tend to like the types higher up on the chart. Here time has expanded into two dimensions. Liking recent SF does not preclude liking early SF.

Certain types of science fiction tend to be associated with one period rather than another, but the picture is not a simple one. I have drawn a diagonal line of equal correlation up and to the right from the zero-zero point, and all points near the line indicate styles of writing that are not limited to the most recent or the earliest years of science fiction.

In the lower right-hand corner is new wave science fiction, which is associated strongly with the 1960s and 1970s ($r = .39$), and near it are three other types also stressed in contemporary SF: fiction based on the social sciences, fiction that is critical of our society, and avant-garde fiction which experiments with new styles. At the other end of the main cluster of types is space opera, a style of super-science space adventure that was quite common in the 1920s and 1930s, but is relatively rare today.

A very prominent feature of the graph is the triad of points near the top, representing classic science fiction from the early days of SF, Golden Age science fiction, and science fiction of the 1940s and 1950s. The placement of this last category is particularly interesting because it is the remaining period of science fiction history covered by the questionnaire. Respondents placed the 1940–1959 period closer to 1920–1939 ($r = .59$) than they did to 1960–1979 ($r = .24$), including it thus among the old days of the field. The typical respondent to the questionnaire was born in 1951 or 1952, so most of this middle period was over before the person appeared on this planet. Since the typical respondent began reading SF at the age of eleven or twelve, the period was entirely over before most of my respondents became fans. For members of the contemporary science fiction subculture, the past has been compressed. Recent distinctions are clearer to them than older ones.

The line of equal correlation identifies those types that either were prominent in an intermediate period, say around 1960, or have been important over the whole span of time covered. Three literature types define what science fiction, traditionally, was all about: stories which take current knowledge from one of the sciences and logically extrapolate what might be the next steps taken in that science, fiction based on the physical sciences, and stories about new technology. Three other types, much nearer the zero-zero point, identify fiction that has been the constant companion of science fiction but is not true SF: fantasy, sagas and epics, and myths and legends. Science-fantasy, properly enough, falls just halfway between these two triads. Five of these seven are associated at almost the identical level with each of the three periods, indicating that they are not restricted to the years in the middle. The exceptions are science-fantasy, which was weaker in the middle period, and fiction based on the physical sciences, which was stronger.

The complex factor of history—too multifaceted to be called a pure fourth dimension—will play a role in each of the chapters of this book. In each, we shall discover new interactions between time and one of the main ideological dimensions.

CONCLUSION

This chapter has introduced my methods of analysis and used them to show that SF literature is, indeed, a world of four dimensions, three of ideology and one of time. The survey was well timed for making baseline measurements of the ideologies, and the differences among them emerged very clearly in my statistical analysis. Although the spectacularly successful movie *Star Wars* had been released fifteen months before, the cultural fallout of the sustained boom in science fantasy it sparked had not yet had a great impact on the subculture of SF literature. All of the good respondents to the survey had been reading the fiction for a long time before *Star Wars*, and because the convention was held in a relatively out-of-the-way city, swarms of neophyte fans did not attend.

My data come also from a time when women were entering the field and when there was a clear perspective on the legacy of the new wave. As Chapter 7 will show, it was possible to chart the ideological patterns of the early women writers using the statistical techniques introduced in this chapter. The new wave was still an issue of great contention in 1978, but the agonizing battles between radicals and conservatives of the late 1960s were long over, so both the distinctiveness and the connections of this movement could be charted validly.

In the following chapters I shall consider each of the spatial dimensions of science fiction ideology. Far from being a monolithic movement promoting technology and the physical sciences, the SF subculture contains three competing ideological perspectives. Not only do hard science and the new wave espouse competing values, but they point toward very different futures. In a sense each is activist, urging us to create a particular kind of future. Fantasy, set between these extreme ideologies, has little to say about the realities of human existence. Instead of portraying problems and opportunities faced by humans in the real world, it escapes to unreal worlds that can be created only by magic.

II

THREE DIMENSIONS
OF SCIENCE
FICTION

3

THE

HARD SCIENCE

TRADITION

In 1929 Hugh Gernsback launched *Science Wonder Stories*, his second SF magazine, with a contest called "What Science Fiction Means to Me." The second honorable mention went to author E. E. Smith, who said that science fiction was literature for scientists, demanding a scientific mind both to write and to read, giving relaxed pleasure and intellectual stimulation to professional scientists. The first honorable mention went to author Jack Williamson, who stressed the excitement and vicarious adventure afforded by SF. He concluded his essay with a vision of unending technological progress: "A new era dawns. Dreams of men reach out to other worlds of space and time. The new unknown of science is calling. The ships of man will follow his dreams as caravans followed the dreams of Columbus. Science will answer the call, with a thousand new inventions— inspired by science fiction."[1]

The winner, awarded fifty dollars, was B. S. Moore, a fan who argued that science fiction was a great tool of scientific education: "I believe that the magazine of true science fiction is a standard scientific textbook. To the one who is seeking the light of scientific knowledge, science fiction is the broad and pleasant avenue toward the goal. For the layman to be well posted on scientific matters is to be well read on science fiction."[2]

Whatever his commercial motives, Gernsback organized the science fiction movement to use as a vehicle for promoting science and technology. To propagate the values and concepts of science, SF must emphasize the most coherent, rational, codified, empirically verified branches of scholarship— the physical sciences.

Gernsback's own fiction, exemplified by the didactic novels *Ralph 124C*

41+ and *Baron Muenchhausen's Scientific Adventures*, were little more than catalogues of mechanical and electrical inventions, decorated with an unobtrusive plot. Although the ideological factions within science fiction took years to coalesce, Gernsback's approach was what today we would call hard science. It gave first priority to scientific authenticity and to the romance of technological progress.

Gernsback expressed his concern for scientific authenticity in many ways. The editorial page of *Science Wonder Stories* carried a list of associate science editors, with the legend, "These nationally-known educators pass upon the scientific principles of all stories." The list for January 1930 included eighteen names in twelve fields: astronomy, astrophysics, botany, chemistry, electricity, entomology, mathematics, medicine, physics and radio, physics, psychology, and zoology. Probably the best-known name was that of Lee de Forest, inventor of the triode radio tube. Other familiar names were Donald H. Menzel, an astrophysicist, and Clyde Fisher, a curator of the American Museum of Natural History in New York. The February 1930 issue of *Air Wonder Stories*, a companion magazine, had five associate aviation editors, and it proclaimed that "these aeronautical experts pass upon the scientific principles of all stories."

From its first issue, *Amazing Stories* carried a slogan on the masthead of its editorial page: "Extravagant Fiction Today . . . Cold Fact Tomorrow." *Science Wonder Stories* expressed a similar sentiment on its editorial page: "Prophetic Fiction is the Mother of Scientific Fact." For a while this magazine proclaimed in bright letters on the front cover that it contained "Mystery-Adventure-Romance." Then in 1930 Gernsback held a contest awarding one hundred dollars "in gold" to the reader who could devise a new motto. Out of a reported 4,362 entries, the winner was Paul D. Mast, who proposed that *Science Wonder Stories* be called "The Magazine of Prophetic Fiction."[3] The honorable mentions were: "Fiction as Strange as Truth," "Science, Romance and Prophecy," "Facts! Through Fiction!" and "Interesting Fiction, Easily Read." Near the end of Gernsback's tenure as editor, *Wonder Stories* bannered on its cover the words "Adventures of Future Science." In 1930 the motto of *Air Wonder Stories* was "The Future of Aviation Springs from the Imagination."

On occasion Gernsback's magazines ran contests to see if readers could discover the errors in particular stories. Introducing Geoffrey Hewelcke's 1928 novelette "Ten Million Miles Sunward," the editor of *Amazing Stories* called it "one of the cleverest stories" but admitted that something was wrong with its assumptions and challenged readers to find the error.

At the beginning of 1935, Hewelcke's story goes, astronomers discover that a massive comet will hit Earth on June 3, 1937, annihilating all life. After much debate by scientists and engineers, the world's industrial resources are dedicated to moving Earth to a new and safer orbit closer to the sun. A series of canals is dug from the Black Sea to the Caspian Sea, which is eighty-six feet lower. By moving thirty million million tons of water three hundred miles Earth is shifted away from the path of the comet.

What was the error? A month after the story ran, astronomer W. J. Luyten of Harvard College Observatory pointed out to the readers of *Amazing* that the method used in the story could not in fact move our planet: "The fundamental flaw of mechanics is that the centre of gravity of the earth will remain in its orbit so long as only interior forces act, and in the case of the Caspian adventure we are dealing with a purely interior force."[4]

The October 1929 issue of *Science Wonder Stories* announced a fifty-dollar Fundamental Error Contest in connection with the story "Into the Subconscious" by Ray Avery Myers. In this tale a simple farmer is regressed through his racial memories by a "subconscious mind searcher" apparatus developed by the world's greatest reclusive scientist. The rustic farmer experiences fragments of the lives of his animal ancestors, until he recalls being eaten in a prehistoric swamp. The error, of course, is that his amphibian ancestor could not have transmitted this memory to its offspring, because dead animals do not reproduce. Note that this would not have been an error if the story had used the fantasy concept of reincarnation, because reincarnated beings may recall past deaths. Whatever one may think of the concept of "racial memory," it at least was supposed to be an authentic scientific idea. When the magazine awarded five modest prizes and eleven honorable mentions, it claimed that over 8,700 letters had been sent in.[5]

The letter columns of Gernsback's magazines carried many analyses of the scientific content of the stories. Often readers wrote in to complain about inaccuracies or to contribute their own peripheral observations that they felt were omitted. Writers sometimes complained about impossibilities in their colleagues' works. On one occasion popular author Miles J. Breuer assailed three short works by W. Alexander: "New Stomachs for Old," "The Fighting Heart," and "The Ananias Gland."

No one (including Mr. Alexander) who is not a biologist, can grasp how excruciatingly absurd the transplantation of stomachs and glands and hearts looks in a story. If *Amazing Stories* were some sort of a burlesque refuse-heap, the sport of innocent clowns, that might get by. But the stories in this magazine are supposed to carry an air of plausibility with them; they are supposed to be built on some sort of foundation that has at least an *appearance* of being scientific.

Green-cheese phenomena should not appear in it, side-by-side with the intel-ligent efforts of people who have worked hard to build up some scientific ideas.[6]

Here is a double irony! First, although physician Breuer considered it impossible, today many organs, even hearts, are transplanted successfully. Second, Alexander's stories are allegories, not meant to be taken literally. Stomachs do get switched in one story, but the doctor only pretends to transplant hearts in another, and there is no question of transplanting glands in the third. When a wealthy Wall Street financier trades stomachs with an Italian slum-dweller, he loses his standing in the community because of his new passion for proletarian food, while the poor Italian goes broke trying to satisfy his new craving for the elegant fare at the Ritz. The pretended trans-planting of a "fighting heart" into a craven coward renders him brave, purely by suggestion. In the third story the Ananias gland, named for an early Christian who was struck dead for lying, is a fictitious organ that controls human veracity and can be adjusted to permit its owner just the right balance of honest truth and socially necessary white lies. Stories such as these do not pretend full technical accuracy but use the intellectual tools of science fiction to explore general human problems.

To prove that his magazines taught science, Gernsback included quizzes in many issues. Each question was followed by a page number where the answer could be found. Here is the quiz from the April 1930 issue of *Science Wonder Stories:*

1. What is the shortest distance of the planet Venus from the Earth?
2. What are some of the physical characteristics which show that modern man evolved from a lower species?
3. What is the period of the revolution of the planet Venus around the sun?
4. How do we analyze the light from a heavenly body?
5. What does the science of ballistics deal with?
6. What is the kind of force which would keep a small celestial body near the earth from being drawn to our planet?
7. About how many asteroids have we been able to observe and classify?
8. What is meant by the fourth dimension?
9. At what period in the history of the earth did the brontosaurians and pterodactyls live?
10. What is the composition of matter as we know it?[7]

The answer to the first question was to be found in a story about an expedition from Earth to Venus. The seventh question was answered in a disaster story about the threatened impact of an asteroid with Earth, and the ninth question was crucial in a story in which the characters encountered living dinosaurs. Thus the facts of science were dramatized as well as communicated. The magazine also published short factual science news reports and a column in which the editor answered readers' science questions.

One story, "Buried Treasure" by Miles Breuer, actually contained a bit of do-it-yourself technology. The story was accompanied by a page that could be removed from the magazine. On one side were printed fifty-six line diagrams; the other side was blank. Readers were instructed to treat the page with "fine oil" until it became transparent, then place the diagrams one at a time over a number and letter block on another page. This permitted them to read a secret code that told part of the story. Unfortunately for the value of this innovation, the magazine printed the deciphered text of the message as well!

Gernsback did much to promote space travel. As early as 1927 an editorial about prospects for spaceflight said, "The only machine so far proposed which stands the best chance of accomplishing the desired results is the Goddard rocket type of machine."[8] Gernsback meant Goddard's early, repeating solid-fuel rocket designs, not the liquid-fuel designs he was then perfecting. *Wonder Stories* published an English translation of Hermann Noordung's comprehensive handbook of spaceflight, *Das Problem der Befahrung des Weltraums*, communicating to a receptive audience many of the facts and ideas that guided the exploration of space.

In my book *The Spaceflight Revolution*, I explained that America's leading aerospace engineering organization, the American Institute of Aeronautics and Astronautics, was originally a tiny spaceflight club founded by David Lasser, who was managing editor of *Wonder Stories*. The June 1930 issue of the magazine announced this organization, which at first was called the American Interplanetary Society, and extended its "enthusiastic support."[9]

Four years later Gernsback launched his own fan club, the Science Fiction League, proclaiming, "It may be said that science fiction, as a popular movement, has finally arrived."[10] The club's aim was the "promotion of science fiction," including efforts "to enhance the popularity of science fiction, to increase the number of its loyal followers by converting potential advocates to the cause."[11] Thus the Science Fiction League was designed to sell *Wonder Stories*, not space travel. Also sold were league letterheads, envelopes, seals, lapel buttons, and a fancy membership certificate.

Whatever the particular SF project, Gernsback furthered hard science ideology, including spaceflight, at least indirectly. But nothing is perfect or absolute. In a 1926 editorial in *Amazing*, he summarized a key principle of hard science: "We reject stories often on the ground that, in our opinion, the plot or action is not in keeping with science as we know it today."[12] Yet the next year the magazine admitted that this principle was applied with some flexibility. "We firmly believe that, if the stories we publish were restricted to absolute fact, with the imagination of the authors permitted to go only into the realm of cold actuality, much of the interest of *Amazing Stories* would vanish."[13]

Gernsback's successor at *Amazing* was the aged but energetic T. O'Conor Sloane, Ph.D., son-in-law of Thomas A. Edison. While sharing completely Gernsback's belief that SF should promote science and technology, Sloane believed that space travel was impossible, and he predicted in 1933 that man would never reach the moon.[14] In 1930 he noted that burning hydrogen as fuel might provide enough energy to lift a spacecraft off Earth, but he was convinced that human beings could never endure the high accelerations that would be required.[15] Among the angry letters from fans was one from the young John Campbell, who later was the dominant science fiction editor, arguing that someday better propulsion than rockets might be devised and explaining that interplanetary flights could be accomplished with moderate accelerations.[16] Sloane's lack of belief in spaceflight did not prevent him from publishing stories about it, using it as an educational tool. "So since our readers like interplanetary stories, since they increasingly ask for them in letters to us, and since there is any amount of science, mechanical, astronomical and other to be gleaned therefrom, we certainly shall be glad to continue to give them, even in face of the fact that we are inclined to think that interplanetary travel may never be attained. On the other hand, in science, 'never' has proved to be a very dangerous word to employ."[17]

Thirty-five years after founding *Amazing Stories*, Gernsback surveyed the subculture he had created and concluded that there were only about a dozen "real science fiction authors" according to his standards. He named seven: Asimov, Clarke, Clement, Heinlein, Simak, Sturgeon, and van Vogt.[18] Except for Sturgeon, they are popular hard science writers.

THE AUTHORS OF HARD SCIENCE

In the previous chapter's factor analysis of seventy-three authors, the first factor represented hard science. Table 5 lists all twenty-seven authors with factor loadings above .35 on the hard science factor, along with correlations linking each to this type of literature, both in data from the 409 good respondents and in the data from all 595 respondents to the questionnaire.

The table includes a few authors who perhaps should not be there. Laumer,

Table 5. Hard science authors from the factor analysis

Author	Factor loading (N = 276)	Correlation (r) with hard science SF	
		(N = 409)	(N = 595)
1. Asimov	.602	.28	.29
2. Leinster	.596	.33	.30
3. Dickson	.591	.22	.20
4. Williamson	.581	.38	.36
5. Harrison	.572	.23	.24
6. van Vogt	.571	.26	.26
7. Clement	.567	.38	.38
8. Reynolds	.564	.19	.26
9. Pournelle	.562	.29	.31
10. del Rey	.560	.18	.20
11. Smith	.552	.34	.30
12. Laumer	.541	.19	.19
13. Anderson	.509	.27	.27
14. Niven	.501	.35	.31
15. Clarke	.499	.35	.36
16. Simak	.490	.13	.18
17. Campbell	.486	.31	.29
18. Bova	.486	.24	.24
19. Hoyle	.474	.30	.26
20. Wollheim	.456	.23	.25
21. Heinlein	.455	.27	.28
22. Carter	.429	.16	.12
23. Pohl	.412	.29	.28
24. Robinson	.391	.18	.14
25. Haldeman	.387	.14	.15
26. Blish	.361	.24	.20
27. de Camp	.361	.21	.20

Simak, Carter, Robinson, and Haldeman fail to achieve correlations as high as .20 with hard science in either the second or the third column of figures. In the case of Haldeman, the factor loading is almost as high on the new wave factor (.368) as on the hard science factor (.387). Of course, because of the way factor analysis works, any author with strong ties to a few hard science authors will be pulled in, no matter why fans connect him with them.

The authors with the highest loadings are not necessarily the ones associated most strongly with this type of literature, especially since so many authors are bunched very close together at the top loadings, and there are accidental random variations in any such statistics. According to the correlations, Hal Clement is the purest hard science writer, followed closely by Williamson, Clarke, Niven, Smith, and Leinster. Some authors who write a lot of pure hard science are not at the top of the list because they also write other kinds of fiction. Anderson, for example, also writes heroic fantasy. When an author works in two or more different styles, his correlations with each will be somewhat lower than if he specialized in just one.

Figure 4 looks at the hard science authors in another way. Based on responses from all 595 fans who filled out the questionnaire, it maps the twenty-seven writers associated with hard science by correlations greater than .20. The vertical dimension is average preference rating, with high popularity at the top. Many SF authors are less popular than even the least of these

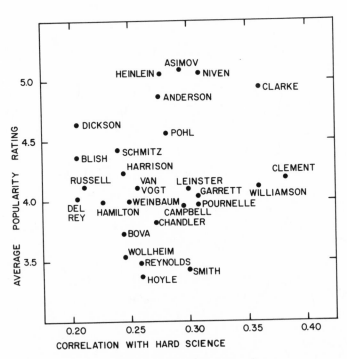

Figure 4. Hard science authors

twenty-seven, so the map covers desirable territory, even though the writers at the top occupy the best real estate.

The horizontal dimension is correlation with hard science. Hal Clement has the most extreme score, showing that his work belongs to the purest hard science. The graph omits all of the more than a hundred other SF authors who do not specialize in this style. They would be graphed off the map to the left.

Many definitions of hard science have been offered over the years. Gernsback gave valid definitions although he did not use the term himself. Perhaps the most useful conceptualizations are those offered by several authors on the list, who have worked successfully in this area. According to Poul Anderson, "the term itself, 'hard' science fiction, originated with the late James Blish who, afterwards, remarked that his original intention had been greatly misinterpreted. Nowadays, what's usually meant by the phrase is writing which is more or less based on 'real' sciences—actual physics, chemistry, biology, astronomy, etc.—and to a considerable extent extrapolates from this, with a minimum of imaginary laws of nature."[19]

Anderson's characterization of physics and the others as "real" sciences echoes John Campbell's opinion that the social sciences have not yet achieved true scientific status. In one essay Campbell wrote, "Psychology and sociology today are definitely not sciences; they're con games."[20] Elsewhere he said that each of the social sciences was a "mess."[21] In 1945, at the height of his influence and editorial powers, Campbell asserted, "Science-fiction characteristically bases its material almost exclusively in the physical sciences— more or less necessarily so, since the physical sciences are the only sciences available to our particular culture . . . Currently, the 'mental sciences' are simply not sciences—which is, of course, why they don't rate as so-called 'physical' sciences."[22] However distressing it may be to the modern quantitative sociologist, many SF fans consider the social sciences soft and the physical sciences hard. Today, when highly technical mathematics dominates sociology journals and when well-stated theories are subjected to highly technical empirical tests, one might argue that the social sciences have hardened up considerably since Campbell and his associates formed their opinions.

Several other authors from the hard science list have defined this ideological division. When a reader wrote to *Isaac Asimov's Science Fiction Magazine*, thanking it for emphasizing "the 'hard-core' science fiction instead of the Fantasy and New-Wave branches," Asimov responded, "It strikes me that the adjective 'hard-core' is used most frequently to modify another noun we need not mention here. I wonder if someone can suggest a better name for the kind of science men like Arthur Clarke, Hal Clement and I write."[23]

When another reader continued the discussion of "hard-core" science fiction, perhaps implying only that Asimov's style represented the heart, or core, of the field, Asimov replied, "Most frequently I call it 'hard science fiction.' I've been thinking we might try 'classical science fiction.' Or maybe we could just call it 'science fiction' and persuade people to call everything else 'sci-fi.' "[24]

Poul Anderson stressed the rationality and realism held as high values by this ideological faction. "Hard science fiction is the kind which, ideally, confines the story assumptions to established facts. The author postulates no laws of nature, as yet undiscovered, which would allow things to happen. He reasons logically, sometimes mathematically, what the likely consequences are of the conditions he is setting up."[25]

One of Heinlein's characters in a 1942 story stated the hero-engineer's creed: "With my slipstick, or on it,"[26] echoing the Greek warriors' maxim, "With my shield, or on it." *Slipstick*, a slang term for slide rule, is now obsolete because slide rules have been largely supplanted by micro-electronic pocket calculators. But the sentiment endures, and what is hard science about if not technological progress? In 1944 Heinlein published in *Astounding* a review of a historical handbook of spaceflight, *Rockets*, by Willy Ley. Heinlein praised this book highly for offering the technical specifications for space travel and warned authors that it contained a wealth of information essential for writing good SF.

A lot of you have been getting away with faulty physics and ridiculous contradictions simply because most of your readers could not check up on you when it comes to orbits, speeds, length of voyage, space maneuvering, et cetera. Willy Ley has changed all that and deserves a good sharp note from the union. But from now on you had better watch it.[27]

Jack Williamson, whose experience and creative history reach back almost to the beginning of the subculture, stated: "To me, however, hard science fiction is really linked to science. It's about what is not yet true, here and now, but what might be possible, elsewhere or elsewhen. Fantasy, on the other hand—some of it called science fiction—deals with the outright impossible. Exploring the possible, we're accepting change. I like to think of serious science fiction as a response to progress in science and technology."[28]

For Harry Harrison, a metaphor from space technology might describe hard science: "What I write most of the time, with rare exceptions, is what the British call 'solid-fuel rocket science fiction'—where all the pieces meld together and you extrapolate a new world."[29]

Often hard science writers do more than devise hardware and calculate transit orbits; they extrapolate new worlds. The concern for intellectual craftsmanship, for logic and rationality, for developing a story around a scientifically plausible set of assumptions was well expressed by frequent collaborators Jerry Pournelle and Larry Niven in their description of how to design a planet. "Most hard science fiction writers follow standard rules for building worlds. We have formulae and tables for getting orbits right, selecting suns of proper brightness, determining temperatures and climates, building a plausible ecology. Building worlds requires imagination, but a lot of the work is mechanical. Once the mechanical work is done the world may suggest a story, or it may even design its own inhabitants."[30]

HAL CLEMENT, HARD SCIENTIST

Donald H. Tuck called Hal Clement the epitome of the hard science writer, saying he "is one of the few to transfer the scientific attitude and methodology to science fiction, making scientific facts integral parts of his stories."[31] And P. Schuyler Miller, book reviewer for *Analog*, said, "Hal Clement is probably our foremost exemplar of *quantitative thought* in science fiction. And this is the key to the best of the 'hard' science fiction with which he—and Analog— have been identified."[32]

Some of Clement's best work is about alien environments and the exotic physical phenomena that occur in them, although he has been faulted for populating other planets with creatures that are unusual in their biology but utterly human in their psychology.[33] Clement's 1951 novel *Iceworld* concerns an interstellar detective named Ken who infiltrates a ring of drug runners. His mission is to discover what planet is the source of a new, highly addictive narcotic. The source, it turns out, is a world so cold that air freezes, where normal technological devices break down and where the mere touch of a hand is sufficient to trigger explosive reactions in the supercold lifeforms, which amazingly survive these conditions through absolutely exotic chemistry.

Iceworld is really Earth, and the dangerous narcotic is tobacco. Our planet seems exotic because it is viewed by a spacefaring species that evolved on a vastly hotter world than this. After showing Ken's terror and nausea at the sight of the ice planet, Clement explains that this reaction was natural, considering how unnatural Earth must seem to him. "Earth, really, is not as bad as all that. Some people are even quite fond of it. Ken, of course, was prejudiced, as anyone is likely to be against a world where water is a liquid—

when he has grown up breathing gaseous sulfur and, at rare intervals, drinking molten copper chloride."[34]

Unable to tolerate cold for long, the drug runners have set up their base on the sun side of the planet Mercury. When Clement wrote, astronomers and SF writers believed, incorrectly, that Mercury always kept the same hemisphere toward the sun, just as the moon does with Earth. Although hard science authors try to achieve the highest possible scientific accuracy, and try to avoid violating principles of current knowledge, they can hardly be blamed for not foreseeing future developments in science. Thus Clement had his aliens dwell in a hot valley on the side toward the sun, concentrating its heat with terraces of mirrors, to bring their living accommodations up to tolerable temperatures without expending great quantities of artificially generated power. To give an example of the scientific detail Clement provided, these mirrors are not made of glass, which would have melted under the conditions on Mercury, but of iron, which is dark in visible wavelengths but an adequate reflector in the infrared.

Clement's masterpiece, perhaps the greatest hard science novel, was *Mission of Gravity*, published in installments by *Astounding* in 1953. The story takes place on the planet Mesklin, a world outside our own solar system that might actually exist. Ten years earlier, when Clement was first writing for *Astounding*, the magazine had carried a factual article by astronomer R. S. Richardson, reporting that close examination of the motions of the double-star system 61 Cygni indicated the presence of an unseen third body. Named 61 Cygni C, this body was perhaps sixteen times the mass of Jupiter and was promptly identified as a planet.[35] Astronomers today, however, doubt the accuracy of the observations. Clement renamed the massive body Mesklin and tried to deduce a reasonable set of environmental conditions that would lead to an interesting story.

To accompany the third installment of *Mission of Gravity*, Clement wrote an article, "Whirligig World," explaining how he had designed an interesting planetary environment from the few facts presumed to be known about 61 Cygni C.[36] If Mesklin is far more massive than giant Jupiter, will it also be larger? Perhaps not, because the extreme pressure at the center will compress the material significantly. Even if Mesklin is only a little larger than Earth, won't its day be much longer than twenty-four hours? No, because the large planets in our own solar system rotate much faster than Earth. Compressed by its own gravity to moderate size despite its great mass, Mesklin would have an even shorter rotation period because the angular momentum of surface materials must have been conserved. Will Mesklin be round like Earth? In fact, Earth is very slightly oblate rather than a true sphere, and Jupiter is noticeably oblate, narrower through the poles than across the equator, flattened by the effect of its high speed of rotation.

If Mesklin is very heavy and compressed, its surface gravity must be extreme, far greater than any human could endure. But if Mesklin rotates rapidly, the gravity at the equator will be offset by centrifugal force. To the extent that the planet is highly oblate, the equator will be much farther from the center of gravity than are the poles. The planet must be a world of widely varying gravity. In consequence, its surface will have a tremendous range of natural conditions. For the sake of an interesting story, Clement designed Mesklin so that the equatorial gravity was only three times Earth's normal gravity, permitting humans to land (though with great discomfort) and establish direct contact with the natives. At the poles, Clement calculated, the force of gravity is a crushing 665 times Earth normal!

Because of Mesklin's large, eccentric assumed orbit and the weakness of its suns, the planet will be very cold. Therefore, Clement realized, the inhabitants' physiology must be based on different chemical reactions from those that give life to humans. With the expert help of Isaac Asimov, who taught biochemistry at Boston University, Clement sketched the general features of a plausible Mesklinite. Postulating a reasonably likely hydrogen atmosphere and methane oceans, he devised lifeforms that used these chemicals and adapted to the crushing gravity.

In the story, scientists from Earth and other planets have sent an astronomically expensive automatic research rocket to one of Mesklin's poles to study the physics of superhigh gravity and to learn how to control gravitational forces. When it is time for the rocket to lift off and deliver its valuable load of data to its makers, nothing happens. The only way to retrieve the data is to enlist the aid of the Mesklinites. Contacted at the equator, sea captain Barlennan, skipper of an ocean-going raft called the *Bree*, accepts the mission. The story follows him through the full range of gravities, across thousands of miles to his goal.

To make it possible for Barlennan to survive at the pole and to give the story more interest, Clement has this stalwart centipede of a sea captain be a native of higher latitudes, who is unfamiliar with any force as weak as three gravities. His crew has never seen anybody throw an object, are terrified of rising up on their hind legs or of getting under any solid object, and are accustomed to an environment where a fall of six inches is fatal even for their strong bodies.

The novel is filled with incidents that illustrate scientific principles of the environment; one example will suffice to show how the physics of high gravity produce interesting events. Traveling down a long, low-gravity river, the *Bree* encounters people who use canoes rather than rafts. Never having seen such light, efficient boats, they obtain one through trade, intending to tow it home. As the force of gravity increases along the voyage, the canoe rides just as high as ever in the methane "water." The weight of liquid displaced increases at the same rate as the weight of the canoe. But a few thousand miles from the equator, the canoe suddenly collapses. The pressure gradient from the surface to its keel has become so steep that the sides of the canoe cannot sustain the great force exerted against them. Now Barlennan knows why his own people use rafts in the higher-gravity regions.

Clement used great care in designing his planets, and he has sometimes been critical of the worlds created by other authors. An article by James Blish about conditions on Mars departed from Clement's understanding of scientific knowledge at the time, so Clement wrote a critical letter to the magazine, which drew some agreement but also counterarguments from Blish.[37] In "Whirligig World," Clement said that science fiction is most fun if treated as a game played between the writer and the reader. The reader's object is "finding as many as possible of the author's statements or implications which conflict with the facts as science currently understands them."[38] The writer's object is to produce an entertaining story with as few such errors as possible.

On several occasions Clement expressed the creed of hard science. In *Unearth*, a magazine for new SF authors, he wrote:

I have always admitted that the *science* part of science fiction means more to me than the fiction, but even I have to grant that there is a difference between a science article and a story. I personally get a lot more fun out of working up the possible permutations of a scientific theme than out of the somewhat trivial job of making characters perform appropriate actions—yes, I know it shows. My reason, if there is any beyond a purely subjective bias, is that the science is really all that determines what *can* happen.[39]

Humanistic or technophobic readers may prefer the other types of science fiction, in which authors examine the harm science can cause, or they ignore science altogether. Some might argue that the strictures of hard science drain the life out of literature and preclude poetry. Clement felt otherwise. "It remains my firm opinion that using 'known' science and coherent extrapolations thereof in science fiction not only fails to restrict the imagination, but provides it with take-off points unlikely to be noticed by the non-scientist and the anti-scientist."[40]

CORRELATES OF HARD SCIENCE SF

Table 6 lists sixteen types of literature that correlate significantly with preferences for hard science, based on data from the 409 good respondents. It provides an expert, quantitative definition of hard science. The six variables at the top of the table are so closely associated with hard science that collectively they practically define it. Certainly, hard science SF is based on the physical sciences ($r = .66$), and often the stories are about new technology ($r = .51$). Many of these stories take current knowledge from one of the sciences and logically extrapolate the next steps ($r = .47$). Indeed, logic is a prime value for fans of hard science, and the authors often provide a rational

Table 6. Correlations (r) between preferences for hard science SF and for related types $(N = 409)$

Literature type	Correlation (r) with hard science
Fiction based on the physical sciences	.66
Stories about new technology	.51
Factual science articles	.49
Stories which take current knowledge from one of the sciences and logically extrapolate what might be the next steps taken in that science	.47
Stories in which there is a rational explanation for everything	.46
Factual reports on the space program and spaceflight	.43
Golden Age science fiction	.33
Classic science fiction from the early days of SF	.31
Science fiction of the 1940s and 1950s	.29
Stories about robots	.29
Science fiction of the 1920s and 1930s	.27
Stories in which the main character is cool and unemotional	.23
Space opera	.23
Stories in which the main character is clever and intelligent	.22
Stories about war	.21
Action-adventure fiction	.20

explanation for everything that happens ($r = .46$). Closely tied to the preference for hard science is a preference for factual writing about the same subjects. Thus hard science correlates highly with factual science articles ($r = .49$) and with factual reports on the space program and spaceflight ($r = .43$).

The respondents' concern for facts, rationality, and logic in the hard science ideology probably extends to the real world as much as to the fiction. The hard science viewpoint expects to find a rational explanation for everything. Murray Leinster, an author with very close ties to hard science, offered an almost perfect expression of the ideology: "In a real world, everything follows natural laws. Impossible things do not happen. There is an explanation for everything that does happen. The explanation links it to other things. There are no isolated phenomena. There are only isolated observations, and sometimes false observations. But everything real is rational."[41]

According to Table 6, hard science is about both science and technology. Some authors in the sociology of science and technology say that the two have little to do with each other; some science fails to produce new technology, and some new technology is not based on scientific discovery.[42] With this in mind, we might ask whether science fiction treats science and technology as a unit. Are these inseparable concepts, or is basic research quite a different human endeavor from engineering invention?

Hard science SF correlates almost exactly as strongly with stories about new technology ($r = .51$) as with stories that take current knowledge from one of the sciences and logically extrapolate what might be the next steps taken in that science ($r = .47$). The .04 difference in these coefficients is not statistically significant. As it happens, the correlation between new technology and new science is essentially the same ($r = .51$).

We can look at the connection between new technology and new science by examining the correlations linking each with a long list of science fiction authors. Figure 5 does this in the form of a map, graphing the two sets of coefficients against each other. The vertical dimension is the correlation between each author and stories that extrapolate new science. The horizontal dimension is the correlation between each author and new technology. I have included 122 authors for whom 100 or more of the 409 good respondents gave ratings on all three variables.

The picture is very clear. The dots representing the authors fall along a narrow diagonal line from lower left to upper right, indicating that these two types of literature are essentially synonymous in respondents' minds. The correlation an author gets with new science is almost identical to the one he gets with new technology. Correlational analysis can even be used here to

THE HARD SCIENCE TRADITION

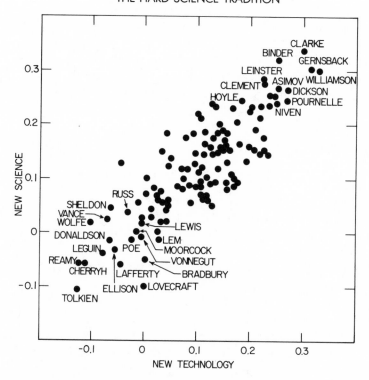

Figure 5. The science–technology dimension

measure the correlation between two sets of correlations. This expresses in a single figure the picture shown by the graph. Measured this way, the correlation between new science and new technology is .85. Most of the coefficients in this study do not approach the theoretically possible 1.00 because the data are noisy; respondents do not express their preferences with perfect accuracy and precision on the seven-point scale. By correlating correlations, I have based the coefficient on much better information than usual—the signal-to-noise ratio is especially favorable. Therefore the .85 coefficient is a much better estimate of the real connection between new science and new technology than the .51 correlation calculated directly from preferences for the two types of literature.

The hard science authors are those at the top right, including Gernsback, Clarke, Williamson, Binder, Leinster, Asimov, Dickson, Pournelle, Niven, Clement, and Hoyle. The authors at lower left, who include some of the leading new wave and fantasy writers, represent something like the opposite of hard science. Their stories express antitechnology sentiments, or they violate physical science with impunity, or they ignore science and technology altogether.

Figure 5 shows very clearly that the correlates of hard science, new science and new technology, delineate a dimension that runs straight through the entire field. All the authors, whether at one of the ends or near the middle, are very close to the science-technology axis, whether or not they are hard science.

THE GOLDEN AGE OF HARD SCIENCE

Table 6 shows a quite respectable correlation ($r = .33$) between hard science and Golden Age science fiction. An Age of Gold is a time of greatness, of cultural efflorescence, lit by a divine spark that no longer burns today. Although some may seek a future aureate era, generally the gold is assumed lost in the past. Ours is an age of mere iron or, at worst, of plastic. Among the 409 good respondents, Golden Age SF correlates most strongly with classic SF ($r = .77$), with SF of the 1920s and 1930s ($r = .68$) and of the 1940s and 1950s ($r = .65$). Two variables that correlate with the Golden Age at about the same level as hard science are space opera ($r = .35$) and action-adventure ($r = .31$). Thus the vanished Age of Gold was dominated by these more active kinds of literature as well as by their cerebral cousin, hard science.

While the strongest correlations simply place the Golden Age of SF in the past, critics and historians have tried to date it more precisely. James Gunn said it began in 1939 with the debuts of four of the greatest writers: van Vogt, Sturgeon, Heinlein, and Asimov.[43] Asimov agreed:

> There is one "Golden Age of Science Fiction" that has actually been institutionalized and frozen in place, and that is the period between 1938 and 1950, with its peak years from 1939 to 1942.
>
> John W. Campbell, Jr., became editor of *Astounding Stories* in 1938, changed its name to *Astounding Science Fiction*, changed its style, and found new writers or encouraged older writers to expand their horizons.[44]
>
> During the Golden Age, he and the magazine he edited so dominated science fiction that to read *Astounding* was to know the field entire.
>
> In that sense, the Golden Age endured till 1950, when other magazines, such as *Galaxy* and *The Magazine of Fantasy and Science Fiction*, entered the field.[45]

There is a widespread consensus that Campbell's ascendancy marked the beginning of the Golden Age, but some commentators disagree. In 1977 John J. Pierce contended:

THE HARD SCIENCE TRADITION

Among some older readers of science fiction, there is still talk of the Golden Age of the 1940's when, under the late John W. Campbell, the genre first began to take itself seriously—and win the beginnings of serious recognition.

But the Golden Age is really *now*. More people are reading science fiction than ever before, and they have better science fiction to read than ever before. The growing acceptance of sf and the increasing quality of writing in the genre are even more important than the much-publicized college courses.[46]

Others say that the Golden Age is not a period of time but a state of mind. Writing as Robert Randall, Robert Silverberg and Randall Garrett considered the sense of wonder, then lamented as a lost virtue of science fiction. But, they contended, this sense of wonder was really the ecstacy a person experienced on first encountering SF, regardless of the year. When was the Golden Age? "When did you feel that 'sense of wonder?' Yeah. *When you first started reading science fiction!*"[47] Peter Scott Graham has been variously quoted as saying that the Golden Age of science fiction is twelve and that it is thirteen.[48] The point is the same whichever number is chosen. The Gold comes from the age of the judge, not from the vintage of the fiction judged.

Writing in *Amazing Stories* in 1935, before the standard Golden Age, Oliver Saari tried to encourage the editor against harsh criticism he had been receiving from people who praised the "good old days" and condemned the present. Saari noted that the "good old days" of the late 1920s had been criticized as well, "but I am convinced that in four years of time, the good year nineteen-hundred and thirty-five shall be prated over as the unimpeachable 'golden age.' "[49]

History, I think, has proven Saari wrong, and nobody suggests today that mid-1930s *Amazing* was much better than rotten. But the general point is a good one. Fans agree with the majority of historians and critics that the Golden Age is far in the past, but the qualities that create the sense of wonder are found in every decade; each is in some way a Golden Age.

ROBOTS AND BLAZING ROCKETS

The correlation between hard science and stories about robots is noteworthy and must indicate a basic harmony between this narrow topic and the basic values and perceptions of the ideological faction.

Authors Asimov and Binder, each of whom separately wrote a story titled "I, Robot," correlated creditably, .32 and .37 respectively, with stories about robots. Asimov is perhaps the best-known SF writer, and I shall discuss his robot stories at length. One of the most prolific and beloved SF writers of the 1930s, Eando Binder was a name used by two brothers writing together, Earl Andrew and Otto Oscar Binder. Indeed, the pen name can be read as "E and O" Binder. But Earl left the collaboration, and all the later stories were written by Otto. A third Binder brother did some illustrations for SF magazines.

Eando Binder was not sufficiently well known to be included in the factor analysis of seventy-three authors, but with the 409 good respondents, he has a modest correlation with hard science ($r = .20$), and the correlation between Binder and factor scores for Factor I is quite high ($r = .41$). In Figure 5 he is one of the authors at the science and technology extreme.

Eando Binder wrote a series of short stories and novelettes about Adam Link, robot. In the first of these, "I, Robot," this metal humanoid with a sponge iridium brain is falsely accused of murdering his creator, Dr. Link. Despite his habit of saving humans from drowning, fires, and auto accidents, he is not exonerated until the third story in the series. Adam Link is strong, intelligent, and especially sensitive. He frequently broods about the sad fate of Frankenstein's monster. People fear Adam at first and later poke fun at him. Continually, he must assert that robots, too, are human. Why, he wonders, cannot people realize, "as Dr. Link once stated, that the body, human or otherwise, is only part of the environment of the mind?"[50]

In a later story Adam falls in love with a human woman and invests his money in her slum-clearance project. But he finds that he must renounce his love because a human friend will be a better mate for her. Despondent at his loss, Adam contemplates suicide. The solution to his problem is a technological one—he builds himself a female counterpart, Eve Link. In later stories the Links defend America from the Japanese, then repel an even more dangerous invasion from the star Sirius.

The Czech word *robot* was introduced into English in the 1921 play *R.U.R.* by Karel Capek. Paul A. Carter pointed out that many American SF writers ignored the fact that in Czech, *robot* has connotations of *forced labor* and *worker*.[51] In the play oppressed manufactured workers (robots) rebel against their capitalist makers and in the end discover their own humanity. Carter is right in complaining that American writers discounted completely the Marxist message in *R.U.R.*, but science fiction authors like Binder successfully incorporated other messages more appropriate to their own culture in stories about robots. The 1938 story "Helen O'Loy" by Lester del Rey suggests that robots can know love as profoundly as any human being. "Farewell to the Master," by Harry Bates, on which the film *The Day the Earth Stood Still* was based, suggested that robots may be superior to humans, without having that fact be sinister.

The master of robot stories is Isaac Asimov, who is known not only for his many tales about robots, but also for the Three Laws of Robotics. These are overriding commands built into all robots—rules they absolutely cannot violate—which not only assure that robots will be beneficial to humanity but which convinced humans to accept mechanical men in their society. First stated in the 1942 story "Runaround," these laws are:

1—A robot may not injure a human being, or, through inaction, allow a human being to come to harm.

2—A robot must obey the orders given it by human beings except where such orders would conflict with the First Law.

3—A robot must protect its own existence as long as such protection does not conflict with the First or Second Law. [52]

Several of Asimov's stories explore the interesting implications of these laws under unusual circumstances. In "Runaround" two men have landed on the sun side of Mercury, where it is too hot for them to survive more than a few minutes in the open, even protected by spacesuits. The vital photocell banks, which shield their base from the blazing sun, are breaking down. Unless they can obtain more selenium to complete a repair, they will die. Without being careful about how they state the command, they send a new-model robot, Speedy, some distance across the surface to get selenium from a pool of this metal. Unfortunately, Speedy has been designed with an especially strong Third Law, and the men's command to him, which depends for its completion on the Second Law, is not stated with an explicit high priority. When Speedy approaches the selenium, he finds that the pool is deadly and will destroy him if he enters it. With a weak command and with strong programming for self-protection, he is caught in what psychologists call an approach-avoidance conflict. He must go in, but he cannot go in. He can neither complete his mission nor abandon it. So he "goes crazy" and begins running around the pool at a safe distance, singing.

The men cannot do Speedy's job for him, and they will die unless they can free him from his psychological trap. Eventually, one of them realizes that only the First Law is powerful enough to resolve this conflict between a weakened Second Law and a strengthened Third Law. So he intentionally exposes himself to mortal danger, forcing Speedy to save him. Then Speedy can be sent under a better command to a safer selenium deposit. Roboticide, committed by intentionally creating "mental freeze-out," "robot block," or "roblock," like Speedy's, is the mystery of Asimov's 1983 novel, *The Robots of Dawn*.

Asimov says that the Three Laws emerged from his first robot stories, rather than being defined beforehand. Indeed, he credits John Campbell for seeing that the laws were implicit in his stories and for encouraging him to make them explicit. [53] What makes the Three Laws especially interesting for us now is that they are formal propositions describing complex behavior, applications of the hard science ideology to psychology and sociology.

The stories of Campbell's Golden Age overflow with assertions about social science, but with rare exceptions the leading authors of the period knew nothing about the actual social sciences. What they presented as social science was in part an extension of the hard science perspective on human affairs and in part the authors' political persuasions. Sometimes, as in van Vogt's novel *The World of Null-A*, the source was a pseudoscientific cult (see Chapter 8). Campbell was the key influence in coordinating and drawing forth social science fiction, but the leading authors also brought their own perspectives and prejudices to the creative labor.

Asimov has disclaimed any knowledge of psychology, [54] but the first robot story in which he formally stated the Three Laws also exemplified a standard psychological concept, the approach-avoidance conflict. The dominant theme of Asimov's stories is precisely human behavioral science. Asimov postulates that rational laws, like those of the physical sciences, explain and limit human action—"Laws of Humanics," he once called them. [55] His first great story, "Nightfall," concerns an inhabited planet in a multiple-star system, where night comes only once every thousand years when all the suns happen to be on the same side. From this interesting physical-science premise, Asimov deduces the social-science hypothesis that when the terrifying dark of night comes and the stars appear, *everyone* goes mad and civilization falls.

The fall of civilization is the background of Asimov's Foundation stories, which won a special Hugo award in 1966 as the "best all-time series." According to SF historian Sam Moskowitz, the plan for the Foundation series developed in conversations between Asimov and Campbell, shortly after Asimov was inspired by reading Gibbon's *Decline and Fall of the Roman Empire*. [56] Asimov believed that a galactic Dark Age would produce regional economic and cultural disaster, long breakdowns in communication, and seemingly endless local wars. His Foundation series tells of the attempt by a secret group of scientists to reduce the duration of the Dark Age from thirty thousand years to a mere millennium. How can they predict and manipulate the future? Through the science of psychohistory, brought to its highest level of development by a social scientist named Hari Seldon.

Today, the term psychohistory refers to more or less psychoanalytic studies of important historical figures. For Asimov, however, psychohistory is not a vague, qualitative analysis of the interaction of creative individuals and the groups they lead, but a highly mathematical science for predicting the course of civilizations. He "quotes" a future book, the *Encyclopedia Galactica*, to provide a formal definition:

> PSYCHOHISTORY—. . . Gaal Dornick, using nonmathematical concepts, has defined psychohistory to be that branch of mathematics which deals with the reactions of human conglomerates to fixed social and economic stimuli . . .
>
> . . . Implicit in all these definitions is the assumption that the human conglomerate being dealt with is sufficiently large for valid statistical treatment. The necessary size of such a conglomerate may be determined by Seldon's First Theorem which . . . A further necessary assumption is that the human conglomerate be itself aware of psychohistoric analysis in order that its reactions be truly random . . .
>
> The basis of all valid psychohistory lies in the development of Seldon Functions which exhibit properties congruent to those of such social and economic forces as . . .[57]

(The ellipses in the quotation are Asimov's own; I am sorry he did not see fit to state Seldon's Theorems.)

Charles Elkins correctly noted that in Asimov's stories, "The logic of history is equated with the logic of the natural sciences."[58] Asimov does not merely transfer concepts like momentum and force from physics into sociology, he takes the position, sometimes called by sociologists social physics, that exact formulas can be stated that describe, explain, and predict human behavior. These laws exist at present only in fiction.[59] In his robot stories, as well as in the Foundation series, Asimov presents his laws as examples of what might be true. They are primarily vehicles for exploring social relations from a hard science viewpoint.

In Asimov's robot detective novel, *The Caves of Steel*, Lije Baley, a human policeman, and R. Daneel Olivaw, a robot detective, team up to solve a baffling murder, a political assassination of the utmost significance. Much of the story revolves around the relationship between Baley and Olivaw—their competition and their growing understanding of each other. On a deeper level the theme is the relationship between people and machines and, on a still deeper level, the relationship between people and the things we use, including other people. Potentially, a happy ending can be reached when Baley and Olivaw—or any two beings—come to understand each other both as *objects* and as *subjects*. In using each other, they can create a division of labor in which each recognizes and values the ways in which the other is different and can be used to achieve more than either could alone. In confronting each other as persons, they can learn the other's motivations and perspectives, achieving a measure of friendship while preserving their separate needs and unique identities.

The murder that Baley and Olivaw investigate directly concerns the Three Laws, and Asimov postulates similar laws that may delimit human behavior. In one discussion between Baley and a robotics expert, machines that follow the Laws are referred to as Asenion robots.[60] The adjective looks rather scientific, like the chemical term *anion*, but because it is capitalized, it presumably is derived from the name of a great fictional scientist. Some wags might want to pronounce it like *asinine*. The word actually refers to Asimov; it originated as a typesetter's error in a letter to the editor,[61] a confusion noted in Lester del Rey's 1952 robot story, "Instinct," in which a character of the far future is not sure whether the inventor of the first robot was Asimov or Asenion.[62]

The victim in *Caves of Steel* is an extraterrestrial sociologist who has devised a scheme for human betterment and who, incidentally, has created the robot R. Daneel Olivaw in his own image. The murderer must have been from Earth, so an interplanetary political crisis threatens. The victim was being kept under extremely tight security, and it seems that the murderer could not have gotten to him in any ordinary way. He must have crossed a wide expanse of open territory, shot the sociologist with a ray gun, then left, again across the open. This seems impossible, because over the centuries all Earthmen have so thoroughly adapted to life in enclosed cities that they cannot psychologically endure open spaces—humans are universally afflicted with absolutely debilitating agoraphobia. A robot could have crossed the open space, but because of the First Law, a robot could not have killed a man.

Eventually Baley concludes that the murder was committed by a man and a robot. The robot brought the gun across the open territory, not knowing it was participating in a murder. The man was allowed to pass through the security cordon because he had no weapon. The remaining problem with this theory is that the only Earthman on the scene at the time of the murder was Baley's boss in the police department, who has passed a test showing that he is incapable of killing another person. Baley solves this dilemma by showing that his boss fired the ray gun at what he thought was only a robot, Olivaw; he was unable to see clearly because he had lost the archaic spectacles he wore as an act of defiance against advanced technology.

Note that this whole story makes sense only if we accept Asimov's assumption that humans are constrained by laws just as rigid and binding as the Three Laws of Robotics. This is the hard science view of humanity, expressed in its purest form. It is a tribute to Asimov's sensitivity that a subtheme in his robot stories is the human potential to transcend such laws through love and understanding. According to the statement quoted above, psychohistorical predictions might not hold if the people who are the subjects of the scientific analysis were themselves aware of psychohistory.

Other items in Table 6, after the one about robots, harmonize with this perspective on human nature, expressing hard science notions that might be applied to real people as well as to the fiction. People who like stories that have a rational explanation for everything may wish for such rational explanations in their own lives. Robots are cool and unemotional, at least in principle, and the best of them are clever and intelligent, just like the characters in stories favored by hard science fans.

But three items near the bottom of the table seem to point in a very different direction. Stories about war seem to focus on the ultimate human irrationality, on the stupidest and most emotional of destructive behavior. Action-adventure fiction concerns such topics as war, and typically each story contains more than one fight to the death between individual characters. Space opera, the SF equivalent of horse opera (cowboy tales) and soap opera (domestic melodramas), consists of fantastic adventures set against a fanciful interplanetary background. Common in the SF magazines of the 1930s, space opera often used the physical props of hard science without the underlying intellectual themes. In no time at all the space opera hero can invent a space dreadnought to defend Earth against alien invasion, as in Campbell's story "When the Atoms Failed." Or, just when he needs an interstellar battleship, one is available for him to steal, so simply constructed that he can operate it after but a moment's inspection of the controls, as in E. E. Smith's "Galactic Patrol." Yet on close inspection it turns out that his ship does not work on any realistic scientific principle, and many conditions of his environment are completely contrary to known science. Brian Aldiss wrote, "Space opera was heady, escapist stuff, charging on without overmuch regard for logic or literacy, while often throwing off great images, excitements, and aspirations. Nowadays—rather like grand opera—it is considered to be in decline, and is in the hands of imitators, or else has evolved into sword-and-sorcery."[63]

Space opera correlates only weakly with hard science ($r = .23$) and is tied as strongly to sword-and-sorcery ($r = .25$). Space opera and action-adventure are nearly synonymous, as the .43 correlation linking them shows. The categories at the bottom of Table 6, I think, are neither attributes of hard science nor direct expressions of its ideology. Rather, these three items are parts of the bridge from hard science to the fantasy cluster. We will encounter them again in Chapter 5.

TO THE STARS THROUGH DIFFICULTIES

The hard science faction passionately wants humans to become masters of space and time. Its authors dream of civilizations around other stars and in other centuries, and their stories often take us to these distant locations. But actual technology is impotent to reach across the galaxy or across the ages. Indeed, current science places absolute barriers in the way of such voyages. Therefore hard science writers have invented literary devices to substitute for plausible technological devices. To reach worlds filled with wonder, they have postulated interstellar spaceships and time machines.

The hard science ideology suffers from a basic contradiction. On the one hand, it tries to adhere to current scientific knowledge to make the stories plausible. On the other hand, it wishes to accomplish feats far beyond the capacity of current technology to maximize the characters' scope for action. Thus it is both rational and optimistic, but often these two values conflict.

Many of the most popular early science fiction stories postulated intelligent life on other planets and placed exotic human civilizations in cities lost in the jungles of Africa or South America. But by the first issue of *Amazing Stories*, real-life geographic exploration and scientific research had severely undercut the plausibility of such settings. Since anything might be possible beyond the reach of the explorer's boot and the astronomer's lens, science fiction followed the receding frontier of human knowledge and found fictional means for crossing the gulfs of interstellar space and intermillennial time.

Sam Moskowitz said the great leap to the stars was made by E. E. "Doc" Smith: "The imagination of the science-fiction world stagnated within the confines of our solar system until 1928, when Edward E. Smith's *The Skylark of Space* lifted mental horizons to the inspiring wonder of the galaxy."[64] Smith himself admitted that the tales could not be written unless a few scientific errors were permitted.[65] For example, his characters are forced to reject Einstein's theory that it is impossible to travel faster than the speed of light.[66] Furthermore, the data in Smith's stories do not compute. In the middle of *The Skylark of Space* the villain's spaceship achieves the velocity of 7,413,000,000 miles per second after just two days of flight, which I calculate would have required a lethal acceleration of seven million times the force of Earth's gravity. Calculated the other way around, the acceleration suggested by the passengers' experience (something like six gravities) would have achieved only 3 percent of the speed of light, far too slow for the star-spanning adventures Smith created.[67]

Campbell's hard science ideology impelled him, then a very young author, to complain in print about Smith's faulty science.[68] Campbell set up equations based on information in the Skylark stories which, when solved, implied that Smith's ships could not have exceeded one hundred miles per second, even given the complete transformation of copper into kinetic energy that their engines supposedly achieved.[69] P. Schuyler Miller later contributed more detailed mathematical calculations to Campbell's side of the debate.[70]

In the December 1930 issue of *Amazing Stories*, Smith responded to Campbell, writing with great elegance about the impossibilities in stories by such competitors as Edmond Hamilton and Campbell himself. He admitted the acceleration problem but defended his stories against the other accusations. He suggested that new scientific discoveries might find even more powerful sources of energy within the structure of subatomic particles than were currently known.[71] In this he expressed an underlying optimism that the human stories SF writers want to tell must be scientifically possible. Unless one assumes that interstellar voyages can be completed in a few months, it is very difficult to invent plots concerning individual human beings.

Some subsequent fiction by other masters of the field has described interstellar flight achieved within the limits of current knowledge. Heinlein's "Universe" and "Common Sense" take place on a slow-moving, city-sized interstellar ship launched toward Proxima Centauri at a small fraction of the speed of light, taking generations to complete its voyage. Van Vogt's "Far Centaurus" sends a crew of four men on a five-hundred-year trip to Alpha Centauri, preserving them against the centuries in suspended animation. In "Proxima Centauri," Murray Leinster follows correct formulas for acceleration but vaguely postulates superior atomic engines that can sustain one-gravity acceleration for a full seven years. Each of these stories exploits the technical premises for dramatic effect, but there is a limit to the number of interesting similar tales that can be written. And the technology postulated takes us only to the nearest stars in the neighborhood of the sun, not to the ends of the galaxy.

Jack Williamson's 1934 novel *The Legion of Space* is a rescue story that would not work if the laws of normal physics were observed. The heroine, abducted to Barnard's Star, must be saved immediately to avert the destruction of Earth. Each leg of the interstellar round trip must take no more than a few weeks, or the story collapses. But Williamson cannot ignore the scientific problems, because his readers are aware of the general principles of space flight. So he postulates a superinvention that can circumvent natural laws as currently understood, engines capable of warping space, called *geodynes*. The flight from Earth to Pluto takes only five days:

Five days—with the full power of the *geodynes*, whose fields of force reacted against the curvature of space itself, warped it, so that they drove the ship not through space, to put it very crudely, but around it, making possible terrific accelerations without any discomfort to passengers, speeds far beyond even that of light. Speeds, a mathematician would hasten to add, as measured in the ordinary space that the vessel went *around*; both acceleration and velocity being quite moderate in the hyperspace it really went *through*.[72]

This literary device became *overdrive* in Leinster's stories "The Disciplinary Circuit," "The Manless Worlds," and "The Boomerang Circuit." Leinster said that overdrive works by reducing the effective mass of a spaceship while conserving its kinetic energy, thus multiplying velocity by a large factor.[73] These stories drew a letter of protest from Poul Anderson, who cited contemporary physics to demonstrate that the speed of light would still be the limiting velocity.[74] Leinster also used another device, a matter transmitter that sends objects over great distances in the same way radio sends sounds and television sends pictures. Then his hero developed a hybrid of overdrive and the matter transmitter, a transmitter-drive, which permits a ship to project itself instantaneously a great distance ahead, without requiring a matter receiver to reconstitute it at the destination.[75]

For his Foundation series, Asimov employed a means of interstellar travel so quick and cheap that it permits the development of a Galactic Empire, a single political and economic unit covering the entire galaxy. The ship leaves a planet by ordinary propulsion—rockets, for example—then carefully prepares for a hyper-space jump in exactly the right direction. It ducks in and out of hyperspace, arriving almost instantly at a point near the destination. Navigation is difficult, calculations must be exact, and intervening objects must be avoided, so long voyages require several such jumps. Without these limiting assumptions, the drama of long, arduous voyages would have vanished from the universe in which Asimov set his stories. He described his mode of interstellar travel:

The Jump remained, and would probably remain forever, the only practical method of travelling between the stars. Travel through ordinary space could proceed at no rate more rapid than that of ordinary light (a bit of scientific knowledge that belonged among the few items known since the forgotten dawn of human history), and that would have meant years of travel between even the nearest of inhabited systems. Through hyper-space, that unimaginable region that was neither space nor time, matter nor energy, something nor nothing, one could traverse the length of the Galaxy in the interval between two neighboring instants of time.[76]

The conquest of time did not produce extensive quantitative debate among hard science authors and fans, but it often required rethinking the laws of temporal logic. Of course, time travel into the future may be accomplished simply through suspended animation—complete hibernation that stops the aging process as well as the hero's consciousness—as in L. Sprague de Camp's novel *The Stolen Dormouse*. Travel into the past, and round trips to and from another time, require utterly unknown scientific principles. In Mark Twain's *A Connecticut Yankee in King Arthur's Court*, a blow to the head sends the hero into the past, and suspended animation returns him. In H. G. Wells's famous book *The Time Machine*, the hero's vehicle travels in the "fourth dimension" but Wells gives not the slightest hint of how this is accomplished.

Unless the time traveler is simply an unobtrusive observer, travel into the past produces paradox. On a recent television show Asimov acted out the classic example: he traveled back to Czarist Russia and murdered his grandfather—thereby causing himself never to have existed and never to have killed his grandfather and therefore to have existed and gone back to kill his grandfather and therefore, paradox!

But even the transmission of information back in time produces paradox. And if free will truly exists, a person might well freely *imagine* a piece of information which would have the same effect as information sent into his mind from the distant future. This raises the serious social-scientific question of whether any individual can change history through the action of personal will and genius. H. G. Wells thought not.[77] In *Lest Darkness Fall*, L. Sprague de Camp explores the question of whether a modern man could use his knowledge to prevent the fall of Rome. He concludes that history could be changed. But this would mean that time machines could multiply themselves across the ages, transforming everybody into a time traveler and every event from a fact into an improbability. If time travel were easy, as Arthur C. Clarke once noted, "our past history would be full of time travelers."[78] Extensive time travel would utterly destroy the coherence of events and transform the universe into a blooming, buzzing confusion. De Camp suggested an assumption that has become something of a literary convention, explicit or not, in many stories: time travel is possible and history can be changed only at certain *very rare* weak points in the fabric of existence.[79]

Jack Williamson's novel *The Legion of Time* concerns the struggle between alternate possible futures to determine what happens at one such point. So long as the crucial event that leads either to one future or to the other is in doubt, both futures exist in a shadowy way. Because each implies the non-existence of the other, it is impossible for them to war directly on each other. Instead, they must send images and ships backward in time to that portion of the past they share in common. The heroine, Lethonee, is a woman of one of the futures, and the hero, Dennis Lanning, is a man of our own century.

The crucial event appears minor, not an obviously earth-shattering occurrence like the death of Lincoln or the birth of Hitler. For Lethonee to live, on August 21, 1921, at 5:49 PM, a young boy must fail to pick up an attractive, oddly colored pebble. If he picks it up, he will use it in his slingshot to kill a bird and will later fail to play a key role in history. If instead he picks up a dark object lying next to the pebble, he will discover that it is a magnet, will wonder about its mysterious attraction for his pocket knife, and will grow up to be a scientist. After a lifetime of effort, dedicated by that chance encounter with the magnet, he will invent a radically new principle in physics rendering cheap, safe atomic power available.

Here Williamson shows a deep understanding of the issues of technological history he raises. If the boy picks up the pebble rather than the magnet, the scientific discovery will be made nonetheless. But it will come later and will fall into evil hands, leading to the evil future in which Lethonee never lived. Williamson weaves both the malleability of history and technological determinism into the same thesis. The mere invention of a new device or scientific principle does not rigidly determine history. The social context in which it appears is important also. In the story Lethonee's opponents steal the magnet, and Lanning's heroism is directed at replacing it on the hillside to be found by the boy.

Williamson's alternate futures imply the possibility of alternate presents. The classic story based on this idea is Leinster's "Sidewise in Time." A rare upheaval of nature causes fragments of other presents to switch places with each other, producing a patchwork world of zones scintillating in and out of contact. The alternate todays diverged years before when the crucial event fell one way for one time line and the other way for another. The story takes a professor and his students away from the America we know to Americas colonized by the Vikings, by the Romans, by the Chinese, by no one—and to another where the Civil War ends in deadlock. The premise that natural disasters or intentional disruption can scramble the times, so that pieces of different centuries suddenly exist alongside each other on Earth, is also explored in *Time Storm* by Gordon R. Dickson and *October the First Is Too Late* by Fred Hoyle.

Many stories have explored quickly a single aspect of the paradox of time travel. In "Other Tracks" by William Sell, time travelers contrive to advance the technology of the past so that their own day has the components necessary to complete their time machine. Heinlein's story "By His Bootstraps" has the hero travel through time repeatedly, playing five separate roles in the drama, encountering himself again and again as his life doubles back on itself. Heinlein explored this topic again in "All You Zombies," a tale that uses time travel and a sex-change operation to let the hero/heroine become his/her own parents. Such a person is a living paradox, brought into existence by himself/herself with no antecedents.

Jack Williamson's "Minus Sign" contains a battle between two military spaceships, in which the behavior of each ship seems irrational to the other. Only at the end does the crew discover that in fact there is only one ship, which encounters itself while traveling backward in time. Since it encounters itself going in the opposite direction, each time it perceives itself as shooting first and asking questions afterward—in other words, as an aggressor. A slightly different failure of understanding occurs in "Brooklin Project" by William Tenn. A secret government project to develop time as a weapon inadvertently changes the past radically, but the researchers fail to recognize the disaster because they have been profoundly changed by their own experiment. Their world continues to seem normal to them, but in fact it is becoming stranger and stranger.

CONCLUSION

Hard science SF, based on the physical sciences and advanced technology, extrapolates new discoveries and inventions through stories that provide rational explanations for much of what happens. In human terms, the universe charted by astronomers seems cold and empty. It is hard in this demythologized age for people to see the promise of future civilizations or personal destinies in the skies, let alone the traditional heaven. Yet hard science SF fills the universe with hope and excitement, imagining possibilities that go far beyond the data of scientists and the limited assumptions of mundane citizens. Though loyal to fact and logic, this variety of science fiction dares to dream great dreams.

In stories about time travel and about interstellar travel, hard science transcends its own self-imposed limitations. While holding fast to the value of rationality and demanding that even the wildest events have reasonable explanations, it breaks through the bonds of the ordinary. These stories revolve around rational consideration of radical physical possibilities. They are, as Groff Conklin once called the fiction of A. E. van Vogt, "stories of the Impossible clutching the Rational by the throat and astonishing it to death."[80]

Many hard science critics, including Lester del Rey and Hal Clement, have admitted that faster-than-light travel and voyages back in time violate known physics. [81] Editor Robert W. Lowndes once said, "Any time-travel story that appears in a science fiction magazine has to appear under a sort of special dispensation, if the editor is trying to avoid pseudo-science, for time-travel is sheer fantasy."[82] But science fiction needs such stories, both because they carry forth the hard science commitment to explore novel ideas in a rational manner and because they may achieve the sense of wonder that has been a goal of all science fiction. In their 1946 anthology *Adventures in Space and Time*, Healy and McComas said: "Is a time machine possible? Escapists that we are, all of us yearn for past or future—anything to carry us out of the dull or unbearable present. We cannot help being charmed with the idea, even while we are aware of the grave complications such a machine might have on the pattern of events."[83]

Even T. O'Conor Sloane, an extreme hard science editor who wanted each story to be a schoolbook lesson, had to admit that the rules of physical science must be bent occasionally: "To give life to science-fiction stories it is quite the accepted and acceptable thing to use what are really impossibilities and illogical to carry out the story. If the attempt was made to keep down to prosaic fact no one would read them."[84]

The new wave, examined in the following chapter, abjures the hard science conception of rationality based on physical science in favor of aesthetic truth, intensity of experience, and radical social vision. Where the hard science ideology demands thoughts like rocks, the new wave seeks feelings that flow. If the poetic symbol of this chapter is an industrial diamond, then the symbol for the next is a human tear.

4

THE

NEW

WAVE

New wave science fiction emerged as a cultural movement in the mid-1960s, but its elements existed long before. The first circle of new wave writers was centered on the British magazine *New Worlds*, edited by Michael Moorcock and introduced to American readers by anthologist Judith Merril. But it would be a mistake to say that the new wave began in Britain then washed across the Atlantic to the American shore. Individual authors in the United States were developing a new agenda for science fiction and would have become visible in any case.

I will leave to literary historians the task of weighing the influence of the British new wave on American science fiction. Michael Moorcock said that the aims of the *New Worlds* circle "had little to do with what Judith Merril and Harlan Ellison, for instance, later came to term the 'New-Wave' in U.S. science fiction."[1] Damon Knight, who has been called by a detractor the self-appointed "American guru of the so-called 'New-Wave,' "[2] said that his periodical anthology, *Orbit*, "has never had anything to do with the stylistic experimentation of the *New Worlds*/New-Wave scene."[3]

But, then, few authors and editors have been willing to declare themselves members of the new wave. The movement was loosely organized and never printed membership cards. Ted White, who alternately criticized and promoted the new wave when he was editor of *Amazing*, observed "that there is no true New Wave, in the sense of a single school of thought. Instead, there has been an explosion of ideas and ways of expressing them among a diverse group of writers—writers who often disagree with each other about their goals and desires for the field and for science fiction in general."[4] White said that the label new wave was applied after the fact to writers who shared only the single characteristic of differing from the traditional norms of science fiction.

I think history will decide the label has meaning nonetheless and that the authors in this cluster in my correlations did collectively transform SF in the late 1960s and early 1970s. The old wave was a diverse collection of styles and ideas, so there is no reason to demand that new wave be a monolith. Waves are composed of many little splashes in resonance with each other. Robert Silverberg, comfortable with the hard science approach but frequently identified with the new wave, has tried to find conceptual order in the chaos. In 1969 he wrote:

> Summarizing the conflicting viewpoints is no simple thing. The older writers, who are by no means closely organized or in any general agreement among themselves, appear to stand for straightforward, direct prose style, plots that demonstrate the ability of a strong and sympathetic protagonist to surmount all obstacles, the story situations that spring from an accurate understanding of the aims and methods of science. The younger writers prefer experimental storytelling methods that put no premium on easy clarity; they disdain standard plot formulas, regarding them as irrelevant to modern s-f; they see no reason why a story's central character must be "strong" in a physical or a moral sense, or why he must necessarily triumph over obstacles instead of being crushed by them; and they have so little interest in the aims and methods of science that they prefer to call themselves writers of "speculative fiction" rather than "science fiction."[5]

Writers deeply committed to the older conventions were especially likely to view the new wave as a monolith. Lester del Rey, who once dismissed the movement as a mere "New Ripple,"[6] saw it as a rejection of the scientific optimism that lay at the heart of traditional SF: "The philosophy behind New Wave writing was a general distrust of both science and mankind. Science and technology were usually treated as evils which could only make conditions worse in the long run. And mankind was essentially contemptible, or at least of no importance. There was an underlying theme of failure throughout. Against the universe, the significance of mankind was no greater than that of bedbugs—if as great."[7]

At least three times John Pierce fulminated in print against the new wave. In his view, "Everything about the New Wave betrays a lack of inner conviction, a 'world without values.' "[8] He said that the new wave accepts the *insig-*

nificance premise, "the idea that the universe is unknowable and life is meaningless," which leads to an "emphasis on the primacy of evil, on anti-heroes, on plotless stories, the rejection of science in favor of mysticism, and the worship of ugliness and disaster."[9] He found this nihilism most apparent in the works of J. G. Ballard, a member of the *New Worlds* circle:

> First, a total rejection of the scientific approach to the universe—which he presented as something completely incomprehensible and vaguely menacing. Second, a total disinterest in the fate of mankind—human life is seen as a "disaster area," as inevitably ruled by chance and therefore meaningless. Nor does any Ballard protagonist make the slightest effort to come to grips with the problems of existence—complete surrender and quasi-suicide are offered as the only course.[10]

The anger of some traditional SF readers toward some of the new wave's antiheroes may have come from their own need for heroes. Much of traditional SF offers larger-than-life heroic images of adults designed to guide and inspire boys as they mature. Writing about the superscience *Skylark* novels by E. E. "Doc" Smith, C. M. Kornbluth described the nature of much traditional SF: "What are these wild adventures . . . ? These mighty conquests, these vast explorations, these titanic battles? They are boyish daydreams, the power fantasies which compensate for the inevitable frustrations of childhood in an adult world."[11] If this is an apt description of what Pierce was defending, then the new wave is not nihilist but merely adult. Instead of inculcating society's values through overblown stereotypes of impossible heroes, its protagonists are sensitive explorers of both the illusions of conventional society and the possibilities for radical adventures.

One hard science writer and literary critic, James Blish, tried to describe the new wave and at the same time castigated it:

> It has consisted mainly of the following elements: (1) Heavy emphasis upon the problems of the present, such as overpopulation, racism, pollution and the Vietnam war, sometimes only slightly disguised by s-f trappings; (2) Heavy emphasis upon the manner in which a story is told, sometimes almost to the exclusion of its matter, and with an accompanying borrowing of devices old in the mainstream but new to science fiction, such as stream of consciousness, dadaism, typographical tricks, on-stage sex, Yellow Book horror and naughty words; (3) Loud claims that this is the direction in which science fiction must go, and all other forms of practice in the field are fossilized; (4) Some genuinely new and worthy experiments embedded in the mud.[12]

In 1968 Donald Wollheim reported that advocates of the new wave "insist that the 'old' science fiction belongs to the past, is stereotyped, and no longer represents the whirl of modern times, the revolution of new thinking and the mind-tingling innovations that seem to be prevalent in all the arts these days."[13] No fans of new wave, Alexei and Cory Panshin judged that SF fell into an uncreative period in the late 1950s and early 1960s.[14] Writing from the vantage of 1968, new wave author Barry Malzberg agreed:

> It is my contention that the majority of modern magazine science fiction is ill-written, ill-characterized, ill-conceived and so excruciatingly dull as to make me question the ability of the writers to stay awake during its composition, much less the readers during its absorption. Tied to an older tradition and nailed down stylistically to the worst hack cliches of three decades past, science fiction has only within the past five or six years begun to emerge from a long, dead period which occurred otherwise during what was probably the most interesting and significant decade of our national history. It has been able to emerge from its category trap only because certain intelligent and dedicated people have had the courage to wreck it so that it could crawl free. One must destroy, it seems, in order to do anything useful.[15]

Damon Knight wondered if the problem was more basic than a short dead period, perhaps an essential flaw in the hard science approach or in the writers who pursued it. "Language and engineering are demanding and, perhaps, essentially contradictory disciplines; again and again in science fiction we meet the engineer who knows his subject, has story-telling gifts, is ambitious and productive; can build and service a hi-fi rig—and has a seventh-grader's understanding of that equally complex instrument, the English language."[16]

THE NEW WAVE FACTOR

The second of the four factors that emerged in my factor analysis of authors clearly represents the new wave. Table 7 lists all twenty-six writers who achieved loadings above .35 for this factor. Some of the authors listed have already been mentioned as advocates of the new wave, including Malzberg, Ellison, Knight, and Merril. Experienced SF readers may feel that some names are out of place on the list. Of course, statistical analysis occasionally produces a false result just through random factors adding up to a large coefficient. But several authors listed were most active long before the mid-1960s when the new wave got its name, among them Sturgeon, Vonnegut, Huxley, Orwell, Bester, and Bradbury.

Table 7. New wave authors from the factor analysis

Author	Factor loading (N = 276)	Correlation (r) with new wave SF	
		(N = 409)	(N = 595)
1. Ellison	.637	.52	.49
2. Silverberg	.568	.39	.33
3. Knight	.562	.26	.22
4. Russ	.550	.35	.36
5. Dick	.549	.37	.33
6. Wilhelm	.547	.40	.41
7. Sturgeon	.531	.15	.14
8. Malzberg	.527	.41	.42
9. Aldiss	.520	.31	.28
10. Lafferty	.518	.20	.22
11. Budrys	.514	.24	.21
12. Tiptree	.504	.28	.31
13. Vonnegut	.498	.39	.38
14. Spinrad	.491	.38	.41
15. Delany	.477	.39	.36
16. Huxley	.458	.24	.27
17. Merril	.436	.36	.31
18. Orwell	.417	.27	.27
19. Brunner	.401	.28	.26
20. LeGuin	.396	.26	.22
21. Pohl	.393	.12	.10
22. Davidson	.390	.19	.15
23. Bloch	.383	.19	.22
24. Bester	.374	.15	.12
25. Bradbury	.371	.25	.24
26. Haldeman	.368	.26	.27

Other authors correlated with new wave, with r for N = 409 in parentheses, are: Wolfe (.38), Burgess (.37), McIntyre (.36), Lem (.33), Reamy (.32), Moorcock (.30), Benford (.27), Sheldon (.27), King (.27), Poe (.24), Donaldson (.24), Wylie (.23), Zelazny (.23), Vinge (.23), Varley (.22), Eklund (.22), Lovecraft (.21), Farmer (.20).

This analysis is not concerned with whether these men were members of a formal literary movement. Rather, the correlations express similarities in their styles and ideological values, determined by charting respondents' preferences. All the authors in the factor have some qualities in common, regardless of when they wrote and what label they applied to themselves.

There has been strenuous objection in the past to including respected earlier writers like Bradbury among the lesser lights of the new wave.[17] Such quibbles have often come from opponents of the new wave who do not want to see high-quality fiction included in the category. One could debate endlessly about which authorities should be allowed to define our terms. In a quantitative ethnography such as this, I defer to my respondents, whose answers inform us about the dominant conceptualizations of the science fiction subculture. In my respondents' estimation, Bradbury's style is about as close to new wave as is LeGuin's. Neither is as close to the center of the ideological factor as Ellison. Bradbury is closer to the new wave than he is to any other main faction.

Perhaps authors like Sturgeon, Vonnegut, Huxley, Orwell, Bester, and Bradbury can be called precursors of the new wave of the late 1960s. Lacking any other accepted term for the entire factor represented in Table 7, we can call all of it new wave. Then the movement of the late 1960s becomes the crest of the wave, which exaggerated elements already present in the works of these earlier authors.

The footnote to the table lists eighteen authors who might be included in the new wave but who do not appear in this factor for one reason or another. Each has a correlation above .20 with new wave. Only three of these names, Moorcock, Zelazny, and Farmer, were sufficiently well known to be included in the factor analysis of seventy-three authors. Farmer calls himself a highly eclectic writer who has tried many styles,[18] even writing a book about Tarzan, Edgar Rice Burroughs's character.[19] Zelazny and Moorcock are pulled toward Factor III as well as toward Factor II, the new wave group. Zelazny achieves a loading of .29 on the sword-and-sorcery or fantasy factor, compared with .31 on new wave, while Moorcock gets a loading of .22 compared with .24. In fact, both write both kinds of fiction. Moorcock is the more important one to discuss, because he was the key figure in organizing the British new wave around the magazine he edited, *New Worlds*. Sidney Coleman has described this multifaceted writer: "There are at least three Michael Moorcocks. Moorcock 1 is a prolific hack, author of an unending stream of sword-and-sorcery novels . . . Moorcock 2 is the energetic promoter of avant-garde speculative fiction. Moorcock 3 is a talented writer of science fiction."[20]

CHARACTERISTICS OF THE NEW WAVE

The new wave has often been described in terms of its literary ambitions, its concern for style and expression. Richard Lupoff said, "The new wave writers have thrown away such old and constricting shibboleths as plot, character and setting."[21] Another relatively unsympathetic critic, Alexei Panshin, felt that "the New Wave seems to be in favor of literary experimentation, non-linearity and a reemergence with the so-called 'literary mainstream.' "[22] Robert J. Hughes described the English new wave as a "blending of imaginative, speculative writing long characteristic of science fiction, and the introspective, impressionistic and sometimes surrealistic style of the modern poet."[23] For Judith Merril, the new wave is marked by the use of experimental techniques taken from other genres of contemporary literature.[24] The very experimental, surprising quality of the writers, she said, provides much of the interest for the reader: "I can't tell you where they're going, but maybe that's why I keep wanting to read what they write."[25] L. Sprague de Camp and Catherine Crook de Camp looked back on the new wave as a rejuvenating influx of modern techniques from twentieth-century high-culture literature: "In the 1960s, several younger writers sought to adapt to imaginative fiction the unconventional narrative techniques pioneered half a century earlier by the Irish writer James Joyce in his huge experimental novel *Ulysses* (1922). These methods include the stream of consciousness; the rapid shift of scene through time and space; the detailed, literal realism of the 'slice-of-life' story; and the avoidance of the structured plot of the well-wrought tale."[26]

The chief characteristics of the new wave can be delineated and some associated phenomena found through correlations between respondents' preference for new wave science fiction and preferences for other items in the questionnaire. Table 8 gives the correlation coefficients above .20 among the 409 good respondents, tying the new wave to terms describing literature types.

As the commentators might have predicted, there are strong correlations between new wave writers and avant-garde literature that experiments with new styles. The ten with the highest coefficients are Malzberg ($r = .43$), Ellison ($r = .40$), Spinrad ($r = .40$), Wilhelm ($r = .38$), Merril ($r = .35$), Vonnegut ($r = .34$), Dick ($r = .34$), Lem ($r = .33$), Aldiss ($r = .33$), and Delany ($r = .30$). The commentators might also have predicted that new wave science fiction itself would correlate with avant-garde, and indeed, Table 8 shows that it does at a high level ($r = .65$). This, then, is the central defining characteristic of the type: it emphasizes literary and aesthetic values, seeking to create the art of the future rather than the science of the future.

Table 8.   Correlation (r) between preference for new wave science fiction and
for related types (N = 409)

Literature type	Correlation (r) with new wave
Avant-garde fiction which experiments with new styles	.65
Fiction based on the social sciences	.40
Science fiction of the 1960s and 1970s	.39
Fiction that is critical of our society	.38
Fiction which deeply probes personal relationships and feelings	.37
British science fiction	.34
Feminist literature	.31
Stories in which the main character is sensitive and introspective	.29
Fiction concerned with harmful effects of scientific progress	.27
Poetry	.27
Ghost stories	.26
Tales of the supernatural	.26
Utopian political novels and essays	.25
Stories in which the main character is an average person	.24
Horror-and-weird	.23
Stories in which the main character is strange and unusual	.23
Science fiction art	.20

An excellent example is Samuel R. Delany's massive novel *Dhalgren*, the
personal journal of The Kid's sojourn in Bellona, a nearly deserted American
city. Delany exalts words rather than scientific facts and labors to express the
most intense experiences he can imagine. When a second moon appears in
the sky, the characters name it George after their favorite black rapist rather
than trying to chart its orbit and find a rational explanation for its sudden
appearance, as hard science heroes would have done. When the sun bloats
to cover half the sky, no scientific explanation is suggested. There are only
dramatic hints of some unknown catastrophe to suggest why Bellona alone
has lost its people and gained extravagant skies.

The implicit explanation is literary rather than scientific. Bellona exists so
that The Kid can experience everything intense and aesthetic and provocative
that a former mental patient and future poet could dream. Bellona has been

stripped of all the artistically uninteresting features of ordinary cities. What remains is a playground for the wild deviants who had been its underlife or who were attracted by the rumor that Bellona was out-of-sight. The book is radically sensate—The Kid feels and describes everything in vivid and often psychedelic detail. When he argues with his friend George the rapist, his vision alters: "His eyes will explode like blooming poppies, Kid thought. His teeth will erupt like diamonds spat by the mouthful. His tongue will snake the yards between us, nearly touch my mouth before it becomes pink smoke. Steam in two columns will hiss down from his nostrils."[27]

Some readers may take comfort in the theory that these images are symptoms of The Kid's psychosis, but really they are Delany's poetry. The Kid is sent to an alien world to bring us the sharpest sensations. For him, time "leaks; sloshes backwards and forwards, turns up and shows what's on its . . . underside."[28] The book begins in midsentence, "to wound the autumnal city,"[29] and ends in mid-sentence: "Waiting here, away from the terrifying weaponry, out of the halls of vapor and light, beyond holland and into the hills, I have come to"[30] Whether these are the two ends of a single sentence, meant to bring the book to closure, I cannot say.

An apparently incoherent collection of flashing experiences, Dhalgren achieves a high level of unity by reflecting upon itself. It is written on three levels. First, it communicates direct, immediate, passionate sensation. Second, it comments upon the sensations from various philosophical perspectives, suggesting possible meanings and interpretations. Third, it comments upon itself as literature.

Momentarily oppressed by the color gray, The Kid becomes fascinated by a plastic wineglass when "the glare on the interface between plastic and wine suddenly diffracted like an oil-slick and the glass was full of color." An inch away on the page is printed a marginal note added by The Kid to explain the circumstances under which he wrote the description of his visual experience: "Writing this while taking a crap: small consolations—expected a really unhealthy turd, baloney yellow and spinach black after a node of mucus. Mercifully what came was mostly liquid and left the water too murky to examine."[31] The reader gets not only the sensuous depiction of the original experience, but also the experience connected with the act of writing. Elsewhere, even the proofreading of the manuscript becomes part of the action.

The book includes lectures on aesthetics, philosphy, and human relations. Tak, one of The Kid's male sexual partners, contends that Bellona really is a case of science fiction. He says it perfectly exemplifies the three conventions of SF: "First: a single man can change the course of a whole world . . . Second: The only measure of intelligence or genius is its linear and practical application . . . Three: The Universe is an essentially hospitable place, full of earth-type planets where you can crash-land your spaceship and survive long enough to have an adventure."[32] Whether or not Bellona fulfills these qualifications, *Dhalgren* does not fulfill traditional definitions of science fiction unless one counts literary criticism as a science! If that is permissible, then the novel can be said to extrapolate what might be the next discoveries in that field and thus qualifies as traditional SF. But, as suggested by the high correlation linking Delany with the new wave ($r = .39$), it splendidly fulfills the definition of new wave.

The new wave interest in literary style also is well exemplified by Norman Spinrad's tour de force, *The Iron Dream*, which was recently banned in Germany. This book purports to be a novel by Adolf Hitler titled *Lord of the Swastika*, one of the most popular works in the sword-and-sorcery genre.[33] Hitler, it must be understood, did not lead the Nazi Party to power in Germany, nor did he launch the Second World War, preside over atrocities, or kill himself in 1945. He abandoned the tiny Nazi Party in 1919, came to the United States, became a magazine and comic illustrator, and turned to writing science fiction after mastering the English language. *Lord of the Swastika* supposedly won the Hugo award for best novel of 1954, which would surprise many science fiction fans who thought there was no Hugo for 1954, although they were awarded for 1953 and 1955. Spinrad has produced the novel that *our image* of Hitler might have written, complete with Hell's Angels and atomic bombs (unfamiliar to the real Hitler) and characters plainly based on Himmler, Hess, Goebbels, and Göring (whom Hitler did not know in 1919 when he supposedly emigrated).

The true lord of the swastika, hero Feric Jaggar, was born of racially pure parentage into a future world genetically corrupted by atomic radiation and psychically corrupted by the evil Dominators, whose personalities sap the wills of ordinary humans just as radiation saps the genes of the race. Upon reaching adulthood, Jaggar leaves Borgravia, a land overrun by inferior genetic mutations, and enters the High Republic of Heldon, the only fit residence for this blond, blue-eyed, genetically perfect specimen. Rising from obscurity, he strides toward the absolute power he must have in Heldon if he is to annihilate all mutations and restore the earth to purity. His symbol is the swastika, and his weapon, with which he personally wins battles, is a Great Truncheon, a magical phallic mace comparable to Siegfried's sword. Jaggar indeed is the kind of fantasy hero Hitler might have imagined, virile and courageous, leading his motorcycle Swastika Squad through purple prose and gushing gore to conquer Parrotfaces, Blueskins, Lizardmen, Harlequins, Bloodfaces, and Dominators: "Gunning his engine, Feric led the SS column down the avenue, an irresistible juggernaut of cannon, machine-gun bullets and truncheons, every last Helder fired to transcendent heroism by utter racial revulsion for the crazed and debased perversions of what was once human germ plasm that rioted and drooled and urinated obscenely all around them."[34]

THE SOCIAL SCIENCES

The literature type with the second strongest link to new wave is fiction based on the social sciences. The correlation between this variable and avant-garde is quite low ($r = .22$), considering the powerful connections of both types with new wave. This suggests that the two types reflect quite different systems of values, different ideological concerns, if not competing factions. Perhaps they provide powerful axes of variation for the entire genre, comparable to the science-technology axis described in the previous chapter. Figure 6 presents the correlations between each of these new wave attributes and those authors who are sufficiently well known to provide reliable statistics. Authors correlated at or above .20 with new wave by the 409 good respondents are represented by solid dots and are labeled. The open circles represent other authors.

Figure 6 does display a relationship between avant-garde and social science, because the authors are ranged in an oval rather than a circle, from lower left to upper right. The new wave writers, appropriately enough, are clustered in the upper right. But the oval is very loose, nothing like the tight band found in the graph of new science and new technology in the previous chapter. Therefore, these two attributes of new wave are rather weakly associated with each other and represent somewhat different sets of values.

Given that fiction based on the social sciences is somewhat remote from avant-garde, what does it mean? One way to find out is to look at correlations linking this variable with other types of literature. Social sciences are most strongly linked with fiction that deeply probes personal relationships and feelings ($r = .50$) and fiction that is critical of our society ($r = .47$). Also closely related are stories in which the main character is sensitive and introspective ($r = .40$), feminist literature ($r = .33$), and utopian political novels and essays ($r = .30$).

New wave interests in literary technique, personal feelings, and the social sciences have combined to produce several interesting stories about future developments in psychoanalysis and psychotherapy. Notable are novels by Ursula K. LeGuin and Roger Zelazny, which postulate innovations in psychoanalytic dream analysis. *The Lathe of Heaven* by LeGuin tells of a patient whose dreams magically influence reality and of his analyst, who unsuccessfully tries to improve the world by manipulating these effective dreams.

THREE DIMENSIONS OF SCIENCE FICTION

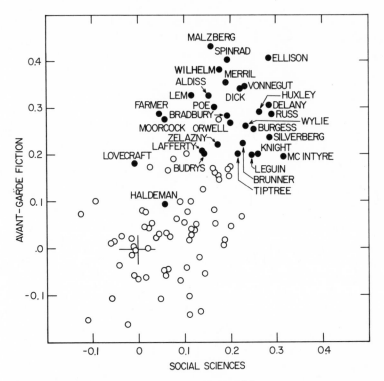

Figure 6.   Prime attributes of the new wave

LeGuin has highly praised Zelazny's similar story "He Who Shapes."[35] This short novel concerns a "neuroparticipant therapist" who shares and shapes the patient's dreams to make the analysis more thorough and efficient. Psychoanalysis is one of the "softest" branches of social science, and many social scientists reject the psychoanalytic approach completely. Zelazny's hero, Dr. Charles Render, has published an essay opposing the application of "hard" quantitative measurement (psychometry) to the human psyche. For him, psychoanalysis is an art demanding high skill and native talent, not something amenable to the rationalized technologies favored by hard science SF: "The quality of psychoparticipation phenomena can only be gauged by the therapist himself, at that moment outside of time and space as we normally know it, when he stands in the midst of a world erected from the stuff of another man's dreams, recognizes there the non-Euclidian architecture of aberrance, and then takes his patient by the hand and tours the landscape . . . If he can lead him back to the common earth, then his judgments were sound, his actions valid."[36]

Although stories such as this frequently find their plots in the arrogant or selfish machinations of a psychotherapist, they are basically sympathetic to the psychoanalytic approach. The methods of Freud and his disciples are very literary forms of mental exploration, naturally producing images and symbols favored by new wave writers. Psychoanalysis has its opponents, among them the rival therapists who follow behaviorism, some of whom have launched broad attacks on the validity of psychoanalytic treatment.[37] In an almost political sense, these two approaches are opposites. Psychoanalytically oriented therapies try to help a person explore himself in a relatively free and self-expressive fashion to achieve liberation from oppressive complexes. Behavior modification programs try to eradicate unwanted symptoms, often treating the patient as an incorrectly adjusted machine rather than as a person, to achieve desired control and conformity. Liberation versus control. In the first, the doctor is an artist, while in the second he is a mechanic. I will not say which is better.

A *Clockwork Orange,* by Anthony Burgess, which explores psychological control, is written in an avant-garde style designed apparently to put into extreme poetic relief the inhumanity of a mechanistic society. This novel is the autobiography of young Alex, told in a futuristic, Russianized teen talk called *nadsat.* Alex and his three *droogs* (friends) rape and pillage. Although ultraviolent, they are lovable barbarians, the most human characters in a hypocritical, mechanized society. Their aimless, assaultive passion contrasts with the cold and subtly cruel culture around them. As villains, they are the only possible heroes in an evil world. Alex's favorite hobbies are mugging drunks, raping *sharps,* and listening to classical music. During a rampage Alex is betrayed by his droogs and locked up for homicide.

After an *oozhassny* agony in the cold, gray *staja,* Alex is offered release if he submits to a form of behavior modification that will condition him against violence in an experimental program favored by the government. The doctors use real present-day techniques generally called aversion therapy or aversive counterconditioning.[38] Alex is injected with a drug that makes him sick then is forced to watch movies of extreme violence so that his nervous system will automatically respond with nausea and revulsion whenever he contemplates violence. When Alex complains that the experience is horrible, the doctor promises there will be many more sessions equally unendurable. "Of course it was horrible . . . Violence is a very horrible thing. That's what you're learning now. Your body is learning it . . . You are being made sane, you are being made healthy."[39]

Alex's aversion therapy involves no willing cooperation from the subject, no renunciation of his past misbehavior, no realization of his moral duty, no apology, no begging for absolution, no mercy. He is treated as a twisted lever in the social machine, to be forced back into the correct shape. The treatment is completely impersonal, based on the simple theory that Alex was conditioned to be deviant and now must be reconditioned. After the sessions are over, Alex is made the star of a scientific demonstration showing state officials how effective aversive counterconditioning is. He licks the shoes of a man who abuses him, showing how thoroughly he has been reshaped. The prison chaplain complains. "Choice . . . He has no real choice, has he? Self-interest, fear of physical pain, drove him to that grotesque act of self-abasement. He ceases also to be a creature capable of moral choice."[40] The minister of the interior rejects the chaplain's ethical qualms. "The point is . . . that it works."[41]

Early in the story Alex and his droogs terrorize an author and his wife, giving him a *tolchock* he'd never forget and doing the old *in-out in-out* on her. Alex reads a little of the bleeding man's manuscript, titled A *Clockwork Orange*, before ripping it up: "The attempt to impose upon man, a creature of growth and capable of sweetness, . . . laws and conditions appropriate to a mechanical creation, against this I raise my sword-pen."[42] Much later, after conditioning, Alex staggers unaware to the same doorstep, begging for help because he can no longer defend himself against the violence that fills his world. At first he and the author fail to recognize each other. Alex sees the published version of A *Clockwork Orange* and comments, "It seemed written in a very bezoomny like style, full of Ah and Oh and that cal, but what seemed to come out of it was that all lewdies nowadays were being turned into machines."[43]

Alex tells the writer that the doctors inadvertently conditioned him not only against violence but also against sex—and even against classical music, which they played as background to the violent films he was made to see while deathly ill. The writer tells Alex he has become a perfect victim, a perfect symbol of what the new, mechanistic society demands of its citizens. "They have turned you into something other than a human being . . . a little machine capable only of good."[44]

While Alex sleeps, the writer conspires with political friends to use Alex as a tool against the regime that conditioned him. By locking his door and playing loud classical music, they hope to force him to a politically useful suicide. Driven into a fit of conditioned agony, he leaps to a likely death.

But he survives, and so does the cynical government, which makes him its hero.

Early in his first-person narrative, Alex states the theme of the story, which is identical to that of the writer's book but phrased in nadsat. He believes himself a kind of hero, fighting for free will against the bureaucrats and social engineers who seek scientific legitimation for their power, who want all people to be under their absolute control. "Badness is of the self, the one, the you or me on our oddy knockies, and that self is made by old Bog or God and is his great pride and radosty. But the not-self cannot have the bad, meaning they of the government and the judges and the schools cannot allow the bad because they cannot allow the self. And is not our modern history, my brothers, the story of brave malenky selves fighting these big machines?"[45]

FICTION CRITICAL OF OUR SOCIETY

Ursula LeGuin has said, "The main function of the artist in modern society is to be and remain a heretic. I think if he's not a heretic, he's not an artist."[46] All science fiction fulfills this dictum, although perhaps the new wave does so most thoroughly. Hard science authors feel that our culture is not sufficiently bold in challenging the universe, and they sometimes criticize bureaucrats, capitalists, and ordinary citizens for selfishness and lack of vision. But the new wave questions our entire system. This means they must radically reexamine ordinary modes of thought and critically analyze societal institutions.

While hard science emphasizes rationality, the new wave often defends irrationality against the numbing chill of too much logic and against enslavement to the definitions of reality promulgated by bureaucrats and technocrats. Harlan Ellison jabbed at the nasty establishment in his story, " 'Repent Harlequin!' Said the Ticktockman." In a world poisoned by good sense and order, the Harlequin is a rebel prankster, striking back against gray sobriety with an aerial attack, showering the time and motion study workers with:

Jelly beans! Millions and billions of purples and yellows and greens and licorice and grape and raspberry and mint and round and smooth and crunchy outside and soft-mealy inside and sugary and bouncing jouncing tumbling clittering clattering skittering fell on the heads and shoulders and hardhats and carapaces of the Timkin workers, tinkling on the sidewalk and bouncing away and rolling about underfoot and filling the sky on their way down with all the colors of joy and childhood and holidays, coming down in a steady rain, a solid wash, a torrent of color and sweetness out of the sky from above, and entering a universe of sanity and metronomic order with quite-mad coocoo newness. Jelly beans![47]

Many other new wave stories have similar themes, notably Ray Bradbury's "Carnival of Madness," published in 1950, fifteen years earlier. The story takes place in the year 2249, and the law forbids fantasy, saying "nothing to be produced which in any way suggests ghosts, vampires, fairies, or any creatures of the imagination."[48] Two rebels, Stendahl and Pikes, conspire against this bleak edict which, Stendahl says, was imposed by men who wished to end all forms of escape from the world they ruled. Stendahl and Pikes achieve a fleeting triumph, brief as that gained by the Harlequin, when they recreate Poe's House of Usher and use its robotic demons to murder leading technocrats of the regime.

A concern for relationships and feelings, as well as criticism of stultifying social institutions, animates nearly every new wave work. Novel insights cannot really be communicated unless the style of writing is somewhat special, either so experimental as to be completely avant-garde or merely a sensitive instrument controlled by the writer. These qualities are not limited to American new wave writers, as the example of Anthony Burgess demonstrated. They are shared by some who write in languages other than English, as the following book by a native of Poland proves.

Stanislaw Lem's *Memoirs Found in a Bathtub* purports to be a manuscript found in the ruins of the Third Pentagon, far in the future, telling of a man's fruitless wanderings in a vast Building populated by spies, traitors, madmen, and other varieties of bureaucrat. Lem probably called the Building a Pentagon to facilitate publishing the book in the East Bloc; otherwise, nothing about the setting or the characters is distinctively American. The man hunts for meaning in a surreal, meaningless environment extrapolated from the alienation and bureaucratization that many social critics feel mark modern society. The protagonist is a new agent, coming to get his mission. First he can't find anyone to give him orders, then the orders are written in a code he can't understand, and finally the orders are stolen.

Everything is a code meaning something other than what it says, and everyone is a double or triple agent. The Building exists because there is an Antibuilding. There is no telling which is the Pentagon, and which the Kremlin. Conceivably, the man is Poland and the Building is the Soviet Union. Or the man is any human and the Building is any society. Everything is in code, and every decoded message is just another code. Everything also is completely random.

The one apparently genuine character the protagonist meets is a priest assigned to betray him, who suggests they intentionally play out the assigned denunciations, thereby exercising free will and thereby remaining true friends, whatever they actually do to each other. The priest wonders if the Building and the Antibuilding have so thoroughly infiltrated each other that there is only one Superbuilding:

> Perhaps there were originally two sides which, locked in mortal combat, eventually devoured one another. Perhaps, too, this is not a madness of men, but of an organization, an organization that grew too much and one day met a remote offshoot of itself, and began to swallow it up, and swallowed and swallowed, reaching back to itself, back to its own center, and now it loops around and around in an endless swallowing . . . In which case, there need be no other Building, except as a pretense to hide its autophagia.[49]

PERSONAL RELATIONSHIPS AND FEELINGS

The fresh emphasis on personal relationships and feelings brought to science fiction by the new wave has sometimes injected life into otherwise exhausted subjects. A prime example is *Beyond Apollo*, by Barry N. Malzberg, a novel that finds something radically new to say about the first interplanetary flight. This theme was already worn out by 1930, and only regained a little life around 1950, when a few hard science authors updated the technology of the heroes' spaceships. Malzberg updated the heroes.

Beyond Apollo is the psychiatric autobiography of Harry M. Evans, copilot of the first expedition to the planet Venus. The first Mars expedition failed in an obscure but horrible way, and now the space program's last chance also ends in madness. Evans will not give a coherent account of what happened on the flight. Did the Captain, archetypal science fiction hero, commit suicide in utter despair, or was he murdered by Evans, or did vile Venusians twist the minds of both? The novel's ambiguities, which are never clearly resolved, may be a statement about the confused meanings and motivations of the original Apollo flights. The ambiguities underscore the uncertainty of the future and the purpose of the real space program and of the technological society it represents.

Both the Captain and a psychologist named Forrest try to make Evans answer these questions. Evans seems to feel that he has answered, or at least tried to the limits of his ability to answer, but the answers are not satisfactory. Perhaps Evans finally gives the Captain a good answer, but one that makes the Captain's life meaningless; it may, in part, be responsible for his disappearance. Dr. Forrest demands clarity. He tested the ill-fated Mars crew, and he took responsibility for choosing Evans and the Captain for the Venus mission. He will use every psychiatric technique available to wring the truth from Evans, even at the cost of the man's death. But Forrest may be incapable of understanding the truth or even of recognizing it, because, as he says of himself, "I was not a humble man . . . I was not a man for having second thoughts! I believed in rigor, order, logic, and control, and converted these beliefs into my own self-assessment."[50]

The book is written in sixty-seven short chapters plus an epilogue. The first chapter, in its entirety, says, "I loved the Captain in my own way, although I knew that he was insane, the poor bastard. This was only partly his fault: one must consider the conditions. The conditions were intolerable. This will never work out."[51]

On the way to Venus, the Captain makes Evans play a game. Each in turn must answer a difficult question posed by the other, giving absolute truth in fifty words or less. The Captain starts with the question, "Why do you think we're on our way to Venus?"[52] This question might mean, "What evidence do you have that this is, in fact, a real spaceflight, rather than an illusion or a simulation?" But Evans tries to answer by stating the motivations behind the expedition. He says, "There's an enormous amount of hardware and administrative bureaucracy which must be utilized and is under severe pressure because of the Mars problem. Also, our going will keep people's minds off our international policy."[53] Wrong answer. Evans tries again. "Because man must explore . . . Man must forage outward and Venus is our California, our Spain, our moon. We must expand ceaselessly and restlessly because our curiosity and courage are the survival quotient of the race."[54] Wrong again. Evans is also wrong when he says, "We went to Venus . . . because our minds were really controlled by Venusians who wanted to lure us there and then kill us."[55] Evans wants to have his turn and ask the Captain about his sex life, so he tries to answer correctly again and again.

Finally the Captain accepts an explanation: "Events . . . control our lives, although we have no understanding of them nor do they have any motivation. Everything is blind chance, happenstance, occurrence; in an infinite universe anything can happen. After the fact we find reasons. We're going to Venus because the dice came up."[56]

Then it is Evans's turn. He asks about the Captain's sex life, but the Captain refuses to answer. At one point early in the narrative, Evans has told Forrest, "The Captain made an unspeakable sexual attack upon me. The rays in space or the pressure of the voyage must have unsettled his mind, and he said he had always had homosexual impulses and by God now he was going to act on them; if you couldn't do what you wanted to do thirty million miles from earth, when were you going to get to do it?"[57] Overcome by his passion, the Captain fell into the toilet and was ejected into space. Mad ravings, Dr. Forrest assumed.

Perhaps this account of the Captain's death is almost correct. The unspeakable sexual attack may have been the Captain's refusal to answer the question about his sex life. He commanded Evans to answer the question about the mission but then refused to follow the rules of the game when it was his turn to answer. Psychologically, this was an attack on Evans, having to do with a refusal to speak about sex.

The reader is left to ponder what really happened on the expedition. Of course *I* know the real answer. "Why do you think we're on our way to Venus?" Because Malzberg has tricked us into believing that we are. In fact, we are not on our way to Venus, and both Evans and the Captain are figments of Malzberg's imagination. The book is not the diary of a trip to Venus, but an imaginative, poetic exploration of human personality, including some darker facets of the mind that might be behind (in the sense of being the backside of) the real space program.

The fictional Dr. Forrest wants to master Evans's paranoid schizophrenia to learn a nonexistent truth about an expedition to Venus that never happened. For Malzberg, who really exists, paranoid schizophrenia is a main theme of the book, coequal with the meaning of spaceflight beyond Apollo. In the introduction to another story, Malzberg stressed the aesthetic quality of psychosis, saying, "I've long been a fan of schizophrenia."[58]

The controversy sparked by *Beyond Apollo* fairly exploded when the novel won the John W. Campbell Memorial Award in 1973. In the letter column of *Analog*, Poul Anderson angrily criticized the award committee, saying Malzberg directly contradicted the values for which Campbell had worked all his life. Although Anderson did not go into detail, the character of the Captain clearly represents a decayed version of the old hard science or space opera hero, such as Campbell had created in his own earlier fiction and preferred in the stories he published in *Astounding/Analog*.

In Anderson's view, *Beyond Apollo* did not deserve the award. He said it was "undeniably well-written but gloomy, involuted, and technophobic, perhaps the three qualities which John most strongly opposed."[59] He complained further about one criterion for the award, as announced by the committee, "realistic recognition of man's fallen state, a requisite of good literature." Man is not fallen, according to the hard science and heroic fantasy ideologies that Anderson represents.

The dispute over the award was in great measure a confrontation between the new wave and the old wave. But literary craftsmanship and aesthetic inventiveness transcend ideological divisions. The chief rejoinder came from one of the award judges, Harry Harrison, an author very similar to Anderson: "We are attempting to advance the quality and standards in the field of literary endeavor to which John Campbell devoted his life. It is irrelevant to attempt to guess whether he would have published the winning books or not."[60]

FEMINIST LITERATURE

During the years when the new wave washed into SF, male dominance of the field was for the first time challenged by an influx of thousands of women fans and a few dozen women authors. I discuss this change in detail in Chapter 7, so here I shall only note the fairly strong association between new wave SF and feminist literature ($r = .31$). A single example of the literature will show how a woman science fiction writer can connect metaphors of science with criticism of contemporary society from a feminist perspective.

Kate Wilhelm's novel *Fault Lines* begins as Emily Carmichael is trapped in bed by the collapse of her California house under the impact of an earthquake. Waiting to die or be dug out, she reviews the seventy years of her life in vignettes arranged by mood rather than chronology. The title carries several meanings. The novel traces the *lines* of Emily's genealogy, which like her home is fractured by fissures and *faults*—deaths, divorces, driftings apart. The faults are infractions as well as social fractures. Emily lays the blame (fault) on rigid ideologies (lines). People are torn apart, wrenched from each other, and sometimes ripped to pieces because they are too afraid to be honest, and success goes to fakes rather than to genuine souls.

But the fault lines are creative as well as destructive. Until her recent forced retirement, Emily has been the editor of the *Golden Gate Review*. She describes her talent as like that of a diamond cutter, chipping at fault lines to perfect the manuscripts she publishes. Emily was born in the great San Francisco earthquake, a geological upheaval that split her terrified mother from her geologist father.

Geology is an important metaphor for the novel, yet Emily herself is not science-minded. She idolizes her long-gone father, who was a successful teenage gold prospector and later a professor of geology. Yet she disapproves of her son, who has inherited her father's orientation to the science of the Earth. She argues bitterly with him, thinking to herself that she knows best and that the life he has chosen is stultifying and oppressive. Emily recalls, more than once, a beautiful moment when he was a child and danced at the seashore in celebration of life. But now he takes science, rather than human feelings, into the sea. He, in turn, blames her for never providing him with a father or legitimacy and for letting her home overflow with disreputable artists. She rejects his fascination with the physical sciences, believing it to be a doomed, obsessive quest for cold certainty. Emily's son, about to lose his wife, boasts for science, "We have to learn everything and then we can make predictions, have some kind of control, and the world will be a safer place."[61] Emily thinks this is an ideology of estrangement and self-delusion, betokening lack of real wisdom.

The novel often accuses science from the perspective of the literary culture. One of Emily's acquaintances tells a ridiculous "story about an archaeologist who dug up bits of Sears Roebuck pottery and pieced them together night after night while the Indians sat in a circle watching silently, solemnly."[62] But this is not a book in praise of the past against a technocratic future, because Emily has always despised fundamentalism and the traditional roles of women.

In childhood, when she was taken to visit her mother's family, whom her beloved father hated, Emily refused to learn to stitch, crochet, knit, or darn. Although she was whipped again and again, she refused to conform to the old patterns. Maury, a close friend, once told her, "You make no concessions at all to customs, to mores. You are an anarchist, you live in a world without standards, and few others can function in such a world." When Emily replies that she is quite successful as a person and as an editor despite her refusal to act the traditional female role, Maury says there remains a good reason why people condemn her. "Because you threaten the system and if the system fails, civilization collapses."[63] Wanda, a conventional woman, complains, "You've been able to live your life like a man, with no responsibilities at all. If we all lived like you do, there wouldn't be any civilization."[64]

Emily "thought of the fall of civilization because a person, especially a woman, gets out of line early and never finds her place in it again, and even comes to doubt the importance or necessity of the line."[65] Perhaps this is the fault line of the title: an ideological line concerning the proper manner of maintaining genealogical lines. The line is faulted in the sense of blameworthy, because it condemns women to an existence not fully human, and now is faulted in the sense of broken, because Emily has refused to accept it.

As she sees it, Emily triumphs in her story because she remains true to herself. Yet the novel is not a simplistic tract. Wilhelm examines the human meaning and the tragedy of being an independent, sensitive woman in the twentieth century. There are no easy solutions. Despair is a constant companion, held at bay only through love of life. Once Emily asks, "Maury, is there anyone you know who hasn't fucked up his life real good?"[66] He shakes his head. Another time she admits to her old publisher, who always respected her professional competence, "I have the feeling I'm adrift in the sea . . . Every time I think I can see something to cling to, it turns out to be part of an octopus, and it's going to take me under."[67]

Fault Lines describes a woman—and a society—with nothing to cling to but courage. Old supports, such as traditional sex roles or science and technology, are of no value. There is not even a hint that new supports, other than life itself, might ever be found.

HARMFUL EFFECTS OF SCIENTIFIC PROGRESS

Table 8 shows a moderate correlation between the new wave and fiction concerned with harmful effects of scientific progress ($r = .27$). I suspect that the relationship between these types is somewhat stronger than the coefficient says. All our computed correlation coefficients are estimates, some of which may be too high, and others too low. The pilot study questionnaire sent to fanzine editors produced a much higher correlation between these two variables ($r = .40$), and the Iguanacon questionnaire on science fiction films produced a coefficient almost identical to that in the pilot study ($r = .37$). All three sets of data indicate that the harmful effects of scientific and technological development constitute an important theme for the new wave, one of the ways in which it is critical of our society.

A technophobic new wave novel especially rich in symbolism is *Frankenstein Unbound* by Brian Aldiss, a leading member of the *New Worlds* circle.[68] Like Mary Shelley's novel *Frankenstein*, this imaginative sequel is a cautionary tale, warning humanity to beware of the hubris of science. In an interview Aldiss said, "Science fiction *should* be subversive, it shouldn't be in the game of consolations, it should shake people up."[69] In another interview he said the new wave "slams out hard at belief in imperialism and technology as life-enhancers."[70]

Nowhere is that more true than in *Frankenstein Unbound!* The protagonist is Joseph Bodenland, a deposed presidential adviser in the year 2020, vaguely trying to endure a world racked by racial war. Atomic bombs, the Promethean fire of modern science, have produced time-slips—like Dickson's time storms or the jostling zones of Leinster's "Sidewise in Time"—which throw fragments of different ages and possibilities in and out of contact with each other.

For Bodenland, the increasing magnitude of the atom-triggered temporal dislocations signals the end of a myth, "the overshadowing belief of our time—that ever-increasing production and industrialization bring the greatest happiness for the greatest number all round the globe."[71] The second chapter consists entirely of an editorial from the *Times*, which says, "The Intellect has made our planet unsafe for intellect. We are suffering from the curse that was Baron Frankenstein's in Mary Shelley's novel: by seeking to control too much, we have lost control of ourselves."[72]

Bodenland writes to his absent wife that he can no longer think straight; his own intellect has received too great a shock. The time-slips have undercut rationality. Promethean technological society has tried to make history and in reaction history has become incoherent and is unmaking technological society. He tells her: "Reality is going to pot. One thing's for sure—we never had as secure a grasp on reality as we imagined. The only people who can be laughing at the present are yesterday's nutcases, the parapsychologists, the junkies, the ESP-buffs, the reincarnationists, the science-fiction writers, and anyone who never quite believed in the homogenous flow of time."[73]

Pieces of other Earths appear and disappear around Bodenland's house, and he drives off to explore one in his well-armed atomic Land Rover. Trapped by another slip, he finds himself in a Switzerland of 1816, a fantastic Switzerland in which there is not only a group of visiting English authors—among them Mary Shelley—but also all the characters of *Frankenstein*. For a while two stories proceed in parallel. Part of the time Bodenland tries to make contact with Victor Frankenstein and stop him from carrying out his plan to make a race of perfect humans out of pieces of corpses. But Bodenland also meets Mary Shelley—along with Percy Bysshe Shelley and Lord Byron— and the two share love and wisdom across the centuries. At this point, she has put down her novel half-finished, and he tells her it is crucial that she complete the book. He seeks guidance from her on how to avert the apparently real Frankenstein tragedy progressing in the world where they met. For Bodenland, and for Aldiss, *Frankenstein* is a compelling symbol, "because Frankenstein was the archetype of the scientist whose research, pursued in the sacred name of the increasing knowledge, takes on a life of its own and causes untold misery before being brought under control."[74]

This does not mean that Bodenland finds early nineteenth-century Switzerland an ideal society by virtue of its simple technology. The civilization of two centuries later has a more developed sense of justice and personal freedom, as he discovers painfully when kept in jail for months on mere suspicion. There is a multifaceted pessimism in *Frankenstein Unbound*, much like the attitude Aldiss once said was characteristic of his circle of writers: "At the Heart of the *New Worlds'* New Wave—never mind the froth at the edges— was a hard and unpalatable core of message, an attitude to life, a scepticism about the benefits of society or any future society."[75]

Step by step, Bodenland becomes more involved with Victor Frankenstein and just fails to stop the scientist from creating a bride for his first monster. Then he kills Victor and takes his place in the drama. He drives his atomic Land Rover after the monsters in a wild chase across the Arctic ice. On the way he passes Peenemünde, the secret base where that real Frankenstein, Wernher von Braun, created the first long-range guided missile, the V-2. Von Braun's German spaceflight enthusiasts developed this ultimate delivery vehicle for lethal warheads in order to go to the moon.[76] Aldiss wants us to feel that rocket engineers seek to reach the stars by climbing a mountain of corpses, just as Victor Frankenstein sought to make better humans by stitching together pieces of cadavers.

At the end Bodenland comes upon the pair of monsters at the edge of a strange city, perhaps belonging to a future age inhabited by a culture of Frankenstein monsters. Ripped by blazing tracers from Bodenland's heavy gun, the dying monster-man prophesies: "Though you seek to bury me, yet will you continuously resurrect me! Once I am unbound, I am unbounded!"[77] Indeed, by 2020, the bicentennial of Mary Shelley's novel, the Frankenstein principle has become unbounded. The atomic war has transformed all space and time into precariously animated monster-worlds, stitched together from fragments of natural worlds. Mary Shelley warned us about the harmful effects of scientific progress, and *Frankenstein Unbound* suggests there may be no way to regain control over science or to morally redeem the soul of our damned species.

The potential danger of high technology was a very common theme in science fiction long before the new wave. Two of the best-loved stories from the Golden Age of *Astounding Science Fiction* concerned the threat of Armageddon from nuclear plants gone out of control. Heinlein's 1940 story "Blowups Happen" concerns the race to develop both technical and social means to manage atomic energy before the world's one vast nuclear power generator explodes. Lester del Rey's 1942 story "Nerves" follows the medical and technical staff of a runaway isotope factory as they struggle to contain an atomic reaction inexorably developing toward cataclysm.

Although both stories illustrate vividly the prospect of atomic doom, their mood is exciting rather than depressive, optimistic even though leading characters are brought to the brink of exhaustion and nervous breakdown. In the end courageous, intelligent men tame the atom. These heroes are not alienated from science and technology but intimately involved with them, mentally calculating mathematical formulas while they grapple directly with radioactive materials, clad in suits of armor and guided by phenomenal expertise. Thus these stories are paeans to man's ability to shape his destiny through technology, not technophobic warnings against progress.

POLITICS OF THE NEW WAVE

The June 1968 issue of *Galaxy Science Fiction* carried competing advertisements for and against American participation in the Vietnam War. Seventy-two science fiction personalities, including thirteen of the authors on my list, announced, "We the undersigned believe the United States must remain in Vietnam to fulfill its repsonsibilities to the people of that country." Another eighty-two people, including twenty-five of the authors on my list, said, "We oppose the participation of the United States in the war in Vietnam." In the Iguanacon data the thirteen hawk authors have a mean correlation of $r = .23$ with hard science SF, but only $r = .05$ with new wave. In contrast, the twenty-five dove authors correlate on average $r = .21$ with new wave but $r = -.01$ with hard science. Thus in 1968, when the new wave had just burst upon SF, it was associated with liberal political views, in contrast to the conservatism of hard science.

Chapter 2 showed that the new wave was significantly associated ($r = .29$) with political liberalism, as measured by a simple political scale taken from the NORC General Social Survey. In addition to the NORC question, the Iguanacon surveys included a simpler one I had used in the pilot study: "In general, how do you classify yourself with respect to current political issues? Radical? Liberal? Moderate? Conservative?" Among the 409 good respondents, these two political questions were highly correlated ($r = .80$), and the simpler question was connected to new wave at essentially the same level ($r = .28$) as the NORC item ($r = .29$). But in the pilot study the simple four-response political item achieved a really powerful correlation with new wave ($r = .52$).

The 1974 pilot study was done four years earlier than the Iguanacon surveys, and the respondents were born on average seven years earlier. I suspect that the discrepancy in the coefficients linking liberalism and new wave represents change, not error. In the late 1960s, when the fanzine editors formed their first impression of new wave, it was considered very radical—propagandizing against the Vietnam War and in favor of all the radical cultural experiments of that revolutionary decade. But people and nations change. By 1978 the new wave had matured, and the political issues of the 1960s had faded from America's consciousness. Just as student revolt had disappeared from college campuses, political battles had all but disappeared from science fiction. Indeed, the status of women in our society may have been the only conventional political issue at all relevant for participants at Iguanacon. By the time of this convention, new wave was perceived as somewhat closer to the political center than my fanzine editors had seen it.

Yet the new wave remained noticeably on the left. Ellison, who publicly supported the Equal Rights Amendment at Iguanacon, was certainly identified as liberal ($r = .32$). He is proud of his "deep and outspokenly anti-Establishment commitment and activities in the civil rights movement and anti-Viet Nam struggles."[78] Among others on the left were Tiptree ($r = .26$), Silverberg ($r = . 23$), Russ ($r = .21$), Spinrad ($r = .21$), and McIntyre ($r = .21$). Russ and McIntyre were associated with feminism in respondents' minds, as I shall discuss in Chapter 7. McIntyre has lectured to the Science Fiction Writers of America on how to avoid sexism in the use of pronouns.[79] Among the authors correlated with the political right were Rand ($r = .29$) and Heinlein ($r = .21$).

Figure 7 looks at the politics of nine authors, seven of them identified with

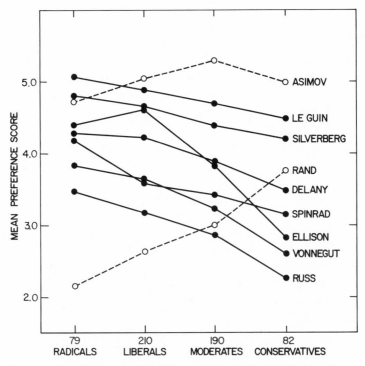

Figure 7. Politics of respondents and preferences for nine authors.

the new wave. Each dot on the author lines represents the author's mean popularity in one of four groups of respondents, distinguished by the four-response political item. Asimov, who does not correlate significantly with the political questions, and right-wing Ayn Rand are included for comparison. Each of the seven new wave writers gets a higher average rating from respondents on the left than from respondents on the right. Ellison seems a bit more favored by the 210 liberals than by the 79 radicals, perhaps hinting that some radicals feel his commercial success constitutes "selling out" to the establishment.

The fact that new wave offers radical alternatives does not necessarily mean it completely rejects the tenets of hard science. Among the 409 good respondents, the association between preference for hard science and preference for new wave is very weakly negative ($r = -.11$). As mentioned earlier, there may be a slight positive bias built into all the preference correlations, but even if one takes account of this factor it is hard to see how the real association could be any more negative than about $-.15$.

For many science fiction fans, the question is not whether they should like hard science *or* new wave. They already like hard science, or they would not be members of the subculture; the question is whether they like new wave too. The new wave certainly is an ideological faction of authors concerned with some contemporary issues of style and social issues. Fans who like them may simply be a bit more cosmopolitan than others, able to appreciate these somewhat argumentative and poetic works along with the classics of the field.

We can explore this fine point in ideological analysis by looking at the authors favored by new wave fans, the 156 respondents who rated new wave either 5 or 6 on the preference scale. Thirty-three writers achieved mean ratings over 4.50 with this subset of fans, and fifteen of them have substantial correlations with new wave ($r = .20$ or over, $N = 409$). Six authors on the list are more identified with hard science, and six with sword-and-sorcery. Ursula K. LeGuin and Harlan Ellison are tied for first on the list, with mean ratings of 5.18, but Isaac Asimov is a close third with 5.12. Fritz Leiber, associated with sword-and-sorcery, and Larry Niven, a hard science writer, are tied for fifth at 5.08, followed by new wave authors James Tiptree, Jr. (5.07) and Robert Silverberg (5.03).

The well-known author showing the greatest ratings difference is Robert Heinlein, who got a mean preference score of 5.05 from all 595 respondents but 4.92 from the 156 new wave fans. Among the 165 respondents who rate new wave at 2 or lower, Heinlein's mean popularity score is 5.23, highest of any author. Many fans and critics consider Heinlein to be a thoroughly illiberal right-winger,[80] an opinion fueled by his public support of a strong

THREE DIMENSIONS OF SCIENCE FICTION

defense and of economic libertarianism.[81] Ted White has commented, "One of the party lines of the so-called new wave movement of the late sixties was the belittlement of Heinlein, both in terms of his impact upon the field and his worth as an author."[82] Yet even among new wave fans, only eleven writers got higher ratings than Heinlein. Those who prefer the new wave do not substantially reject traditional science fiction; instead they seek ideological breadth and cosmopolitanism.

FACTOR ANALYSIS OF THE NEW WAVE

To gain perspective on the subfactions within the science fiction ideologies, I used the technique of factor analysis. When I tried this with hard science, in a series of computer runs not worth detailing here, I failed to find evidence of subfactions. At best, the analyses separated some of the older authors from more recent ones and distinguished those who also wrote fantasy from those who did not. In contrast, the new wave is divided into real subfactions. For factor analysis I selected the 266 good respondents who were familiar with at least twenty-five new wave writers, and the twenty-seven authors most associated with the ideology. An exploratory computer run produced seven factors,[83] although only four significant groups really stand out: precursors, feminists, machos, and fantasts.

Aldous Huxley and George Orwell, as a pair, correlate most highly with utopian novels and essays $(r = .34)$, undoubtedly because of their dystopias, *Brave New World* and *1984*. They also correlate with fiction that is critical of our society $(r = .27)$, fiction concerned with harmful effects of scientific progress $(r = .27)$, and with mainstream literature $(r = .25)$. Clearly these are precursors of the new wave, not current members.

As a group Ellison, McIntyre, Merril, Russ, Tiptree, and Wilhelm correlate most highly with feminist literature $(r = .46)$, and they show distinctive associations with fiction that deeply probes personal relationships and feelings $(r = .34)$ and stories in which the main character is sensitive and introspective $(r = .25)$, two variables that express traditional feminine values. Ellison, loaded lowest on this factor, is the only man in the group. This factor of new wave is the only one rated higher by women fans than by men $(r = .23)$.

Farmer, Haldeman, Silverberg, Spinrad, and Vonnegut represent a distinctively masculine contingent of the new wave, the macho subfaction. In many respects this group expresses the same ideology as the feminists. Both are associated with the political left, coincidentally to the same degree on the NORC question $(r = .23)$. Both are associated with avant-garde fiction that experiments with new styles $(r = .22, r = .30)$, both are correlated with science fiction of the 1960s and 1970s ($r = .35$, $r = .26$), and both are tied to fiction concerned with harmful effects of scientific progress ($r = .23$, $r = .21$). But where the feminists are preferred by women, this group is preferred by men ($r = .27$), and it is linked to stories in which the main character is brave and aggressive.

Finally, LeGuin, Moorcock, and Zelazny in one factor and Lovecraft and Poe in another represent new and old sections of the bridge from new wave to the fantasy cluster. They correlate with tales of the supernatural ($r = .21$, $r = .39$), sword-and-sorcery ($r = .20$, $r = .26$), and fantasy ($r = .27$, $r = .22$). Poe and Lovecraft are most strongly associated with horror-and-weird ($r = .51$), a style of writing that evokes the pessimism and the interest in psychological probing of the contemporary new wave.

Another perspective on the structure of the new wave can be gained by factor-analyzing types of literature rather than authors. Fifteen types are correlated with new wave in the whole group of 595 respondents. Because the results of factor analysis depend on the choice of items, and this mapping is of concepts rather than writers, the divisions will not be exactly the same as those just mentioned. However, the four factors produced by an unrestricted analysis make complete sense, as listed in Table 9.[84]

Table 9. Factor loadings of eleven literature types (N = 409)

Literature type	Factor I	Factor II	Factor III	Factor IV
Tales of the supernatural	.84	—	—	—
Horror-and-weird	.79	—	—	—
Ghost stories	.77	—	—	—
Fiction which deeply probes personal relationships and feelings	—	.69	—	—
Fiction based on the social sciences	—	.60	—	—
Feminist literature	—	.45	—	—
Fiction that is critical of our society	—	—	.61	—
Utopian political novels and essays	—	—	.52	—
Fiction concerned with harmful effects of scientific progress	—	—	.50	—
Avant-garde fiction which experiments with new styles	—	—	—	.86
New wave science fiction	—	—	—	.58

The first factor groups three types of literature that correlate only weakly with new wave: tales of the supernatural, horror-and-weird, and ghost stories. Obviously, this is the peninsula of the fantasy cluster that extends in the direction of the new wave. The second and third factors also each group three items, coming rather closer to the heart of new wave. Factor II connects psychology and social science to feminism. Factor III is critical of contemporary society and interested in considering radical social alternatives. Finally, Factor IV connects the new wave itself to the avant-garde. Four items, although individually connected slightly to new wave among the 595 respondents, did not appear in any factor: science fiction art, poetry, mainstream literature, and British science fiction.

CONCLUSION

The new wave is a large, fairly cohesive ideological and stylistic faction of authors who present alternatives to traditional science fiction and to contemporary society. It is tied in some way to the fantasy cluster, and its main internal division is between feminist and macho writers. The term new wave has come to mean something broader than the short-lived movement of the late 1960s. Until the science fiction subculture develops a more comprehensive term, new wave can be considered the generic name for the cluster of styles and values explored in this chapter. Some might object to the label "new" for a movement that has endured for two decades, but there is a scholarly precedent: musicologists still refer to certain music of the fourteenth century as *Ars Nova* or "new art."

Some writers whom my correlations identify with the new wave have called the division between the old wave and new wave artificial and have said that to the extent there ever was a division within SF, the factions have rejoined. Ellison wished we "could get past the senseless animosity of journalese conveniences like 'old wave' and 'new wave.' "[85] Delany called the rupture more propagandistic than real.[86] Yet the correlations in this chapter tell us that a distinct set of values about life and literature is expressed most forcefully by the new wave. This is not just the perspective of young writers or a generational phenomenon, because hard science SF and all parts of the fantasy cluster are alive and well. Something entered SF in the 1960s—or emerged from hiding within SF—something important that has become a permanent part of the genre.

Paul Walker said the experimental stylists of the new wave improved the quality of SF writing and characterization. "And more importantly, they opened the floodgates of the 1960s and let all the social turmoil of the age pour into the genre."[87] Terry Carr said the new wave revived science fiction's sense of wonder by providing "a new consciousness, more flexible attitudes, a realization that science fiction has come alive again as a possible contributing force to changing the future."[88] For Damon Knight this has meant not only a revitalization but a reconciliation, as SF rejoined the traditions of good literature and social criticism it may have abandoned under the influence of men like Gernsback.[89]

Hard science writer and editor Ben Bova contended that when new wave washed onto the mainland of science fiction, it irrigated but did not permanently flood the field. "The New Wave–Old Wave controversy evaporated some time ago when writers on both sides started taking the best features of each to make their stories stronger and better. Which is the way most 'artistic' quarrels end: in synthesis."[90] Yet the quarrel did not end in a uniform, homogenized literary genre. Divisions remain, and this chapter has demonstrated that the social and stylistic ideology of the new wave remains a major division of science fiction.

5

THE

FANTASY

CLUSTER

The territory of fantasy lies between the culturally antagonistic nations of hard science and new wave. Several hard science writers are also known for stories of action-adventure, and antique space opera paves the bridge to fantasy. On the other side, horror-and-weird spans the gap from the new wave to the fantasy cluster. One can view all the fiction described in this book as a vast supercluster of fantasy in the usual meaning of that term. In a famous definition, Sam Moskowitz implied that the science in the fiction was only a trick for facilitating stories that are in essence fantasy: "Science fiction is a branch of fantasy identifiable by the fact that it eases the 'willing suspension of disbelief' on the part of its readers by utilizing an atmosphere of scientific credibility for its imaginative speculation in physical science, space, time, social science and philosophy."[1]

Others have seen an inseparable bond between science fiction and fantasy. Fletcher Pratt argued, "All fiction is fantasy!"[2] Anthony Boucher, cofounder of *Fantasy and Science Fiction*, said, "What SF fans really like is fantasy, but they don't like it called that."[3] Samuel Merwin, editor of *Startling Stories*, once said, "Granted, fantasy, the macabre and such have little to do with science. But even in its purest sense science fiction is fantasy wearing a tight girdle."[4] That is, SF follows various restrictive conventions, the "atmosphere of scientific credibility" mentioned by Moskowitz, to achieve the purposes of fantasy. Merwin once tried to distinguish the two and, finding it difficult, concluded, "Stf is a sector of fantasy. An attempt by the author at some sort of quasi-logical explanation seems to us to be the badge of science fiction as distinct from other branches of fantasy."[5]

Thus SF is unfanciful fantasy—fantasy that pretends to be reasonable.

Merwin saw in this apparent contradiction an opportunity for SF to be something more than mere entertainment: "Science fiction is great at times, not because it applies science, but because it allows the trained human imagination to leap beyond the bounds of science convincingly. In short, it is magic—and as long as it *is* magic, we're for it, all equations notwithstanding."[6]

For Poul Anderson, science fiction is distinguished from other varieties of fantasy by a special assumption: "It is the basic scientific one, that the universe makes sense, that the rational and exploratory human mind can come to an understanding of things."[7] He agrees with Merwin and Moskowitz that even the best and most archetypal SF stories often describe worlds and events that are rather remote from our experience. But if the story is science fiction rather than raw fantasy, there is a connection. "In science fiction, however wild the story postulate, we find an implication that it ties in somehow with what we do know of science; that it's describable in rational terms."[8]

Narrative can be divided into three categories. First, there are stories of the *actual*. To the extent that it is possible to know the world, or at least to describe it from a particular vantage, histories, ethnographies, biographies, and news reports tell about things as they actually are. Second, there are stories of the *possible*. They describe situations and characters believed not to exist at present, but governed by familiar laws and arising from processes which we believe may exist. Of course, deciding what is possible is a matter of judgment. Robert A. W. Lowndes argued, in various issues of his magazine, *Future Science Fiction*, that a science fiction writer was justified in treating his own religious beliefs as facts on which he could base a science fiction story, while religion in which the writer did not believe could only be the basis of fantasy.[9] The third category is that of the *impossible*.

In the first issue of *Fantasy and Science Fiction*, then titled *The Magazine of Fantasy*, publisher Lawrence E. Spivak defined fantasy as "the wondrous recounting of the impossible-made-convincing."[10] An advertisement for a short-lived rival magazine, *Fantasy Fiction*, tried to distinguish the two types: "Science fiction requires that the reader adjust himself to the idea that the writer is dealing with what may be possible; fantasy requires an adjustment to the known impossible for purposes of amusement at a good story."[11] In the second issue of *Fantasy Fiction* Lester del Rey said, "Fantasy depends on the reader being willing to fool himself during the story and believe in what he knows is impossible; science fiction depends on the author being able to fool the reader during the story into believing what he thinks may be possible."[12]

A parallel distinction often made between science fiction and fantasy is that the *causes* of crucial events are conceptualized quite differently in each. Every kind of fiction lets its characters exercise free will occasionally, but in science fiction there is another, defining source of action—the natural world operating according to rational, mechanical principles. Fantasy, in contrast, tells of many events caused by supernatural agents—the deeds of gods and demons. According to L. Sprague de Camp, a leading author in both styles, science fiction is "based upon scientific or pseudoscientific assumptions," while fantasy is "based upon supernatural assumptions."[13]

For Richard Kyle, science fiction and fantasy are both subcategories of imaginative fiction. This is a good typology. The overarching category of fantastic literature that includes SF is called imaginative fiction; the smaller category of fantastic literature that stands alongside SF is called fantasy fiction. This avoids confusion caused by using the term *fantasy* for concepts on two different levels of generality. Kyle defines the three terms, preserving the idea that SF should be rational in the sense that events have mechanical causes, and stating in different form the idea that fantasy may tell of the purposeful actions of supernatural beings:

> *Imaginative fiction:* The branch of literature in which the events that occur are not—so far as it is known to the author—possible in the real world.
> *Science fiction:* The branch of imaginative fiction in which all things are subject to law.
> *Fantasy fiction:* The branch of imaginative fiction in which there is an agency from which all law and power devolves.[14]

Some proponents of the hard science ideology reject such supernaturalism. In 1953, introducing the first issue of his last science fiction magazine, *Science-Fiction Plus*, Hugo Gernsback said he intended to publish a purist's magazine, without any taint of fantasy:

> Let me clarify the term Science-Fiction. When I speak of it I mean the truly scientific, prophetic *Science*-Fiction with the full accent on SCIENCE. I emphatically do not mean the fairy tale brand, the weird or fantastic type of what mistakenly masquerades under the name of Science-Fiction today. I find no fault with fairy tales, weird and fantastic stories. Some of them are excellent for their entertainment value, as amply proved by Edgar Allan Poe and other masters, but when they are advertised as Science-Fiction, then I must firmly protest.[15]

But readers' complaints to magazines, demanding that fantasy be excluded, were often greeted with counterarguments, including the frequent observation that there is no consensus over where to draw the line. One reader told Samuel Mines, editor of *Startling Stories*, "If I can't believe a story as perhaps possibly occurrable, or if it doesn't impress me as being realistic, then it's not science-fiction." Mines disagreed and resisted the readers' call for a purge:

> Out the window goes 90% of the great imaginative stories of all time. The delicate fluttering wings of fantasy are not for you. Your ears are not attuned to the music of the spheres, they hear only the dull grind of clashing gears, the ponderous rhythm of the equations, the squeak of the slide rule. Strip literature of its gauzy wings and you have textbooks; eliminate the dreamers and you are left with clods. Is this your blueprint for the arts—for life? Perish forbid. [16]

The editor of *Thrilling Wonder Stories* was more direct, telling Joe Kennedy to "crawl back into the bolt bin and pull the lid down firmly into place after you," when Kennedy submitted the following limerick:

> A magazine seldom a bore
> Began using fantasy more.
> But the fans hollered "No!
> This old hog-wash must go!
> Or else there is gonna be war."[17]

Several editors and authors have noted that the line between the possible and the impossible does not run along the traditional border between SF and fantasy, so any attempt to separate the genres would be difficult and probably unproductive. In 1951 the editors of *Fantasy and Science Fiction* resisted distinguishing the two kinds of fiction of their magazine's title: "But if the line is to be drawn, we feel strongly that it should come at a different point than the usual one. Extrapolation of probable science, as practiced notably by such as de Camp and Simak, can be legitimately called *science* fiction; space-warps, galactic drives, BEMs [Bug-Eyed Monsters] and time machines are as purely fantasy as werewolves or vampires."[18]

This comment reminds one of the issues raised at the end of Chapter 3. The hard science ideology demands that science accomplish some things which are as yet impossible. So science fiction postulates fantastic, magical means of doing the impossible but gives them seemingly rational engineering names. As the de Camps see it, tradition, not possibility, defines the limits of science fiction: "Whether the things in the story are possible does not necessarily tell us which class a story belongs in. There is more evidence for the existence of werewolves than there is for the possibility of time travel. Yet a werewolf story is classed as fantasy, while a time-travel tale is considered science fiction."[19]

Thus the distinction between fantasy and science fiction is a matter of heated contention, which perhaps cannot be settled without some agreement on literary values and on the actual nature of the universe. Some fans and critics try to separate fantasy from SF, but others fuse them. However clear the line or deep the chasm between the two, the forms of fantasy discussed in this book are intimately related to standard science fiction, and an analysis of SF would be incomplete without this chapter.

STRUCTURE OF THE FANTASY CLUSTER

I will begin my quantitative analysis of the fantasy cluster by returning to the calculations in Chapter 2. Recall that Table 4 identified four main components of the cluster: action-adventure, sword-and-sorcery, fantasy, and horror-and-weird. The great factor analysis of seventy-three authors located the cluster in Factor III, defined by sword-and-sorcery and fantasy. Table 4 placed the cluster *between* hard science and the new wave, with bridges linking it to each of the two rival ideologies. Sword-and-sorcery and fantasy mark the heartland of the cluster, and the first of these may have the greater influence on the SF subculture.

I have already provided some definitions of terms, but here I will define the components of the fantasy cluster more precisely. The meanings of action-adventure and horror-and-weird are conveyed by their names. The first refers to action-filled stories of adventure; the second, to weird stories eliciting horror. Table 10 provides detailed definitions of fantasy and sword-and-sorcery through their correlations with other types of literature. The connection between the two types is quite high ($r = .66$), but their ties to some other forms of literature vary considerably. Fantasy correlates at or above .20 with only sixteen other types, while sword-and-sorcery correlates at that level with twenty-two. Among the forms showing a slight link to sword-and-sorcery but not to fantasy are classic SF, Golden Age SF, and space opera.

I will dissect the term science-fantasy later, but its high correlations in the table demand comment now. Appendix B shows that science-fantasy is one of the most popular types of literature, standing fifth in the main list of forty, better liked on average than any of my three ideological types. Science-fantasy is a highly ambiguous term, used by various writers to mean rather different things. A correlation with fantasy is inevitable, because it contains the same

THE FANTASY CLUSTER

Table 10. Correlations (r) between preferences for fantasy, sword-and-sorcery, and related types (N = 409)

Literature type	Correlation (r) with	
	Fantasy	Sword-and-sorcery
Sword-and-sorcery	.66	—
Science-fantasy	.65	.57
Stories about magic	.61	.57
Myths and legends	.58	.48
Sagas and epics	.47	.55
Stories set in a universe where the laws of nature are very different from those found on our world	.44	.42
Tales of the supernatural	.44	.28
Horror-and-weird	.43	.38
Stories about barbarians	.40	.66
Ghost stories	.35	.23
Occult literature	.35	.27
Poetry	.28	.15
Science fiction art	.27	.24
Action-adventure fiction	.27	.42
Stories about alien cultures	.22	.20
Stories in which the main character is strange and unusual	.22	.18
Comic books	.22	.28
Stories in which the main character is brave and aggressive	.18	.23
Classic science fiction from the early days of SF	.15	.20
Space opera	.14	.25
Golden Age science fiction	.14	.20
Stories in which the main character is strong and tough	.09	.23
Stories about war	.06	.22

key word. Superficially, science-fantasy appears to name both SF and fantasy—the best of both worlds—so anyone who likes either ought to like this combination. But James Blish does not like the term for this very reason: "Science-Fantasy may not yet have become a swear word, but it is certainly a contradiction in terms."[20] In a letter to that preeminent combination magazine, *Fantasy and Science Fiction*, Blish noted that H. G. Wells coined the term *science-fantasy* for science fiction itself, but that it has degenerated into a compromise style:

> It has seemed to me that in recent years the term "Science Fantasy" has been subject to a lot of abuse. When Wells invented the term, he meant us to understand that he was indulging in a free fantasia *from known facts*, which he tried very hard to get right. In present usage, "Science Fantasy" stands as a warning that the author reserves the right to get the facts all wrong. Why, then, use the word "science" at all? The usage is an affront to the word; the stuff is fantasy, period.[21]

I have already shown the powerful connection between fantasy and stories about magic, which have a .65 correlation in Table 10, and I will have more to say about this later. It is quite reasonable that myths and legends are more closely tied to fantasy, and sagas and epics to sword-and-sorcery, but all four variables are closely connected. The correlation linking myths and legends with sagas and epics also is very strong ($r = .54$). These two items refer to traditional forms of fantasy, which played vital roles in the culture of preliterate and feudal societies. Perhaps the fantasy cluster performs similar functions for modern societies.

Myths, according to the dictionary, are traditional stories set in lands very different from our world and revolving around gods, spirits, and other supernaturals. Legends recount events that may have taken place on Earth in the remote past. Sagas are heroic prose narratives, while an epic is a narrative poem in elevated style recounting the deeds of a legendary or historical hero. In my data, myths and legends correlate more strongly with fantasy than do sagas and epics, while the reverse is true in correlations with sword-and-sorcery. Sagas and epics correlate with stories about barbarians more strongly ($r = .48$) than do myths and legends ($r = .38$). Those who do not appreciate sagas and epics may imagine that they are stories of blood and thunder (or thud and blunder), in which the hero is stupid but brave, but Poul Anderson said, "The ideal held forth is far less frequently reckless bravado than it is endurance and common sense."[22]

These strong correlations suggest that the traditional forms may represent an axis of variation running through the fantasy cluster. In Chapter 3 I showed that new science and new technology, aspects of the hard science ideology, were not only highly correlated ($r = .51$) but also represented a powerful, defining dimension of all science fiction and related genres. I graphed each

of 122 authors with these two variables and found a very tight axis of variation.
A similar analysis of the new wave attributes, avant-garde literature and social
science, showed a much looser pattern. In the same way, graphing myths
and legends against sagas and epics, which are strongly correlated ($r = .54$),
may result in a similarly powerful dimension.

Figure 8 graphs correlations linking these two types of traditional fantasy
with each of the 121 authors for whom at least 100 good respondents provided
complete data. The picture is not crystal clear. There is a spread of dots from
lower left, near the zero-zero point, upward toward the right. This indicates
a positive correlation between the types represented by the x and y axes. But
the dots are not tightly arranged in a line as was the case in the hard science
analysis. Their spread indicates significant divergence in the meanings of the
concepts.[23]

One of the most interesting items in Table 10 is stories set in a universe
where the laws of nature are very different from those found on our world.

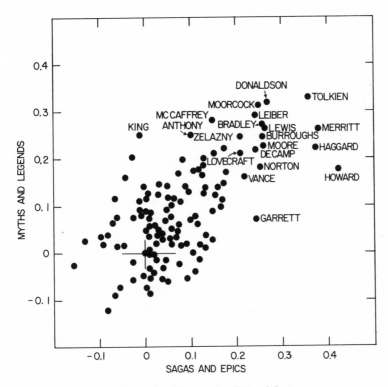

Figure 8.   Forms of traditional fantasy

Although magic surpasses this hint of alien natural law in the coefficients, this item suggests a group of authors and fans who want their fantasy rationalized, who like stories about alternate rather than impossible worlds.

Three items in Table 10 sketch a wider role for magic: tales of the supernatural, ghost stories, and occult literature. "Stories about barbarians" is almost a definition of sword-and-sorcery, as revealed by the high correlation $(r = .66)$ linking them. Other items that express the qualities of sword-and-sorcery are action-adventure fiction, stories about war, and stories in which the main characters are strong, tough, brave, and aggressive. The aesthetic flavor of the fantasy cluster is shown in its ties to poetry and to science fiction art.

Bracketing the cluster are space opera and horror-and-weird. I will identify the leading authors and describe the most representative fiction of the main types within the cluster. The action-adventure coast of the fantasy continent is a bit rugged, so I shall first consider space opera, the bridge leading to hard science. Then I shall cover action-adventure itself, followed by sword-and-sorcery, general fantasy, and finally horror-and-weird at the edge of the new wave.

SPACE OPERA

Among the most popular science fiction published in the 1930s was a large category sometimes called stories of superscience. Against overwhelming odds, heroes save Earth from alien invasion or other perils by the almost instantaneous invention of a death ray, interstellar spaceship, or some other improbable creation. The science was *super* because it went far beyond current discoveries, because it permitted the greatest technological leaps, and because it gave the scientist-hero the power of a superman. In the 1940s this type was retrospectively given the somewhat pejorative name *space opera*. The term was coined by analogy with horse opera, melodramas of the Old West, and soap opera, radio and TV melodramas of domestic life. Leigh Brackett, an author of much space opera and the wife of Edmond Hamilton, who is a popular and prolific author in this style, said that space opera "has developed into a term of opprobrium for any story that has an element of adventure and action."[24]

Ted White, the editor of *Amazing Stories*, which published much space opera in its earlier decades, recently defined the type. " 'Space Opera,' as I understand the term, refers to action-adventure fiction in which other planets (or space itself) are substituted for more traditional locales like the Old West or East India."[25]

Many editors and reviewers have tried to capture the essence of space opera. In 1951 the book reviewer for *Fantasy and Science Fiction* said it consisted of "broad swashbuckling romantic adventure."[26] The editor of *Imagination*, a magazine that in 1954 still carried space opera, referred to it as "suspense-action science fiction thrillers."[27] For editor Groff Conklin, pure space opera was only "about 1/64th of an inch deep."[28] Leonard Isaacs called it "a Western in space drag."[29] This comparison with Western adventure stories was made most forcefully in an advertisement on the back of the first issue of *Galaxy* magazine. The editor wanted to explain that *Galaxy* was going to carry true science fiction, rather than ordinary stories of adventure set in outer space. The advertisement placed the first paragraphs of a hypothetical horse opera and a space opera story side by side to show the limitations of the latter:

Hoofs drumming, Bat Durston came galloping down through the narrow pass at Eagle Gulch, a tiny gold colony 400 miles north of Tombstone. He spurred hard for a low overhang of rimrock . . . and at that point a tall, lean wrangler stepped out from behind a high boulder, six-shooter in a sun-tanned hand.

Jets blasting, Bat Durston came screeching down through the atmosphere of Bbllzznag, a tiny planet seven billion light years from Sol. He cut out his super-hyper-drive for the landing . . . and at that point, a tall, lean spaceman stepped out of the tail assembly, proton gun-blaster in a space-tanned hand.[30]

Although modern critics seem obliged to excoriate space opera as primitive and juvenile, nostalgia occasionally shines through. As recently as 1979, Baird Searles alerted readers to "the good old term 'space opera,' which for you newcomers refers to classic action-adventure interplanetary or interstellar SF."[31] *Analog's* book reviewer, P. Schuyler Miller, has admitted his affection for this style, though he prefers "what you might call planet opera, full of strange worlds, strange creatures, and strange societies."[32]

Because space opera was written as adventure fiction for boys, leaving little room for female heroes, women readers may find it an alien and unfriendly style. Perhaps its authors had to diminish the threat such heroines would pose to the fragile self-esteem of adolescent male readers. Mari Wolf expressed a female perspective, sympathetic as well as critical, noting that the women in these stories were "girls who are usually none too bright but always photogenic. (Space opera may make the girl a system-famed biologist or physicist, but in the crisis she clings to the hero and does the equivalent of the days-when-knights-were-bold swoon.)"[33]

A market for such stories has always existed, and it exists today. For those who can believe in them, they offer the most concentrated sense of wonder to be found in science fiction. As William L. Hamling once wrote, "Part of the interest of the bygone days of the field lay in the glamour of adventure on other worlds in other times—in essence, the space opera."[34]

The type of literature most strongly correlated with space opera is action-adventure fiction, at a quite strong .43. Two other variables are associated above .30 and are nearly synonymous with each other, Golden Age SF ($r = .35$) and classic SF ($r = .33$). These three coefficients identify space opera with some precision. The three authors most highly correlated with space opera are E. E. Smith ($r = .43$), Edmond Hamilton ($r = .34$), and Murray Leinster ($r = .34$). In 1979 Tom Staicar noted, "Everyone knows that 'space opera' has to do with blazing blasters and the spiritual descendants of Doc Smith and Flash Gordon."[35] More than thirty years earlier P. Schuyler Miller wrote: "Dr. Smith should never take offense when he is called the father of the space-opera. Just as in grand opera everything is done on a grander, more sweeping scale than on the ordinary stage, so in a Smith epic the people and events move in a way and on a scale all their own."[36]

The qualities of space opera, at its best and at its worst, can be understood by looking at selected works of Smith and Hamilton, both of whom have produced respected science fiction. The individual who has been most intensely stigmatized for cranking out vast quantities of juvenile space opera was Edmond Hamilton. His largest and most infamous project was the Captain Future series, mainly published in *Captain Future* magazine in the 1940s. Sam Moskowitz described these formula tales for boys as "the pure distillation of stereotyped science-fiction gimmicks brought to bear on a single-character magazine."[37]

A perfect early example of illogical superscience space opera is Hamilton's 1930 novel *The Universe Wreckers*. Scientists discover that a mysterious ray from the planet Neptune is causing the sun to rotate faster. In half a year, they calculate, the sun will spin so fast that it will break into two parts, vaporizing the inner planets and destroying humanity. When they analyze the ray, scientists fortunately discover that it offers a means for propelling spaceships. In a matter of weeks an interplanetary vehicle is invented, assembled, and launched with a crew of four.

This plot synopsis already reveals three standard features of superscience space opera. First, the entire human race, or something of nearly as great value, is at risk. Second, scientific discoveries are postulated that have only the vaguest relationship to current knowledge—mysterious rays and power sources quite beyond ordinary science. Third, great technological leaps are accomplished in very short periods of time by small teams of heroic engineers.

On the way to Neptune, the ship passes very close to Mars, Jupiter, and

Saturn, a highly unlikely trajectory that requires the planets to be in almost perfect alignment. Despite a velocity of five million miles an hour, the craft is nearly drawn into Saturn when the engine is damaged. Of course, this violates our present-day knowledge from experience with space travel past Saturn, but it also contradicts knowledge that was available in 1930. At that speed, nearly 1,400 miles per second, the craft would hardly have been perturbed by Saturn's gravity, engine or no engine. Here is a fourth characteristic of all but the best space opera, the failure to understand even very simple principles of real science.

Hamilton's valiant crew finds Neptune all but deserted, its billions of inhabitants having migrated to the satellite Triton. They learn that two rays stab out from Neptunian bases on Triton. One presses on an edge of the sun to accelerate its spin, the other presses on a distant star to hold Triton in place against the force of the first. Space opera often assumed that some rays were "beams" that would be projected like a beam of light but could also exert pressure like a beam of wood or iron. After the literary conventions were more fully perfected, beams that pushed were called *pressor beams*, and beams that pulled were called *tractor beams*. These concepts bear only the most distant relationship to the findings of real science.

After being captured, taught the Neptunian language, and informed that the whole mad situation is merely a means of giving Neptune a warmer climate, the members of the crew escape, to return to Earth. Luckily, the Neptunians were holding them in a prison cell without a ceiling! They get home just in time to lead a fleet of five thousand brand-new Earth warships against Neptune. All this in just five months!

A great battle around Saturn is won by the Earthlings. Then, after several skirmishes, they destroy the ray aimed at the stars. Unopposed, the ray against the sun drives Neptune's satellite out of the solar system, annihilating all the Neptunians and saving Earth. Sad to say, no one on Earth or Triton realizes that technology capable of speeding up the sun could also move Neptune into a warmer orbit.

The most perfect, influential, and gloriously impossible example of space opera is undoubtedly the Lensman series by E. E. Smith. The wealth of Smith's imagination is documented in a concordance of the seven novels, compiled by Ron Ellik.[38] Many a later writer has built a whole story around an idea that occupied only a paragraph, or even a phrase, in the Lens novels. The first one published, although not the first in the sequence of fictional events, was *Galactic Patrol*. Initially it appears to be a simple story about space pirates, but on closer inspection, one realizes that the pirates represent an evil civilization called Boskone, which has half the galaxy within its grasp and uses fantastic technology of awesome effectiveness to combat the patrol.

Smith's strategy was to show us as many wonders as he could in each Lens story, and to leave us exhausted, thinking we had seen everything. At each climax we supposed we finally understood Boskone and saw it utterly defeated. Then in the next story we would discover that only the most superficial levels of Boskone had been destroyed and that another level, of even greater power and evil, was ready to counterattack. By Ellik's count, the Lens novels reveal seven different levels of the nature of the evil Boskone.[39] Smith sustained the all-important sense of wonder by inventing wheels within wheels, worlds within worlds. This strategy was extremely effective. It suggested, quite directly in some of the stories, that the drab world of everyday life was but a superficial phenomenon, beneath which cosmic struggles raged. At any moment our own uninteresting lives might be caught up in the struggle and become cosmically significant.

The first book introduces not only the evil Boskone, but also the supremely good Galactic Patrol, which sets out to defeat the pirates. The patrol is an elite corps of spacemen and spacecreatures who police the stars for tens of thousands of light years. The novel begins as the young Kimbal Kinnison graduates at the top of his class at the academy. A million men apply for the patrol that year, and only a few thousand pass the tests and initial training. Of these, most wash out along the way and are given subordinate jobs; just a hundred become superelite wearers of the Lens. The Galactic Patrol is an incorruptible force for good, respected and obeyed throughout the galaxy.

The Lens itself, created through secret processes by the superior civilization of the mysterious planet Arisia, gives the Lensmen the ability to read minds, and it has even greater potential, originally unknown to the men of the patrol. Everything about the story is incredible, fantastic, super. In the first half Kinnison goes on a mission to get the technical designs of the pirate spaceships. Escaping with the plans, he is chased across the entire galaxy. At one of the dozens of moments when all hope seems lost, his lifeboat just happens to come upon a derelict pirate ship, which he uses to elude his pursuers. Impossible luck! When he lands on one planet of an alien system and wants to travel to another planet, the reader is casually informed that the patrol's spacesuits are capable of propelling the wearer on rapid interplanetary voyages, so Kinnison simply jumps from one planet to the other.

The second half of the novel follows Kinnison's single-handed conquest of the vast enemy home base, where he dominates the minds of the pirates with superpowers he has learned to derive from his Lens, powers greater than any previous patrol member ever dreamed of. Kinnison is a superman—a doctor even comments at one point that X-rays show he has perfect bone structure—given superpower through magical technologies.

The chief of the pirates, Helmuth, is killed in the final battle of *Galactic Patrol*. Throughout, he has given his vile commands as "Helmuth, speaking for Boskone." Is Boskone simply the name of the pirate organization? Or is Helmuth himself Boskone? Or is Boskone something greater, something behind Helmuth and the pirates, a vast evil hardly touched by the patrol? In the second novel, *Gray Lensman*, Kinnison discovers that Boskone is the malignant species that controls the Second Galaxy and now seeks to add Kinnison's galaxy to its conquests. For much of this story Kinnison is a secret agent, using his super powers to trace the line of command of Boskone's pernicious drug ring, which spreads corruption across the stars.

The high point of his heroism comes when he allows himself to be captured to gain precious information about the enemy's home planet in the Second Galaxy. The inhabitants pluck out his eyes and inject in him a virulent disease, which necessitates amputation of his arms and legs. Happily for Kinnison, a Galactic Patrol scientist has just invented a regeneration drug that allows new limbs to grow, restoring him to perfect health without so much as a scar to record his torture!

Ordinary battles between spaceships, described many times by Smith and other authors of space opera, are generally carried out at surprisingly close range. Dreadnoughts grapple, using tractor beams, crush each other with pressor beams, and blast away with disintegrator rays. When all else fails, an atomic torpedo is always at hand to fire against the foe, or space marines are ready for hand-to-hand combat. Assault on planetary bases requires even greater superscience weapons. In *Gray Lensman* the patrol hurls a planet-sized mass of antimatter at the fortress of Jalte, Boskone's agent in our galaxy. Later Kinnison smashes Boskone's planet in the Second Galaxy by cracking it between two other planets.

Incidents such as these illustrate the extremes of violence and triumph experienced by the space opera hero. Everything takes place on the center stage of history, on the grandest scale, with cosmic forces in play. As the Lens series went on, the reader came to realize that the theme of Smith's novels was nothing less than the moral battle of good against evil, reaching across eternity as well as across all the galaxies.

ACTION-ADVENTURE FICTION

Action-adventure can be conceived either as a category lying between space opera and sword-and-sorcery or as a broader category that includes them. The main characters are brave, aggressive, strong, and tough. On the sword-and-sorcery side they are barbarians engaged in sagas and epics. Like space opera, action-adventure is significantly connected with classic science fiction of the Golden Age.

Over the years, several magazines, including two with the name *Science Fiction Adventures*, have emphasized this style. The first issue of the second of these proclaimed, "The future holds the greatest adventure mankind has yet faced. The entire universe is waiting just around the corner, full of exciting discoveries and mysterious dangers."[40] What makes these types of fantasy more interesting than detective stories, spy stories, war stories, sea stories, and Westerns, is their invention of wondrous worlds and societies. In SF, according to Lester del Rey, "essentially, an adventure story is a conflict of man or men against an exotic environment or culture."[41] This approach demands vivid imagination from the author but calls for less scientific accuracy than does hard science. As one standard rejection slip of 1940 explained, "*Science-Fiction* and *Future Fiction* specialize in the action-fantasy type of science-fiction—good adventure stories based on logical science, but minus any lengthy scientific discussions or technicalities."[42] In 1952 the editor of *Space Stories* announced that his magazine would stress adventure tales:

> The coldly mental story, the complex parable, the tale of social significance is not for us. We offer warmth, excitement, color, action. We build upon science fiction's greatest asset: its imagination-stirring concepts of tremendous distances, colossal speeds, vast empty sweeps of space, unknown, mysterious worlds, unguessable forms of life behind strange, murky atmospheres.
>
> In short, our purpose is to take you out of this world.[43]

Ten years earlier *Planet Stories*—a magazine that Marion Zimmer Bradley said was in the "tradition of Thud, Blunder, BEMs [bug-eyed monsters] and sirens"[44]—stated the same policy: "Each issue of *Planet Stories* will feature yarns of high adventure of the future centuries, weird pulse-quickening tales of far away planets, strange stories of alien worlds and surging action. There will be vivid features, planned for your entertainment, exciting your imagination, filling your leisure hours with moments of romantic adventure."[45]

The three authors most closely associated with action-adventure are E. E. Smith ($r = .36$), Robert E. Howard ($r = .36$), and Edgar Rice Burroughs ($r = .34$). Still very popular with the general public more than thirty years after his death, Burroughs is a sterling example of much that is good in action-adventure. Since he wrote of feudal and tribal societies, it is not surprising that his strongest correlation is with stories about barbarians ($r = .39$), and that his link to sword-and-sorcery ($r = .34$) is equal to that with action-adventure. Most famous as the inventor of Tarzan, he wrote strict science fiction as well, notably in his many books about Mars, Venus, and Pellucidar.

The typical Burroughs plot involves a beautiful woman captured by villains, pursued by the hero, and rescued from dire danger, often with a larger peril, like defeat in war or the destruction of a great civilization, to be avoided. Cultures invented by Burroughs have their own languages, and the stories are peppered with alien words. Two novels, *Thuvia, Maid of Mars* and *Tarzan the Terrible*, have glossaries in the back giving a few particulars of the exotic language. In *Tarzan and the Ant Men* the names of two characters are shown in weird hieroglyphics, although in every edition I have seen, the hieroglyphics are reversed because of a printer's error. The inside covers of the first editions of the Venus novels show maps of the planet, with place names in English and Venusian script. Maps of imaginary territories also appear in some editions of *Pellucidar* and *Tarzan and the Lost Empire*. *The Chessmen of Mars* offers complete rules for playing the Martian equivalent of chess, and Burroughs also devised but did not publish a Martian game of chance. [46]

Most important for science fiction readers are the ten (or eleven) novels about Barsoom, as the Martians call their planet. *Soom* is their word for world or planet. Mercury, Venus, and Earth are called Rasoom, Cosoom, and Jasoom. *Bar* is Martian for the number eight, and Mars is indeed the eighth innermost body of our solar system, if one counts the sun and the satellites at their closest approach to the sun.

For those who wish to examine the Barsoom culture apart from the stories themselves, there is the exhaustive *Guide to Barsoom* by John Flint Roy. In addition to a directory of two hundred characters' names and a gazetteer of a hundred places, this book reports the units of measurement, customs, beliefs, aphorisms, technology, and wildlife of the mythical planet. It also includes the maps Burroughs drew but chose not to publish.

The prime hero of the Barsoom books is John Carter of Virginia, late officer in the Confederate Army. As in many of his novels, Burroughs introduces *A Princess of Mars* with the claim that the tale might be true. He has received the manuscript from Captain Carter himself, a sort of uncle, with the warning not to publish it until twenty-one years after his death. Yet John Carter seems immortal, never aging and recalling no youth. Burroughs was educated at a military academy and spent a few years seeking adventure in the Wild West, and Carter is an idealized version of the author, an exaggeration rather than a complete fabrication. It is in the Wild West that Carter, escaping from wild Indians, has the strange experience that hurls his mind across space to Mars.

On Barsoom Carter meets the green Martians of the nation of Thark, tusked nomads fifteen feet tall with four arms. They ride thoats, great eight-legged beasts colored white, yellow, and slate. The greatest civilized race is the red Martians, although related peoples also come in the colors black, yellow, and white. Red Martians live in city states and empires with names like Ptarth, Zodanga, Dusar, Gathol, and Helium. Carter falls in love with Dejah Thoris, princess of Helium, the daughter of Mors Kajak (king of the city of Lesser Helium) and granddaughter of Tardos Mors (emperor of the nation of Helium).

The red Martians maintain the canals and the atmosphere factories that make life possible on the dying planet. A million years before, oceans had covered much of Mars, and the air was rich. As the oceans dried up and the air thinned, the once-great civilization of the planet sank fitfully into semi-barbarism. Today Mars is divided into many regions that have no communication with each other and that differ greatly in culture and biology. Thus Barsoom presents great scope for adventure.

A problem for much science fiction is that highly advanced technology generally is not compatible with very personal stories. Spaceflight costs billions, so it is not worth rescuing—or kidnaping—a single individual through interplanetary flight. Modern war is won by masses rather than by a few brave individuals. Even science is produced in vast knowledge factories. Fantasy societies constructed on feudal principles, while totally incompatible with high technology, do permit a few supreme individuals to rise above the masses. Burroughs provided a historical excuse for the Barsoomian anachronisms, but much action-adventure SF simply puts swords and spaceships together without any reasonable justification.

A cartoon published in *Vertex* magazine in 1975 poked fun at this practice. It shows two space soldiers talking. Although wearing advanced spacesuits, they carry knives, bows, and arrows. One explains their attack plan to the other, noting that while they will use the latest time warp to get to their target, they must use these primitive weapons to fight.[47] When Burroughs's characters cast aside their radium rifles to duel with swords, feudal honor is said to be at stake.

In addition to strange races of men, Burroughs loved to imagine alien animals. The apes that raise the human child they call Tarzan ("white-skin" in ape talk) belong to a species not known to any zoologist. Equestrians on Mars ride thoats and have zitidars for draft animals. Instead of a dog, one has a faithful calot. There are banths instead of lions, ulsios instead of rats, apts instead of polar bears. Other creatures, such as the horrible but herbivorous plant men, who eat grass through their hands and reproduce by budding, have no close earthly counterparts. True, Burroughs's animals are put together from pieces of familiar creatures—the apt has the fur of a polar bear and the eyes of a bee—but the bits of familiarity amid his wild imaginings only make the impossible seem plausible.

Often Burroughs used fantasy tales to express his personal values, to subtly communicate his own ideology. If I had to distill the Burroughs creed into a phrase, it would be the old Latin motto, *mens sana in corpore sano*—a healthy mind in a healthy body. Tarzan, often played in the movies as an ignorant if affable savage, in the books was a supremely intelligent and philosophical gentleman, master of several languages as well as a perfect physical specimen. Brutish humans and semihumans were inferiors in Burroughs's value system, but so were effete intellectuals. Several characters and incidents in his books depict an excessively mental orientation as inferior to the mixture of good mind (and spirit) in a beautiful and healthy body.

One of the most fascinating of Burroughs's creatures is Ghek the kaldane in *The Chessmen of Mars*, who represents a split between mind and body. Kaldanes are crablike creatures, ninety percent brain, that look like distorted human heads. Over thousands of years they have bred one of the lower animals, the rykor, until it resembles a headless human. Each kaldane rides a rykor, controlling its primitive nervous system by seizing the spinal column with special tentacles. Ghek is extremely arrogant and rather lacking in sympathy, until he gets caught up in human adventures. The purpose of kaldane society is to produce a perfect, bodiless brain that can lie beneath the surface of the planet, meditating forever.

Burroughs criticizes pure intellect again in *Thuvia, Maid of Mars*. The city of Aaanthor, first city of Mars alphabetically if in no other way, is a paradise for pseudointellectuals. The inhabitants' minds are so powerful that they defend their city with phantom bowmen whom they imagine whenever necessary. Morally, however, they are children—bad children. They can easily imagine into existence anything they like, and such power does not encourage good manners. The city is divided into warring philosophical parties, the etherealists and the realists. The former group believes it is disgusting to eat food and only necessary to postulate good health in order to achieve it, while the latter group believes it is necessary to go through the ritual of postulating the existence of food, then eating this imaginary nourishment. Thus does Burroughs parody intellectuality.

In one of his miscellaneous novels, *The Cave Girl*, an overeducated, effete

Boston aristocrat learns physical strength and courage in a primitive environment. As Burroughs describes this character in the first chapter, "It had
been a giant intellect only that he had craved—he and a fond mother—and
their wishes had been fulfilled. At twenty-one Waldo was an animated
encyclopedia—and about as muscular as a real one."[48] But by the end
of the book, this weakling has become a powerful hero. There is hope for
us all.

SWORD-AND-SORCERY

Here is the heartland of the fantasy cluster. Table 11 shows the twenty-five
authors from my list who have significant correlations above .25 with sword-
and-sorcery, along with associations to three related types of literature: fantasy,
stories about barbarians, and stories about magic.

Lin Carter, who is at the midpoint in the list, has defined sword-and-
sorcery as "the sort of action fantasy Edgar Rice Burroughs and Robert E.
Howard wrote."[49] As the table shows, Howard, creator of the barbarian hero
Conan, achieves a very high correlation with sword-and-sorcery ($r = .55$)
and an even higher one with stories about barbarians ($r = .60$). Conan is
pure sword-and-sorcery, but Lester del Rey has suggested calling Burroughs's
Mars and Venus stories sword-and-planet, "sort of a mixture of space opera
and sword-and-sorcery, without sorcery."[50]

Howard, morbid genius of the brutal scene, is the purest example of sword-
and-sorcery. L. Sprague de Camp, who edited and completed Howard's Conan
stories, described this purity: "Heroic fantasy is a type of story of the supernatural laid in an imaginary world—either this planet as it is once supposed
to have been, or as it will be long hence, or some other world or dimension—
where magic works and all men are mighty, all women beautiful, all problems
simple, and all life adventurous."[51]

The Conan stories consist of violent and horrible episodes, one bludgeoning
after another, brains spilled on every battlement. Conan himself shows only
the most perfunctory concern for the welfare of others. He is guided by the
simple, base emotions of rage and lust; revenge is his most complex thought.
The one complete novel in the series, *Conan the Conqueror*, begins with
Conan as king of the mythical nation of Aquilonia by right of conquest.
Usurpers reanimate the mummy of Xaltotun, a long-dead sorcerer, using a
magic gem called the Heart of Ahriman. Weakened by black magic, Conan
loses his throne, then embarks on an erratic quest to get the jewel so that
friendly priests can help him regain his kingdom. Vicarious wish fulfillment is very close to the surface in these stories, and there is little, if any,

Table 11. Authors of sword-and-sorcery and related types (N = 409)

	Correlation (r) with			
Author	Sword-and-sorcery	Fantasy	Stories about barbarians	Stories about magic
1. Howard	.55	.38	.60	.24
2. Moorcock	.43	.37	.31	.29
3. Merritt	.43	.43	.40	.30
4. Tolkien	.42	.48	.26	.28
5. Haggard	.41	.38	.27	.26
6. Bradley	.39	.29	.35	.30
7. Wagner	.38	.20	.35	.05
8. Leiber	.37	.40	.25	.34
9. Kline	.37	.23	.37	.11
10. Burroughs	.36	.27	.39	.16
11. Norton	.36	.27	.25	.36
12. de Camp	.36	.27	.23	.33
13. Carter	.35	.20	.28	.17
14. Garrett	.31	.16	.28	.25
15. Derleth	.30	.22	.18	.12
16. Henderson	.28	.17	.19	.21
17. Cherryh	.28	.14	.16	.21
18. Vance	.28	.24	.17	.21
19. McCaffrey	.28	.24	.21	.30
20. Chandler	.27	.06	.28	.18
21. Schmitz	.27	.19	.21	.29
22. Zelazny	.26	.25	.21	.30
23. Moore	.26	.26	.21	.30
24. Lovecraft	.26	.25	.17	.15
25. Laumer	.25	.02	.20	.16

attempt to justify the raw pleasure of slaughter under any civilized gloss of morality.

I find the well-crafted, rather subtle sword-and-sorcery romances of A. Merritt much more deserving of close analysis than Howard's unmitigated gore, though Merritt gratifies the same repressed impulses. Merritt develops background, themes, and characters with some care, and his stories show structure and symbolism on every level. Thus they provide an escape for the mind as well as for the lusts. In common with Burroughs, he is especially careful to provide a bridge from the world of the reader to that of the saga.

In *The Ship of Ishtar* a modern man is catapulted into the world of Babylonian myth, sixty centuries ago. A feud is kindled between the mighty goddess Ishtar, Lady of the Heavens and of the Earth, and the evil god Nergal, Dark Ruler of the Dead. The fault is human weakness: Zarpanit, priestess of Ishtar, and Alusar, priest of Nergal, fall in love. Aided by Zarpanit's lady-in-waiting, Sharane, the pair meet for lovemaking. But Klaneth, Alusar's assistant priest, prepares to betray the couple, for their love is a great sin against the gods. At times the deities themselves enter the bodies of their priests and priestesses, to speak and act through them. Unexpectedly, both Ishtar and Nergal choose the exact moment of lovemaking to enter Zarpanit and Alusar, bringing the rival deities into unwanted copulation with each other—a disaster of cosmic proportions. Just at this cataclysmic moment, Klaneth reveals the tryst to all the other priests and priestesses.

Zarpanit, Alusar, and their retainers are doomed by the gods to drift forever, always locked in conflict and attraction. Powered by sails and slave oarsmen, their ship moves through a timeless sea. At the bow is a cabin for Zarpanit, Sharane, and their slave girls. At the stern is a cabin for Alusar, Klaneth, and their guards. No one can pass through the wall of magical force that cuts the vessel amidships, except the oarsmen and others who have no part in the great sin. The lovers are killed, but the retainers are doomed to sail into all eternity.

The story actually starts in modern New York when John Kenton receives a block of black stone shipped from an archeologist friend who is excavating the ruins of Babylon. It bears a dozen lines of cuneiform writing, worn to illegibility except for the names of Ishtar and Nergal. On impulse, Kenton smashes the block and finds inside a jeweled replica of the ship of Ishtar. Seized by dizziness, he falls out of this world and finds himself on the actual ship sailing the ancient seas.

The author uses evocative language and intense images to convey a sense of the marvelous and mysterious. It is Kenton's fate to intervene in the frozen cosmic struggle between Ishtar and Nergal, to fall in love with Sharane, and to gain Klaneth as his mortal enemy. The book builds tension through the device of letting Kenton's tie to the ship periodically become so weak that he falls back, unwilling, to his New York home. Kenton's tenuous psychic connection to the ship represents the reader's involvement in the fantasy. At any moment the ship may fade from reality, and both Kenton and the reader will be imprisoned in the mundane world of the everyday.

Dwellers in the Mirage, also by Merritt, not only transports the reader away from civilization to a fantasy land but also hints that within the reader there may lurk a more primitive, free personality for whom this impossibly exotic place is home. The story starts with two friends, Leif and Jim, on an Alaskan camping trip. Odd sounds in the forest hint at unseen wonders, and Jim coaxes Leif to tell him about his terrifying experience two years earlier on an anthropological expedition in the Gobi desert. Leif was instantly accepted as a member of the Uighur tribe, a strange people who felt that Leif shared their bloodline. Leif, a blond, blue-eyed Scandinavian, rejected the wild idea that he could possibly be of Uighur stock and share somehow in their racial memory. But an anthropologist, providing a scientific rationale for the fantasy that follows, convinced Leif there might be some truth in the Gobi tribesmen's superstitions, since many tribes had long ago migrated from Central Asia to Europe.

Leif tells Jim that he went with the Uighur into the desert, where a hypnotic spell caused him to perform an ancient blood sacrifice, offering a young woman to Khalk'ru, the hideous Kraken-God. Grotesquely carved stones came alive in the form of a monstrous squid that ate the girl, and he himself was momentarily transformed into the long-dead barbarian warlord, Dwayanu. Jim listens, half-believing, to Leif's tale as the Alaskan forest groans and rings with unearthly sounds. Perhaps the ancient peoples of the Gobi went not only to Europe but also across the land bridge to the American Northwest.

Marching north through Alaska, Leif and Jim discover a valley whose floor seems at times to be a lake, at other times to be littered with ritual pyramids, and at others to be an ordinary stony field. Inside this mirage they discover a magic realm where hallucinations are stimulated by a high concentration of carbon dioxide. It is populated by elflike folk and by Norse barbarians of great strength. After marrying a good woman named Evalie, Leif falls under the spell of Lur, the beautiful but sinister Witch-Woman. As in the Gobi, but this time completely, Leif becomes lusty Dwayanu, forgetting his wife and Jim. Gone are the restraints of ordinary morality as he sacrifices more women to the Kraken-God and lays waste a peaceful city. Only as Jim lies dying does Leif cast aside the vicious Dwayanu personality that has possessed him and become himself again. Was he bewitched or mesmerized? Or is he indeed a reincarnation of Dwayanu in whom the barbarian remains, ready to burst forth in fury when Khalk'ru calls?

Perhaps the reader wants to express the lusts within himself. To let his sword drink deep in the blood of his enemies, to sacrifice beautiful women to the many-armed monster that hides within his own soul, to find in himself a different person, one free of fears and inhibitions. He may want to become

Dwayanu, to liberate the dwellers in the mirage that is his own psyche, to do in reality what the novel permits him to experience only weakly through vicarious identification.

The magic of these novels is not just in the spells of the fictional necromancers but in their ability to transport the reader away, to provide radical escape. Burroughs invented tales to achieve his own escape after he failed to find real adventure on the American frontier, and thus a special touch of realism flickers in his novels. Purer fantasy may be the creation of writers who always dreamed but never really attempted to live heroic lives. Some say that the writers of such stories must have exceptional needs to flee reality, so they create fictional means of escape, madness-driven vehicles that can transport their sane readers. Damon Knight saw psychopathology and inferiority complexes in Howard, Merritt, and H. P. Lovecraft, who dominates the section on horror-and-weird. "All the great fantasies, I suppose, have been written by emotionally crippled men. Howard was a recluse and a man so morbidly attached to his mother that when she died he committed suicide; Lovecraft had enough phobias and eccentricities for nine; Merritt was chinless, bald and shaped like a shmoo. The trouble with Conan is that the human race never has produced and never could produce such a man, and sane writers know it; therefore the sick writers have a monopoly of him."[52]

FANTASY

Table 12 shows the authors who are significantly correlated above .25 with fantasy, along with two associated types of literature. Two authors on the list might be described almost as anti–science fiction writers: J. R. R. Tolkien and C. S. Lewis. Tolkien, of course, is famous for the Hobbit stories, the saga of a magic Ring that is in some respects comparable to that by Richard Wagner. Tolkien was a historical linguist, and his tetralogy overflows with elements of old European culture—the riddle contest in the first book, for example—and the Hobbits apparently speak Old English (Anglo-Saxon). Lewis, who was a close friend of Tolkien, is best known among SF fans for his trilogy of space novels that are actually vehicles for Christian theological speculation.

Arthur C. Clarke recounted that Tolkien and Lewis, in a debate with him and another prominent member of the British Interplanetary Society, argued that spaceflight might lead to "the destruction or enslavement of other species in the universe" and that space travel was an evil concept.[53] The first novel of Lewis's trilogy, *Out of the Silent Planet*, says that of the sun's planets only Earth fell from God's grace and that it must be quarantined so the other planets, still in the Edenic state, will not be contaminated. The villain of the

Table 12. Authors of fantasy and related types (N = 409)

| Author | Fantasy | Correlation (r) with | |
		Science-fantasy	Stories set in universe where laws of nature are very different
1. Tolkien	.48	.28	.16
2. Merritt	.43	.36	.19
3. Leiber	.40	.24	.26
4. Haggard	.38	.31	.30
5. Howard	.38	.25	.13
6. Moorcock	.37	.29	.28
7. Lewis	.33	.24	.23
8. Bradley	.29	.26	.32
9. de Camp	.27	.21	.28
10. Norton	.27	.28	.19
11. Burroughs	.27	.24	.15
12. Moore	.26	.24	.29
13. Lovecraft	.25	.21	.09
14. Zelazny	.25	.21	.14

second novel, *Perelandra*, is described as a wicked man obsessed with the vile "scientifiction" idea of conquering the universe. The concluding book, *That Hideous Strength*, describes an epic struggle between the scientific forces of evil embodied in a research institute, whose acronym is N.I.C.E., against a few humanistic forces of good embodied in the character of Ransom, a Christ figure, and in the spells of Britain's traditional magician, Merlin.

Despite the potential for technophobia represented by Tolkien and Lewis, the commercial and intellectual successes of American science fiction forced a truce that often reshaped fantasy in the image of SF. To harmonize with the hard science perspective, at the end of the 1930s fantasy began to be rationalized, and supernatural events were redefined "as natural occurrences whose laws we do not yet understand."[54] John Campbell was the leading editor in this dominant rationalistic tradition. In the 1950s *Astounding* carried many articles and stories about psionics—magical "parapsychology" that was given hard science connotations of electronics.[55] He promoted various other pseudosciences in *Astounding* as well, such as Dianetics and mechanical levitators.[56] But from 1939 to 1943 he had his greatest direct influence on fantasy fiction as editor of the magazine *Unknown*, published as a companion to *Astounding*.

The fiction in *Unknown*, and some that spilled over into *Astounding*, is often called science fantasy. As Judith Merril put it, this is "the genre of supernatural science, of the technology of magic, matter-of-fact fantasy, the territory just this side of weird-gothic-horror, fantastic whimsy, and sword-and-sorcery."[57] According to P. Schuyler Miller, "What John Campbell did was introduce the concept of science to the traditionally supernatural, and the result was the 'typical' *Unknown* story."[58] Miller said that traditional fantasy stories rested on actual belief in the supernatural, but because our culture had lost its faith, Campbell "introduced a fantasy of disbelief to replace the old outmoded fantasy of lost beliefs."[59] *Unknown* "accepted the existence of demons and vampires and the like, then clapped on the scientist's—John Campbell's—stipulation that if a thing exists it must be governed by laws, even though we may not know what they are. The stories in *Unknown*, or most of them, dealt with the discovery and use of these laws."[60]

Fritz Leiber, third on the list of authors in Table 12, is a fantasy author very close to the hearts of SF fans, as shown by his high mean score (4.85) in Table A1. Among the 276 expert fans whose responses gave us the factor analysis of seventy-three authors reported in Chapter 2, his mean score of 5.06 places him third, after Niven and Heinlein and ahead of Asimov. Sam Moskowitz said, "Fritz Leiber, Jr., for decades now, has been regarded as the leading proponent and high priest of a movement to modernize, explain 'logically' or 'scientifically,' all the dark forms and various accouterments of witchcraft and superstition that have so dishonorably been passed down by mankind from generation to generation and that now usually evoke laughter rather than horror in a world unsympathetic to their impotence."[61]

A good example of this is Leiber's early novel, *Gather, Darkness!* Years ago, in the aftermath of an interplanetary war, the scientists decide that humanity is not ready for further scientific discovery. They devise means for holding Earth culture at a primitive level until they can figure out how to progress in safety. They create a new Middle Ages, complete with serfdom and monks, but with secular and sacred power in their own hands. Confirmed atheists, the scientists pretend to be priests of the one great God, using hidden technology to accomplish miracles. Among their secret tools of dictatorship are rays that control people's emotions. The avenging angels that fly over the heads of the astonished serfs are really airplanes.

But like all theocracies, that of the scientists becomes a grinding, hypocritical tyranny. Opposition appears in the form of a rival cult, worshiping Sathanas (Satan). The science-based magic of the theocracy begins to fail, sometimes in spectacular ways. Dark, wolfish shapes roam the country-side—witches, warlocks, werewolves! When a great revival ceremony is disrupted by Satanic pranks, even the highest-ranked priests are frozen with fear:

> They felt that the whole materialistic world on which they based their security was going to pieces before their eyes. Physical science, which had been their obedient servant, was suddenly become a toy in the hands of a dark power that could make or break scientific laws at pleasure. Something scratched out the first principle of their thinking. "There is only the cosmos and the electronic entities that constitute it, without soul or purpose"—and scribbled over it, in broad black strokes, "The whim of Sathanas."[62]

Throughout the novel the central characters wonder whether perhaps Satan really exists and his minions possess real magic, unlike the priests' scientifically faked magic. By the end there are seemingly logical explanations for everything that has happened. The witches' familiars turn out to be cloned creatures produced by advanced genetic engineering, cultured from the body tissues of their masters and therefore identical twins with a telepathic bond. The apparitions turn out to be projections from advanced-technology television devices—holograms, a contemporary writer might call them. The Sathanas cult has been organized by a radical party of priests who actually believe in the fake state religion and want to stimulate a real revival. Ultimately, science in the service of witches breaks the power of science in the service of priests, and democracy erupts across the planet.

Campbell encouraged an alternative to this science-faked magic approach, which postulated that real magic is ruled by undiscovered scientific laws. The best example of this rationalized fantasy is *The Incomplete Enchanter*, a series of humorous stories that began in *Unknown*, written by L. Sprague de Camp and Fletcher Pratt. In the stories psychologists develop a new theory of existence, paraphysics, which postulates the existence of alternate universes based on different codes of natural law. The principles on which our own world operates are described by science; other worlds are described by magic. In some worlds, but not in our own, the Law of Similarity holds—*effects resemble causes*. Thus pouring water on the ground might make it rain in a world based on this law. Like science, magic has fixed principles, as Reed Chalmers, discoverer of paraphysics, explains:

> Medicine men don't merely go through hocus-pocus. They believe they are working through natural laws. In a world where everyone firmly believed in

these laws, that is, in one where all minds were attuned to receive the proper impressions, the laws of magic would conceivably work, as one hears of witch-doctors' spells working in Africa today. Frazer and Seabrook have worked out some of these magical laws. Another is the Law of Contagion: Things once in contact continue to interact from a distance after separation.[63]

One can travel from one universe to another by filling one's mind with the fundamental assumptions of the target world. In *The Incomplete Enchanter*, Harold Shea, Chalmers's young assistant, is the first to use incantations of symbolic logic to attune his mind to an alternate reality. He aims for the world of old Irish myth but lands by accident in the world of Norse mythology instead, encountering the gods shortly before their Götterdämmerung. Shea has with him such tools as a flashlight, a revolver, a book of matches, and a *Boy Scout Handbook*. In the Norse alternate reality, where the laws of nature are very different from those found on our world, none of the technological devices works. Shea cannot even read his *Boy Scout Handbook*, because English is unknown to the Norse gods. Magic, however, does work, and Shea sets himself the scientific task of learning the natural laws of the alternate universe so that he can become a powerful magician.

In the second half of *The Incomplete Enchanter*, Chalmers joins Shea in the world described in Spenser's *Faerie Queene*, where the two infiltrate a guild of enchanters in order to help fantastic heroines with whom they have fallen in love. At one point the magicians hold a professional meeting, not unlike an annual meeting of scientists in our world, at which technical papers are read: "Ye Poweres magickal of six selected Water Fay-Human Hybrids," "A neue use for ye Bloud of unbaptized infants," and "Of ye Comparative efficacie of ye Essence of ye Spotted Frogge & ye Common Gren Frogge in sleeping Enchauntments."[64]

HORROR-AND-WEIRD

Many varieties of science fiction try to stimulate the emotion of horror in the reader. For example, at the end of Tom Godwin's famous hard science story, "The Cold Equations," an innocent young girl must be jettisoned into airless space without the slightest hope of survival, because the cold equations of astronautics dictate that the rocket on which she has stowed away will crash if forced to carry her extra weight. But true horror-and-weird is more than just fiction that stimulates fear and revulsion in the reader; it must be based on supernatural assumptions. In 1935 Donald A. Wollheim distinguished this style: "Science fiction is that branch of fantasy which is rendered plausible by the reader's recognition of its scientific possibilities. Weird fiction is that branch of fantasy dealing with supernatural or occult objects, which is rendered plausible by the reader's recognition of the fact that there are people somewhere who did believe or do believe in the truth of the ideas therein, and is willing to concede the truth of these things for a period in which he is reading the story."[65]

Horror-and-weird correlates most strongly with tales of the supernatural ($r = .66$), ghost stories ($r = .64$), and occult literature ($r = .49$). Ideologically, horror-and-weird disagrees with the main premise of the "Unknown" school of science-fantasy, which holds that the supernatural can be understood and therefore controlled. Campbell's writers asserted that science can conquer the unknown and make it safely known. Horror-and-weird doubts that the supernatural is constrained by any humanly intelligible laws. Magic and the supernatural become horrible only when they are inexplicable, inhuman forces acting to defeat us, merciless and unmanageable. Robert W. Lowndes traced horror-and-weird fiction back to the impotence and ignorance of primitive peoples, asserting, "It has its roots deep in the primal feelings of bafflement and helplessness the first conscious men felt before the forces of nature, and the vast expanse of phenomena which, though beyond their limited senses, was constantly revealed to them."[66]

The supernatural, according to horror-and-weird, is quite indifferent to humans. H. P. Lovecraft who has the highest correlation with horror-and-weird ($r = .57$), once said, "All my tales are based on the fundamental premise that common human laws and interests and emotions have no validity or significance in the vast cosmos-at-large."[67] Another time he wrote: "My idea of the essence of a weird tale is that it successfully present a picture of some impressive violation of the established order of things—some defeat of time, space, or natural law, or some subtle intrusion of influences from another imagined order of being upon the familiar order of being."[68]

These principles are perfectly illustrated in Lovecraft's story "The Colour out of Space," published in Gernsback's *Amazing* in 1927. When a meteorite falls on New England, creeping death falls with it. Iridescent, fleeting colors flicker at the edge of one's vision, and the land turns gray. Life and sanity wither. The meteorite is utterly alien. "It was nothing of this earth, but a piece of the great outside; and as such dowered with outside properties and obedient to outside laws."[69] A piece of it is taken to the university, where scientists watch it unaccountably shrink and vanish. "When it had gone, no residue was left behind, and in time the professors felt scarcely sure they had indeed seen with waking eyes that cryptic vestige of the fathomless gulfs outside; that lone, weird message from other universes and other realms of matter, force, and entity."[70]

Contemporary science assumes that the same physical laws which operate here and now in the laboratory apply across the greatest gulfs of time and space. But in Lovecraft's stories other laws may exist, laws that are unimaginably strange, inconceivable, inscrutable. For the sensation of *fear* to be maximally stimulated, not only must horrible things happen in the stories, but the human characters must be singularly unable to deal with them. The typical horror-and-weird protagonist emotes rather than acts, faints rather than thinks, flees rather than attacks. As Fritz Leiber explained, "In supernatural horror fiction the protagonist is generally a helpless victim of cosmic forces, dead afterwards, or only babbling of his escape . . . science fiction protagonists more often solve the dreadful problem facing them and gain knowledge of the unknown."[71]

Lovecraft's tale "The Shadow out of Time" finds horror in time travel. Consider the emotionalism and ideological character of the opening paragraphs:

> After twenty-two years of nightmare and terror, saved only by a desperate conviction of the mythical source of certain impressions, I am unwilling to vouch for the truth of that which I think I found in Western Australia on the night of July 17–18, 1935. There is reason to hope that my experience was wholly or partly an hallucination—for which, indeed, abundant causes existed. And yet, its realism was so hideous that I sometimes find hope impossible.
>
> If the thing did happen, then man must be prepared to accept notions of the cosmos, and of his own place in the seething vortex of time, whose merest mention is paralyzing. He must, too, be placed on guard against a specific, lurking peril which, though it will never engulf the whole race, may impose monstrous and unguessable horrors upon certain venturesome members of it.[72]

What is this thing that may have happened in the Australian desert? What manner of nightmare and terror grip the narrator for twenty-two years? The story is told by Nathaniel Wingate Peaslee, who experiences a marked personality change, almost as if a different person has suddenly inhabited his body, followed by depression, amnesia, and nightmares that recur for years. Perhaps the dreams are real, perhaps the emerging sense of what has been done to him is not a consolidating paranoid psychosis but the truth. Psychiatrists urge Peaslee to seek the meaning of his dreams rather than repress them. He studies old manuscripts, including "the dreaded Necronomicon of the mad Arab Abdul Alhazred."[73] He dreams on and tries to interpret the nightmares. It seems to him that he is having visions of an age in the distant past. Did some horrible, ancient beings called Elders displace the minds of some modern men in order to explore and enjoy our own century? Has his mind been switched for a time with the mind of an alien being who lived millions of years ago? Is his madness really the partial recall of time travel that he has undergone against his will by transmigration of souls—not psychosis but metempsychosis? In some vast ruins beneath the Australian desert Peaslee discovers a book written a hundred and fifty million years before, written *in his own handwriting*.

CONCLUSION

The key to the ideology of the fantasy cluster is the high correlations linking fantasy and sword-and-sorcery with stories about magic ($r = .65$, $r = .57$). While space opera and action-adventure may not invoke supernatural forces, the events typically are so obviously impossible that the characters and machines act as if by magic. A character who possesses magical powers does not need the technical competence prized by hard science nor the social consciousness and psychological insight prized by the new wave. Because magic defies natural law and rests upon supernatural assumptions, it cannot fully be understood.

Either one has magic or one does not. No amount of action or insight can achieve magic in the real world. If an Arthur or a Siegmund finds a magic sword driven into a rock or tree, he is the only hero who can draw it forth. But such rocks and trees do not exist in the landscape we readers inhabit, and no amount of exercise will give an ordinary character the strength to draw forth a magic sword. Only characters who already are magical can get magic. While some fantasy heroes—such as the Hobbits who quest for the magic ring in Tolkien's fables—have to earn their magic, they cannot start from a world without magic. The quest itself is given to them, not invented by them. Either supernormal powers confer the magic directly, or they set a mission that results in magic.

The hard science ideology urges achievement of greatness through intelligence and hard work. It says that the world can be remade through physical science and technology. The new wave ideology urges a new consciousness. Often it, too, is achievement-oriented, but it considers human action impotent unless guided by sensitivity and awareness. At other times the action of the new wave story is entirely internal, and it is precisely a new consciousness that must be achieved. Each of these ideologies urges that we act to change the real world. Thus each is culturally activist, though urging different means to achieve change and seeking different futures.

The fantasy cluster often describes action and awareness, but at base this ideology rejects the idea that the real world can be transformed. Fantasy depicts lives that absolutely cannot be achieved and worlds that cannot be understood fully by any form of human consciousness. While all fiction is to some extent escapist, fantasy seems completely so, giving no guidance for reshaping the world through any kind of activism.

In hard science the protagonists change the world, and in new wave they themselves are changed. In hard science the characters struggle to change their relationships with things; in the new wave the characters grope to change their relationships with other people. In fantasy, no matter what superficial twists the plot takes, nothing changes.

Theodore Sturgeon complained that sword-and-sorcery fails to offer what he feels great fiction must offer, the growth of human awareness through a protagonist who is changed by experience. He said, "The genre's very nature dictates that the sword-swinging protagonist must be the same person at the end of the story as he is at the beginning."[74] The values he expressed are those of the new wave, but they are not the only possible values.

A clue to the alternative set of values that might be applied to sword-and-sorcery and other parts of the cluster is found in two items with extremely high correlations in Table 10: myths and legends and sagas and epics. Some social scientists view primitive myth and ritual as merely awkward attempts to describe and magically influence the natural world—as a primitive form of science that should be discarded as soon as modern science is available. Similarly, hard science critics trying to find realism in the fantasy cluster will condemn the stories when they fail to find it. But many classical sociologists and anthropologists, including Emile Durkheim and Bronislaw Malinowski, have argued that myth and ritual perform very important functions, supporting the solidarity of the tribe and forcefully transmitting the norms, values, and traditions essential to the group's survival.[75]

Thus myth acts but is not activist; in the broadest sense, it is conservative. It conserves, transmits, protects, and promotes traditional ways of thinking and living that have proven successful over generations of trial. Perhaps the fantasy cluster serves these functions for its modern readers. Action-adventure and sword-and-sorcery, for example, may offer macho images of the ideal hero and in so doing support traditional male values. Fantasy comforts its audience and entertains in a way that apparently supports older American and Western values.

By placing its stories in distant lands, fantasy protects current social policy from reexamination. Its magic gives vicarious pleasure through relief from the restrictions and problems of everyday life. In so doing, it makes the conditions of daily life more bearable. But its uninhibited adventures and aesthetic glories take place on planes removed from mundane action. Thus magic permits gratifying fiction about things that cannot and must not be achieved.

Unlike the other two types, fantasy seems to support the status quo. Space opera, at the hard science end of the fantasy cluster, does not suggest realistic inventions, educate readers in correct physical science, or propose careers that readers might conceivably achieve. Horror-and-weird, at the new wave end, expresses, as some new wave stories do, an abject hopelessness about saving humans from damnation. Even the most apparently gloomy new wave stories serve to warn the reader about real-world issues that must be addressed and thus may energize action despite the impossibility of effective action in the stories. On the positive side, fantasy may serve to decorate readers' lives with aesthetic experiences, just as it inspires artists to decorate the covers and pages of its books. Uninterested in activism, the subgenres of the fantasy cluster are art for art's sake.

III

THE POWER
OF
IMAGINATION

6

THE EFFECTS

OF

SCIENCE FICTION

I have shown that science fiction is divided into competing ideological factions with distinctly different agendas for the human future. With such dissension in its ranks, does SF have any net propagandistic effects on its readers? Or do the opposing factions cancel each other out, leaving no significant resultant? In this chapter I will show that science fiction promotes spaceflight and the exploratory mind. However, it may fail in the task Hugo Gernsback set for it, propagandizing on behalf of science and technology in general.

In *The Spaceflight Revolution*, a study of the social movement that produced modern rocketry, I demonstrated that science fiction played a crucial role by inspiring the space pioneers. It gave continual encouragement to young people and to engineers who wanted to conquer outer space. But the SF subculture has always claimed to do more. As Lester del Rey wrote in 1960, "The road to space is paved with good inventions, and most of them are the ideas of science fiction writers."[1]

One chapter in *The Spaceflight Revolution* considered the claim that SF often suggests creative technical ideas that need only be developed slightly to produce useful new machines and procedures. The available evidence was mostly negative. Many of the "inventions" in SF stories were lifted from already published technical reports; they merely popularized an existing innovation. Most of the others were not sufficiently detailed or realistic to guide engineers in producing a workable device.

There is more merit in the hypothesis that SF is a storehouse of deviant ideas of a nontechnical sort and thus that it has become a fertile breeding ground of new social movements. Overflowing with unusual concepts and schemes, the literature allows the reader to consider alien perspectives and unexpected options. Within its three broad ideologies are hundreds of specific ideas that originated in a very wide range of subcultures.

A THEORY OF THE POWER OF WORDS

There are many approaches to the sociology of ideology. In a series of essays, Rodney Stark and I have explored what might be called the pragmatic or utilitarian theory of how words, written or spoken, might shape action.[2] All persons seek rewards and avoid costs. To do this effectively, humans need explanations, statements about how they can obtain rewards at the least cost. Ideologies are systems of explanations about how societies and other groups can achieve rewards and escape costs. How, then, can ideologies influence behavior? Do ideas have power over human minds?

If any one book has influenced history, it is the Bible. And if any systems of ideas and evaluations can influence minds and shape history, they are the religious faiths that have thrived in all ages and all societies. We have been told by clergy and social scientists alike that religion instills morality. But when Travis Hirschi and Rodney Stark examined the effect of religious belief on delinquent behavior among California high school boys, they found that belief had no effect. Religious youngsters were just as likely to commit acts of delinquency as were their irreligious peers.[3] That finding fitted in with the secular biases of many social scientists, Hirschi and Stark found, and the study was widely cited as evidence that religion is moribund and irrelevant to the modern world.

But in Georgia a study found that religious beliefs do keep believing teen-agers from committing the deviant acts performed by those who lacked faith.[4] And nationally rates of crime across geographic areas show strong negative correlations with rates of church membership.[5] Despite the apparent contradiction between them, these findings can be harmonized. A society-level effect can switch the influence of religion on or off. The studies finding a strong religious effect on delinquency have been done in areas with high rates of church membership, while the contrary studies, like the one by Hirschi and Stark, have been done in areas of low church membership.

Apparently religion does not prevent individuals from committing deviant acts if they wish to commit them unless religious organizations are strong in the community. Our theory does not merely say that where many people are unchurched, those irreligious people will be free to deviate. It says that in such areas even religious persons will deviate. When churches are weak and do not have a strong alliance with the secular society, they lack the power to restrain their own members. Good evidence for this was found in a national survey of high school students. In areas where religion was weak, there was little relationship between religion and delinquency. But where religion was strong, there was a strong negative correlation.[6]

These findings harmonized well with the theoretical perspective called control theory that proved most successful in Hirschi's analysis of the original California study.[7] This highly sociological approach emphasizes the power of the social bond—of enduring social relationships between individuals— to restrain deviance. It assumes that persons can often gain immediate gratification and other rewards from violating norms and that they will naturally do so unless something stops them. For example, boys with close attachments to their parents are far less likely to commit acts of delinquency than boys who lack this social bond. This fits exactly the theory that humans act to obtain rewards and avoid costs, because social attachments are highly valuable rewards (providing a wide range of specific rewards as well as being intrinsically rewarding). Delinquency threatens these relationships and thus is costly rather than rewarding for the socially bonded person.[8]

Subsequent research found that religion deters many kinds of deviance when it can act through social networks of people who share religious consensus. Suicide rates are higher in unchurched regions of the country. Even religious deviance itself, in the form of cults, is facilitated by any weakening of the traditional religious organizations. Religion is not salient for friendships unless it is promoted by a vigorous social movement, such as the Protestant born-again phenomenon. That is, respondents who said they had very strong religious beliefs, but who were not part of the intensive born-again social network, seemed completely uninfluenced by their religion in choosing friends or in many other kinds of behavior.[9]

In all of these studies, ideological beliefs and values do not seem to matter in themselves, no matter how strongly the individual proclaims them, unless they are rendered potent by strong social bonds. Even then one may wonder whether religious faith is merely a marker indicating that an individual is incorporated into the conventional society, rather than a real power acting parallel to social forces. In the picture sketched by this research on religion, ideology is epiphenomenal.

The same may be true in the area of sex role ideologies, a topic frequently covered in modern science fiction. In a study that relied on content analysis of stories written by college students, Matina Horner claimed to have found that American women suffered from "fear of success," instilled through childhood socialization and teenage culture. But many subsequent attempts to verify this hypothesis have failed, and the original research design has been criticized as highly inadequate.[10] My own research has failed to find any impact of sex role ideology either on delinquent behavior or on interest in mathematics. That is, women with "liberated" views on sex roles were not more likely than their more traditional sisters to enter the formerly male provinces of youthful misbehavior or mathematical accomplishment.[11] On the other hand, gender differences in love of math seem to be entirely explained by the utilitarian theory that people's interest in mathematics depends partly on how useful it will be to them in their future careers; women have not yet found that mathematics will provide them with opportunities as great as those enjoyed by men.

I doubt that we can understand ideology in terms of ideas or values that have *power* over the minds of people who hear or read them. In modern America people have great freedom to seek cultural expressions that harmonize with their chosen lifestyles, past experiences, and current needs. They read science fiction only if they choose to; few people will ingest many stories from one of the SF factions unless they are rewarded with pleasure. And because enjoyment of science fiction is mainly a solitary activity, the authors do not have an alliance with cohesive social networks that might give their writings the power to change unwilling minds.

Elsewhere I have written about the factors that helped the Nazis rise to power in Germany.[12] Ideology played a role, but I concluded that its function was as a facilitator of social forces rather than as a force itself. Few people read Hitler's book *Mein Kampf* until after he was in charge of the country. The Nazis adjusted their ideological appeals to local conditions rather than converting the masses to a coherent new doctrine of faith.[13]

Recently I have been investigating quantitative data on the American utopian experiments of the nineteenth century, a topic not that far from science fiction, because both involve radical dreams of the future. Several writers on utopianism agree that religious ideology, or something very much like it, gave communes added strength once they had been started.[14] But my own research causes me to doubt this proposition. The largest and most successful "utopia" was that of the Shakers, which in 1850 had about 4,000 members in twenty-one communes across the Northeast. My research in the U.S. Census archives revealed that of the 1,600 new Shaker recruits mentioned in the 1860 census, fully 68 percent were children and many others were single parents with children. Thus, far from being a utopian experiment inspired by ideology, the Shakers were a social refuge for homeless children and some unfortunate adults. Most other alleged utopian movements in American history either failed quickly or, like the Shakers, fell short of modern definitions of utopianism.[15]

If ritual and ideology were really powerful in their own right, the Shaker experience would have been overwhelming in its effect. Daily rituals, rich mythology, and aesthetic symbols conspired to convince the children that the Shaker way of life was by far the most moral and sacred. Yet what happened when the children reached adulthood? Most of them left. Shakers were forbidden to express sexuality in a normal way and to produce children. Individual careers and selfish pursuit of rewards were also forbidden. Even an extremely strong social influence (allied with a transcendental ideology) was unable to restrain the individual search for valued rewards.

Thus there is good reason to suspect that utopian ideologies have little independent power to force people in a new direction. Religious belief, political ideology, and utopianism appear to be *expressive* rather than *instrumental* forms of culture, if we focus only on their coercive power over individual action. Perhaps the same is true of science fiction. It may be an attractive mode of self-expression or private contemplation of what fans already feel, rather than a shaper of new feelings.

Culture includes more than just attempts to exhort others and to express ourselves. It consists of facts, skills, and ideas for accomplishing practical tasks and making decisions about future action. If literature has not the power to persuade people to go along with the author's opinions, it may have the capacity to provide alternatives, making suggestions that the reader can compare with others before taking action. Some recent research on religion provides further observations on this point.

One study of suicide, even after statistical controls for the effect of social bonds, indicated that religion has some power to deter self-murder.[16] Apparently, religious beliefs provide a measure of hope to sustain potential suicides through the period of greatest danger. Questionnaire research in the unchurched Pacific region of the United States (where barely a third of adults belong to churches, half the rate in the rest of the country) indicates that religion has some power to determine attitudes toward abortion, to shape sexual behavior, and to limit the use of recreational drugs.[17] Apparently, religious beliefs provide guidance to help people decide what to do in circumstances of danger, ambiguity, and uncertainty. Again, statistical controls showed that this guidance does not depend upon a person's current social involvement in church and that it does not require religion to be manifested in a strong organization allied with secular society or the state. Thus religion can offer hope and guidance even when it cannot force obedience to its commandments.

For people who invest much time in reading it, science fiction may also offer guidance and hope, and it may serve other related functions as well.

Traditionally, literature has been seen as a force or as the indicator of other social forces. But an alternate view is that science fiction literature is valuable for what it gives people, rather than what it does to them or says about them.

Science fiction is a resource, offering ideas about possible courses of action and interpretations of reality. People are entirely free to adopt or reject these ideas. When SF disseminates a really new idea, many people may adopt it, not because they are forced to but because they find it of value in their own lives. In those cases, science fiction becomes a potent cultural influence, worthy of analysis as propaganda.

SPACE PROPAGANDA

The idea that has perhaps been most successfully propagated by science fiction is that of space travel. My analysis of the impact of SF will begin with this issue, which was promoted in the fiction of the Golden Age.

Concerning the message of science fiction, Lester del Rey has said, "Since the beginning, the single most important theme has been that of getting out into space."[18] All kinds of SF stories have used space and other planets for their backgrounds, and many popular authors have described spaceflight as an exciting and wonderful endeavor. Several pioneers in the social movement that gave us modern rocketry were inspired in adolescence by science fiction. Robert H. Goddard, American rocket inventor, decided that space travel would be rewarding after he read Wells's *War of the Worlds*. Verne's *From the Earth to the Moon* suggested astronautics as a career to both the Russian pioneer Konstantin Tsiolkovsky and the German Hermann Oberth. Also influential for German space pioneers was the novel *Two Planets* by Kurd Lasswitz.[19] Carl Sagan, a leading scientist and the preeminent contemporary propagandist for space, was partly inspired in youth by the Mars novels of Edgar Rice Burroughs.[20]

While SF may promote space travel subtly, implicitly describing interplanetary flight as a means of obtaining valuable rewards, sometimes an author breaks into rapturous prose about spaceflight, expressing the prime emotion of science fiction: the sense of wonder. In Jack Williamson's story "Minus Sign," Rick Drake takes a meditative walk across the surface of the asteroid Pallas: "He shivered again. The dark spatial night had reached out to touch his heart with the bright and chilling finger of its veiled eternal mystery. He felt its awe and dread, yet somehow he was stirred and lifted with a sense of human might and human daring. Humbly, he shared the human greatness that had begun to conquer worlds never meant for men."[21]

Some hard science writers have written textbooks of the spaceflight movement, using the medium of fiction to discuss the technical requirements of spaceflight and the justifications for it. Heinlein's first two "juvenile" novels, *Rocket Ship Galileo* and *Space Cadet*, written in 1947 and 1948, are excellent examples. They were designed to teach young readers that they should go to the planets and offered sound ideas on how to get there and what conditions in space would be like. Each novel follows a group of teenage boys who learn astronautics, then make trips into space. On a more adult level, in Heinlein's story "The Man Who Sold the Moon" a space-dedicated capitalist organizes the first moon flight on a commercial basis. The story describes the economic benefits of spaceflight and tells something about rocket engineering.

The impact of these stories was greatly magnified when they were translated effectively from print into a visual medium. *Space Cadet* became *Tom Corbett, Space Cadet*, one of the most successful television series of the early 1950s. In 1950 *Rocket Ship Galileo* and "The Man Who Sold the Moon" became *Destination Moon*, a hard-sell, educational feature movie about the first moon flight. It achieved a high level of technical accuracy, in part because Heinlein was employed as adviser. *Destination Moon* included an educational cartoon on the principles of rocket propulsion, dramatic demonstrations of weightlessness and hard vacuum, and a lecture on the value of space.[22] Sensing well the mood of America in the 1950s, the film stresses the motive of military security, although the moon mission is carried out by private industry rather than by the air force. Entrepreneur Jim Barnes tells an assembled group of capitalists, whom he wishes to persuade to invest in a moon rocket, "Not only is this the greatest adventure awaiting mankind, but it's the greatest challenge ever hurled at American industry, and General Thayer is going to tell you why." Thayer explains, "The reason is quite simple. We are not the only ones who know that the moon can be reached. We are not the only ones who are planning to go there. The race is on! And we'd better win it, because there is absolutely no way to stop an attack from outer space. The first country that can use the moon for the launching of missiles will control the earth. That, gentlemen, is the most important military fact of this century."[23]

Nineteen years later the first spaceship did reach the moon, propelled as much by a space race with the Russians as by its liquid fuels.[24] Of course, science fiction did not invent the laws of physics or politics that made real moon flights possible, but the ideas it disseminated over the decades influenced the course of real events.

Arthur C. Clarke's 1951 novel *Prelude to Space* is so thoroughly educational that one could even say it is not a work of fiction. Critic Albert I. Berger wrote, "It has been Clarke's often stated belief that science-fiction reading is preparing the public for the age of space flight, an attitude which this frankly propagandistic novel demonstrates to the full."[25] In the book Dirk Alexson, a professional historian, documents the first flight to the moon, carried out by an idealistic private organization. The story begins some weeks before the flight and ends at the moment of launch. In almost every scene Dirk and the reader learn about some technical aspect of spaceflight or hear ideological statements in favor of it. There is hardly any plot in the conventional sense, other than a few moments of interpersonal conflict. The moon flight itself is not described, and only an epilogue, in which Dirk is living out his last years on the moon, tells us that the flight was successful. Yet the book is a marvel, because it communicates intelligibly many of the ideas and values of space-flight.

At a couple of points *Prelude to Space* considers the role of science fiction. In one humorous passage Clarke reports that the chief intellectual opponent to the fictional future moon program is C. S. Lewis, with whom Clarke had actually debated the issue.[26] A little later, two leaders of the moon program, Professor Maxton and Raymond Collins, discuss science fiction with Dirk:

> Collins turned to Dirk with a smile. "I should explain," he said mischievously, "that the Prof has a soft spot for the lurid magazine—*Stupendous Stories*, or whatever it calls itself—that goes in for hyperspace, time-travel, and all that sort of thing. In fact"—he leaned forward conspiratorily—"*once upon a time he used to write for it!*"
>
> Professor Maxton seemed unabashed. "I'm not ashamed of the fact,'" he said cheerfully, "that before Ray was born I was paying my college fees with the aid of my typewriter. Besides someone had to write about space-travel before people would believe it was possible."
>
> "But it didn't work out that way," objected Collins. "Most of those stories were so damned silly, and so badly written, that they had just the opposite effect. Everyone thought that interplanetary travel was stuff for the kids."
>
> "So it was—in the 1940s," said Maxton. "They read about it—and when they grew up, they made it happen. There's quite a field for you literary fellows there, Dirk. When you've finished your history, what about a learned thesis on 'Scientific Romances and Their Effects on the Development of Astronautics'?"
>
> "You mean, 'Science Fiction—Its Cause, Diagnosis and Cure'," interjected Collins.[27]

Certainly, one can name many stories in which space travel heaps nightmares upon human beings, from Wells's *War of the Worlds* to Malzberg's *Beyond Apollo*. But readers may focus more on the fact that space travel brings them a rewarding reading experience than on the ruin it brings to the fictional protagonists. It is quite possible that SF convinces the audience to love space, even if some varieties of it simultaneously teach hostility to other results of science and technology. Furthermore, science fiction may be the main influence on many people's attitudes toward interplanetary travel and an expanded space program.

In 1976 I wrote, "Although science fiction played a vital role in disseminating ideas and values in the earliest years of the Spaceflight Movement, it drew apart from actual space developments in the 1930s. It does not produce many ideas useful in real spaceflight. We cannot be sure if it has an active role to play in producing a positive attitude toward NASA in the general public, and testing such a hypothesis would be difficult."[28] However, surveys of college students and science fiction conventions provided the data needed to confirm what many may feel is a self-evident hypothesis: science fiction promotes positive attitudes toward the space program. The complete findings, reported to the 1981 Goddard Memorial Symposium of the American Astronautical Society, suggested something more surprising.[29] Science fiction apparently does little to promote other areas of technology: its boosting effect seems limited to spaceflight. It is not certain that SF does not promote technology in all nonspace areas, because the surveys contained only a few good, previously tested questions. But the effect of science fiction on space attitudes is very clear.

The first evidence came from my pilot surveys: a 1974 questionnaire filled out by 81 members of the New England Science Fiction Association, a 1974 survey of 130 SF fanzine editors and their associates, and a 1975 survey of 79 participants at the Boskone SF convention in Boston. In 1969 a Gallup poll found that only 14 percent of its national sample wanted appropriations for the space program increased. But 81 percent of the NESFA respondents and 80 percent of those at Boskone wanted more money for the space program.

A study carried out in 1970 by Irene Taviss asked 201 Boston area respondents to rank seven "technological and social programs" in terms of how much they favored each one.[30] They put welfare in first place and the space program in last place, after pollution prevention, crime prevention, mental health, urban housing, and national defense. But when presented with the same question, both the NESFA respondents and the fanzine editors placed the space program second, with pollution prevention in first place. Only 38.8 percent of Taviss's respondents agreed that "in the long run, discoveries made in our space program will have a big payoff for the average person." In comparison, fully 88.7 percent of the 595 respondents to my main Iguanacon questionnaire agreed with this statement.

In a survey I made of 1,439 students at the University of Washington, 166

THE POWER OF IMAGINATION

gave "science fiction novels" the rock-bottom lowest preference rating of 0. They hate SF. Of this group, 51.2 percent agreed with the anti-spaceflight statement, "The United States is spending too much money on space, so appropriations for the space program should be reduced." In contrast, of the 196 students who gave science fiction novels the top rating of 6, who love SF, only 14.3 percent wanted space funding reduced. Figure 9 shows the connection between preference for SF and agreement with the antispace statement for the 1,439 college students. It graphs their feelings about the television shows *Star Trek* and *Battlestar Galactica* as well as their preference for SF novels. Clearly, those who like science fiction want NASA defended against budget cuts.

My Goddard Symposium report examined the data more closely, and sought to determine whether the three ideological factions within SF had

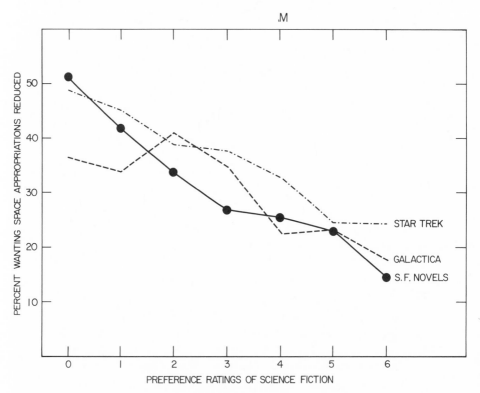

Figure 9. Science fiction and the space program

different opinions about spaceflight. The results were unimpressive. No survey question I have tried detects any antispace feeling among the new wave or fantasy cluster factions. Fans of these styles are just like other SF fans in their attitudes toward spaceflight. There is, however, some indirect evidence that hard science promotes the space program more than the other styles. As Chapter 3 reported, hard science fans are more apt to like factual reports on the space program and spaceflight ($r = .43; N = 409$). All fans strongly support the space program, but hard science fans show a personal interest in it.

In Chapter 4 I examined the preferences of new wave fans for authors of other types of literature. I showed that embracing the new wave did not imply rejection of hard science SF. That is, fans could enjoy new wave fiction in addition to more traditional forms, without any apparent contradiction. To put a name to it, one might say that new wave fans are more *cosmopolitan* in their tastes and that they favor traditional forms of science fiction as much as other fans. New wave is an ideological faction of authors more than of readers. Preference for new wave may indicate a greater tolerance for new ideas and an interest in exploring alternative value systems, but it need not imply rejection of the traditional values of science fiction. Similarly, the fantasy cluster fan may simply add heightened imagination to the traditional SF values such as space exploration.

PROMOTION OF PARAPSYCHOLOGY

Spaceflight is not the only value promoted by the literature. Another is openness to the magic that is so important in fantasy. One of the most common themes or devices of science fiction is that of the "wild talents" possessed by some persons, according to religious cults and occultists. The terms for these phenomena are many: telepathy, teleportation, clairvoyance, ESP, astral projection, psychic healing, psychokinesis, and so on. The names used in science fiction include some with a scientific flavor, notably parapsychology, psi, and psionics. Articles in the popular press often assert that such talents exist, and self-anointed parapsychologists publish what appear to be scientific and scholarly journals and books in the field.[31] But standard academic behavioral science does not accept parapsychology at all, and debunking books and articles appear with some frequency. At present a lively debunking news journal, *The Skeptical Inquirer*, attempts to summarize and disseminate negative evidence. Among those closely associated with this journal are science fiction writers Isaac Asimov, Philip Klass, and Milton Rothman.

The Visual Encyclopedia of Science Fiction mentions fiction about parapsychology by fifty-two of the authors included in my questionnaires: Aldiss, Bester, Blish, Brunner, Budrys, Burroughs, Campbell, Clifton, de Camp, del Rey, Delany, Dick, Dickson, Doyle, Ellison, Farmer, Garrett, Haggard, Heinlein, Hubbard, Keyes, Knight, Kuttner, Lafferty, Leiber, Malzberg, Matheson, McCaffrey, McIntosh, Miller, Moorcock, Moore, Niven, Poe, Riley, Russell, Schmitz, Sheckley, Silverberg, Simak, Smith, Stapledon, Sturgeon, Tucker, van Vogt, Vance, Weinbaum, Wells, Wilhelm, Wilson, Wyndham, and Zelazny.[32] Most of the other authors could have been included if the encyclopedia's essay had been longer. The list is remarkable for its breadth as well as its length. Most styles and all the main ideological divisions are represented. It is logical to conclude that the large number of psi stories in SF literature may have a powerful propaganda effect, spreading acceptance of pseudoscience.

One would certainly expect this kind of magic in stories from the fantasy cluster, and the new wave concern for aesthetics and psychological speculation might bring its writers to parapsychology. But a remarkable number of superficially hard science stories contain ESP. Often some "explanation" rationalizes the magic as technology based on as-yet-undiscovered science. For example, the lens in E. E. Smith's *Galactic Patrol* is a psionic device giving its wearer the power to read and influence other minds. Sometimes a hard science writer postulates that ESP will be the natural next step in human evolution, as Heinlein does in *Beyond This Horizon* and van Vogt does in *Slan*. In his novel *The Alien*, Raymond F. Jones places psychic powers in a gland that can be transplanted into the body of an ordinary human.

Two of the cleverest psi novels were written in the 1950s by Alfred Bester, *The Demolished Man* and *The Stars My Destination*. Each subtly analyzes a type of parapsychology and a kind of psychoanalysis. *The Demolished Man* is about telepathy and Freud's theories, while *The Stars My Destination* is about teleportation and Alfred Adler's system of depth psychology. Bester's novelette, "Fondly Fahrenheit," combines psychosis and psychic symbiosis linking a man and a robot. In stories like these SF has explicated the logic of ESP and thus perhaps has made ESP more plausible for many readers. And plausibility may lead to belief. One of the largest new parapsychological religions, Scientology, founded by SF writer L. Ron Hubbard, emerged from the pages of *Astounding Science Fiction* in 1950.[33]

Table 13 gives the patterns of responses by fans and student groups to my simple ESP question. Of course, many things separate the two groups of respondents beyond mere love of science fiction. But I think that the college students provide a reasonable comparison with the fans, sharing with them

Table 13. Comparison of belief in ESP among SF fans and among students (in percentages)

Opinion on ESP	All respondents		Male respondents		Female respondents	
	SF fans	Students	SF fans	Students	SF fans	Students
Definitely exists	37.8	22.7	28.0	22.6	51.6	22.9
Probably exists	30.3	34.6	32.1	33.6	27.9	35.6
Possibly exists	27.3	37.6	32.7	38.4	19.7	36.8
Does not exist	4.6	5.1	7.2	5.4	0.8	4.7
Total	100.0	100.0	100.0	100.0	100.0	100.0
N	590	1,412	346	735	244	677
	(gamma = .24)		(gamma = .07)		(gamma = .47)	

a high level of education, awareness of cultural trends, and youth. The first two columns compare fans with students, based on responses from the 590 fans who answered the ESP question and indicated whether they were male or female and on responses from the 1,412 students who answered these two questions and also rated SF novels on the preference scale. Members of the SF subculture seem more convinced of the reality of ESP, with 37.8 percent saying it "definitely exists," compared with 22.7 percent of the Seattle college students. The association between SF and ESP can be measured by a correlation coefficient, which here achieves a moderate gamma of .24.

One great and mysterious difference between the fans and the students is that the respondent's sex played a different role in determining attitudes toward ESP in the two groups. For respondents to the main Iguanacon questionnaire, there was a highly significant correlation between being female and believing in ESP (gamma = .42). The Iguanacon pilot questionnaire on SF movies gave the same result (gamma = .36). But among the college students the association between being female and believing in ESP was utterly insignificant (gamma = .03). At present I do not have data to help explain this remarkable difference. The students at the university were such a broad sample of intelligent young people, equally male and female, that I think the answer to the problem is in science fiction itself. Perhaps the women who are attracted to SF are very different from the men. Conceivably the male fans include many hard-headed engineers who reject ESP, while female fans are disproportionately fanciful personalities. I have no proof. In the table the third through the sixth columns of percentages compare fans with students, separating them by sex. There is little difference between male fans and male students (gamma = .07), but a huge difference between female fans and female students (gamma = .47).

Belief in ESP does correlate with preference for certain types of literature. Among the 409 good Iguanacon respondents, the associations linking the ESP question with hard science SF ($r = -.11$) and new wave SF ($r = .12$) are insignificant. Statistically significant if weak correlations tie ESP to sword-and-sorcery ($r = .19$) and fantasy ($r = .20$). The strongest correlations, not surprisingly, are with occult literature ($r = .37$), stories about telepathy ($r = .36$), and tales of the supernatural ($r = .34$). Also correlated are myths and legends ($r = .27$), stories about magic ($r = .25$), and stories set in a universe where the laws of nature are very different from those found on our world ($r = .25$). The four authors most strongly correlated with belief in ESP are women writers of fantasy: Bradley ($r = .23$), Henderson ($r = .25$), McCaffrey ($r = .25$), and Norton ($r = .23$).

Among the students a weak correlation exists between liking SF novels and liking occult literature ($r = .22$). Although neither fans nor students gave very high ratings to occult literature, the average score on the zero-to-six scale was significantly higher for fans (2.13) than for students (1.45). Only 25.5 percent of the fans gave occult literature a zero rating, but 41.5 percent of the students did so. In contrast, 24.5 percent of the fans rated it 4 or higher, compared with only 13.5 percent for the students.

The obvious interpretation of these findings is that SF does indeed propagandize in favor of parapsychology, pseudoscience, and occultism. An alternate possibility is that the science fiction subculture attracts people who are more open to new ideas and magnifies this characteristic in them. Perhaps fans tend to reject conventional wisdom in favor of novel speculations, a trait they seem to love in their authors.

A SUBCULTURE OF FREETHINKERS

Novelty is a prime value of SF. Robert Silverberg said, "What I think sf does uniquely is show the reader something he's never seen before, and only if an sf story does this is it worth anything to me."[34] Often the new vision is a radical perspective on familiar things. As Gardner Dozois once commented, "One of the premier values of science fiction as literature is that it enables us to look at ourselves through alien eyes."[35]

SF takes its readers beyond the limits of current assumptions, rejoicing in unconventional concepts and evaluations. Calling SF "a philosophical, speculative vehicle," Algis Budrys observed, "Science fiction is almost inescapably a vehicle for ideas whose time has not come."[36] No wonder fans toy with notions of ESP and spaceflight. Alfred Bester, who is a foe of superstition and religion but who used ESP in his novels, said, "The appeal of science fiction has always been its iconoclasm. It is the one field of fiction where no cows are sacred, and where all idols may be broken. It stimulates, entertains, and educates by daring to question the unquestionable, poke fun at the sacred, condemn the accepted, and advocate the unthinkable."[37]

Lester del Rey has noted the liberating power of the special assumptions upon which science fiction rests:

> Science fiction is unique in that it is essentially a literature of ideas. With only a few exceptions the general stream of fiction has been forced to depend on the emotional involvement of essentially familiar people and their interactions in basically familiar situations. That makes the use of any really different new idea so hard to weave in convincingly that few writers can succeed. On the other hand, science fiction offers a universe-wide range of possibilities. We can tell the story of a woman who marries a complete alien or a man who sees the end of the universe.[38]

A similar faith in the virtues of SF was expressed in more alliterative language by Forrest J. Ackerman:

> It's a literature of ideas and ideals. A fascinating forum of disciplined discussion.
> Science fiction is a literary laboratory, where the pro's and just-suppose of semantics, cybernetics, soma drugs, Esperanto, automation and automatons, immortality, extra terrestrial life, Utopia vs. Dystopia, and a thousand and one theories and discoveries more amazing than the Arabian Nights are imaginatively extrapolated by authors with inquiring minds.[39]

Seventy-one percent of the respondents to my 1973 survey of the New England Science Fiction Association agreed that "fans are literate loners in an illiterate and group-oriented society. Having more imagination than others and holding views radically at variance with their own culture they band together to find a little comfort."[40] To the extent that SF fans are indeed disaffected freethinkers, one would expect them to be dissatisfied with the society around them, especially with its cultural institutions.

To get evidence on this point, I included in the 1974 survey of fanzine editors five questions on satisfaction taken from a Gallup poll.[41] In the Gallup survey carried out just a few months before my pilot survey, 53 percent of

American adults said they were satisfied with "the future facing you and your family." Only 41 percent of the fans were satisfied with their families' futures. While 71 percent of the general public were satisfied with their standard of living, 65 percent of the fans were happy. On a related matter, 61 percent of citizens, but 50 percent of NESFA members, were satisfied with their family income. Finally, 79 percent of Gallup's sample and 70 percent of the fans were satisfied with their work. These are small differences.

Actually, there is some evidence that SF fans are better off financially than the average citizen. The median income of respondents to my survey was about $15,000, higher than the approximately $12,000 median found in the 1974 NORC General Social Survey.[42] If fans have more money than the average, they should be more satisfied. But satisfaction depends on the correspondence between what people have and what they think they deserve.[43] Fans have a bit more than the average, but they may feel they should have much more than that. Because they are well educated and live in expensive urban centers, their standards may be very high. Members of the subculture consider themselves an intellectual elite, yet society does not reward them for their imagination and brilliance.

At the 1962 World Science Fiction Convention in Chicago, James O'Meara administered an IQ test to 79 volunteers.[44] The range of scores was from 104 to 139, with a mean of 127. This is nearly two standard deviations above the population mean of 100. In the 1974 NORC General Social Survey only 15 percent of respondents had completed college, but fully 54 percent of respondents to the 1974 fanzine survey had done so, and several were still students.[45] Only 6 percent of NORC's respondents had done any graduate work, but 25 percent of the fanzine respondents had a master's degree or the equivalent, and 5 percent had a Ph.D. Fifty-nine percent of respondents to the 1973 NESFA survey were college graduates, while many of the remainder were still working on their degrees. The fan newsmagazine *Locus* reported that of the 247 nonstudent respondents to its 1973 survey of subscribers, "71% had at least a bachelor's degree and 29% had some sort of advanced degree."[46] SF fans are highly educated, but they may feel insufficiently rewarded for their intellectual superiority.

In the fifth satisfaction question in the 1974 fanzine survey, fans expressed their opinion of the American educational system. While 61 percent of Gallup's respondents were satisfied with "the education children are getting today," only 17 percent of the fans were satisfied. Just 29 percent of the general population expressed dissatisfaction with children's education, compared with 70 percent of the fans. This is a vast difference, expressing the disdain of this group for an educational system in which they excelled. This high level of dissatisfaction toward an American cultural institution, compared with the relative satisfaction indicated on the four other questions, emphasizes the fact that science fiction is primarily an *intellectual subculture*, deviant mainly in its attitudes toward intellect and ideology.

A survey of 225 Seattle area voters also included the Gallup question about "the future facing you and your family," along with items about reading SF or watching SF movies and TV shows. Of those who never read SF, only 24 percent were dissatisfied, while of those who read SF often, 48 percent were dissatisfied. Of those who never watched SF, only 22 percent were dissatisfied, compared with 49 percent of those who often watched it. [47]

Perhaps science fiction produces dissatisfaction, especially with the culture communicated through mass education, because it presents vivid images of radical cultural and intellectual alternatives. Or perhaps intellectually oriented persons who are already alienated from conventional society turn to SF for escape, achieving vicarious rewards because its stories convey great honor on characters with whom the readers identify.

The unconventionality of the science fiction subculture can also be found in its attitudes toward religion. America is still a religious nation, but SF is irreligious. As I have mentioned, respondents to the main Iguanacon questionnaire rated the Bible very low, placing it thirty-ninth out of forty kinds of literature (see Appendix Table A2). Of the 198 college students who gave a top rating to science fiction novels, 43.5 percent strongly agreed with the statement, "I definitely believe in God." In contrast 58.2 percent of the 171 who gave the lowest possible rating to science fiction novels strongly agreed. In another study I found that born-again Protestants opposed the SF idea of communication with extraterrestrials. [48]

Table 14 compares the denominational affiliations of persons in six relevant groups. The NORC General Social Survey and the survey of University of Washington students represent very different samples of the population. [49] NORC uses a random national sample of adults, and the University of Washington probably represents an extreme in irreligiousness, because students in the 1970s generally had freethinking attitudes and because Washington is the state with the lowest proportion of church members. [50] The proportion of students reporting "other" affiliation is inflated by the large Asian minority in the West and by the recent fundamentalist habit of rejecting the Protestant label.

The other two groups share many of the attitudes of science fiction fans. The World Future Society is a pop-futurology organization, based in Washington, D.C., with some thousands of members. [51] The Committee for the Future is rather like an extreme faction of the WFS, professing greater op-

THE POWER OF IMAGINATION

Table 14. Affiliations of respondents to surveys (in percentages)

Religious affiliation	1974 NORC national survey	1979 student survey	1972 World Future Society	1973 Committee for the Future	1973 NESFA survey	1974 fanzine survey
Protestant	64.3	39.4	35	25	16	25
Catholic	25.4	23.4	8	16	16	16
Jewish	3.0	3.3	6	8	14	13
Other	0.5	15.4	21	30	7	15
Nonreli-gious	6.8	18.6	30	21	48	31
Total	100.0	100.0	100	100	100	100
N	1,483	1,383	184	80	74	130

Sources: The data from the 1974 survey by the National Opinion Research Center are taken from Davis et al., 1978; data on the World Future Society are taken from Wynn, 1972; the surveys of undergraduates at the University of Washington, members of the Committee for the Future, members of the New England Science Fiction Association, and editors of science fiction fan magazines were conducted by the author.

timism about the future than its parent group. In *The Spaceflight Revolution* I described the CFF as an enthusiastic space-boosting movement that has gradually evolved into something resembling a religious cult.[52] The high proportion of those with "other" affiliations primarily represents the leaders and members of small cults who attended the 1973 CFF convention and who were polled in the survey.

The percentages of Protestants and Catholics in the two sets of science fiction fans are low compared to the NORC data and even compared to the college survey. A high proportion of fans are Jewish, three to four times the proportion in the general population, which is not so surprising, because Jews are disproportionately represented in almost all liberal intellectual movements.[53] The modal religion category is that of the nonreligious, which includes 48 percent of the NESFA respondents and 31 percent of those answering the fanzine survey. I expected to find a large number of nonreligious respondents in NESFA, so I also asked this group to report their parents' religious orientation; slightly over half replied "Protestant," and less than a quarter had nonreligious parents.

If SF fans are dissatisfied with the culture transmitted through the schools and the churches, they also tend to be politically unconventional. The 1974 NORC General Social Survey found that 36 percent of the public does not call itself either Republican or Democrat, but the proportion in the NESFA survey was 55 percent and in the fanzine survey 40 percent.[54] In both cases, Republicans were underrepresented, so one might guess that fans are closer to the liberal or radical end of the spectrum. As I discussed in Chapter 4, I included the NORC question on general political orientation in my questionnaires. Recall that I found the fans of new wave SF to be especially liberal. Now in Table 15 we can see that science fiction fans as a whole are much more liberal than the general population. When the three liberal categories are combined, 28.2 percent of the general public and 45.8 percent of the college students are distinctly left of center politically. In contrast, far more fans are on the left—61.1 percent of respondents to the main Iguanacon questionnaire and 63.9 percent of those to the film survey. In the student survey, preference for SF was associated with political liberalism, but the average difference between lovers and haters of SF novels was only one-third of a point on NORC's seven-point political scale. Table 15 reveals a bigger "extremely conservative" minority of fandom. My ethnography of the subculture revealed a vocal radical-libertarian faction, consisting of Heinlein and Anderson fans and persons who had experimented with Ayn Rand's Objectivist movement.

Table 15. Political views of respondents to surveys (in percentages)

Political orientation	1978 NORC national survey	1978 Iguanacon surveys		1979 student survey
		Main survey	Film survey	
Extremely liberal	1.5	15.5	13.1	1.9
Liberal	9.9	23.2	22.6	15.4
Slightly liberal	16.8	22.4	28.2	28.5
Moderate, middle of road	38.3	14.4	13.4	24.9
Slightly conservative	18.3	14.1	12.2	21.1
Conservative	13.1	6.6	7.7	7.9
Extremely conservative	2.1	3.8	3.0	0.2
Total	100.0	100.0	100.0	100.0
N	1,435	548	337	1,410

Sources: The data from the 1978 survey by the National Opinion Research Center are taken from Davis et al., 1978; the Iguanacon surveys and the survey of undergraduates at the University of Washington were conducted by the author.

CONCLUSION

Of all the innovations presented in science fiction, the ideal of spaceflight is most powerfully and uniformly promoted. Although literature may not have the power to force people to accept its values, science fiction appears to create strong support for the space program. It may succeed in this because the space program is not part of our everyday lives and is not an issue tied to any particular political camp. Thus SF can make the ideas of space exploration and colonization seem attractive without having to fight opposing social or ideological forces.

Literature may have its greatest autonomous impact when it recommends new ideas to readers who have no existing, salient commitments for or against the innovations. While few people may be attracted at first, those who are can act as opinion leaders, because they are the only ones who understand the innovation. SF has promoted spaceflight for generations, and the dreams that percolated for decades in the literature have bubbled over into movies and television programs, reaching far vaster audiences.

Since Sputnik, the news media have reported a succession of real space adventures. But only a hundred or so Americans have so far ventured into space, and very few lives are directly, palpably shaped by spaceflight. Thus science fiction is free to form our image of travel beyond Earth and to tell us what the space program means. Millions of people look toward future civilizations in space because SF has given them the vision to imagine that astonishing goal. In the absence of competing definitions of spaceflight, SF has had this power. When outer space is more fully developed, its practical consequences for human lives and the social influences flowing from the individuals most directly affected may be more powerful than the words of imaginative literature.

Beyond promoting spaceflight, science fiction appears to encourage and support a measure of intellectual deviance. Fans are less satisfied with society, and they are especially dissatisfied with intellectual orthodoxies. They are irreligious compared with other citizens, and they are distinctly liberal in their political orientation. In a way, this aspect of SF works against its ability to persuade readers to accept any one ideological position. Science fiction presents so many competing radical alternatives that it may inoculate fans against dogmatism. Whatever fans find in the fiction, they learn to question. The ideological impact of SF is to be found not merely in the specific opinions it inculcates but also in the resistance to conventional opinion it teaches. SF is a subculture of freethinkers rather than of believers.

Writing about the boom in SF's popularity over the past decade, Norman

Spinrad hypothesized that science fiction has to some extent replaced religion, because it is "the most nourishing and credible source of scientifically credible transcendentalism in the second half of the twentieth century."[55] Spinrad argued that the human spirit craves experience of the transcendental, and that the onward rush of science and technology has diminished the credibility of traditional religions. The sense of wonder afforded by SF is akin to religious awe, and in it people may find at least a taste of the spiritual uplifting and cosmic meaningfulness once gained in church. Spinrad's hypothesis squares with my findings that the subculture dislikes traditional religion yet is infatuated with cultic notions like ESP, especially if given a pseudoscientific gloss, as in parapsychology. Freethinkers in politics as in religion, fans of science fiction are prepared to consider many radical alternatives in culture and social organization.

7

WOMEN

IN

SCIENCE FICTION

Throughout its history, science fiction has developed new ways of looking at the world and has spread new concepts about the physical universe as well as new images of society. In the past two decades, SF has become a major category of popular culture and an important medium for invention and dissemination of radical ideologies. One of the more common topics for fictional exploration today is the perceived disadvantages of traditional sex roles and the implications and possible advantages of novel alternatives. This chapter's examination of the new activism of women in science fiction, as writers and as readers, will show how science fiction may both shape and reflect changing conceptions of the roles available for women in the real world.

WOMEN'S INVOLVEMENT IN SCIENCE AND TECHNOLOGY

If science fiction traditionally has been a literature of speculation about the physical sciences and technological development, then it is important to ask whether these subjects are as attractive to women as to men. If women typically do not like the physical sciences as much as men, or if they are drawn less often to technical careers, then women are less likely to become science fiction fans. The survey of 1,439 students at the University of Washington in Seattle, carried out in 1979, permits a comparison of attitudes toward science fiction and toward related subjects in a fairly representative college population.[1] But first, there is much to be learned from the declared majors of undergraduates and graduate students at this university. If, traditionally, science fiction drew its readership from young men interested in engineering and the physical sciences, then the movement of young women into these fields should measure the possible audience for SF among women today.

In 1979, 52 percent of the university's 16,036 undergraduates and 41 percent of the 2,509 graduate students were women. Except in botany, which is not a high-status field, most of the students majoring in the physical sciences were men. Men especially predominated in those sciences usually associated with hard science SF. According to official reports, the university did not have a single female graduate student in astronomy. Only 8 percent of the 166 undergraduate physics majors and 9 percent of the 116 physics graduate students were female. Women made up just 11 percent of the 115 chemistry graduate students and 18 percent of the 82 in mathematics. These differences undoubtedly reflected the discrepancy in career opportunities for women and for men in these fields; at the undergraduate level 27 percent of the 257 chemistry majors and 35 percent of the 247 mathematics majors were women.

In contrast to the physical sciences, a majority of the undergraduates majoring in the social sciences were women: 70 percent in sociology and 75 percent in anthropology. But in economics and political science, fields which offer more opportunities for high-status careers, men prevailed. More liberal arts majors were women—66 percent among 567 English and comparative literature majors, for example. The sex imbalance was marked in the university's professional schools. Fully 94 percent of the 913 students in the school of nursing were women, while in the school of engineering the field that is most closely associated with traditional science fiction, only 13 percent of the 3,864 students were women.

For whatever reasons, women still do not participate equally in the academic fields upon which most great science fiction of the past was built. This means, first, that fewer women will be disposed to like science fiction of any kind. Second, of those who do become fans, fewer will be drawn to the hard science variety than to the more socially oriented new wave or the more aesthetic and imaginative fantasy cluster. This does not necessarily mean that female fans active in the subculture will like hard science less than the male fans, because an appreciation of this traditional style may be a prerequisite for commitment to fandom. But on balance the sciences will attract fewer women than men.

Recently there has been much debate about and some research on the factors that discourage women from entering careers in mathematics and the physical sciences. Among the most powerful factors are the sex-role stereotypes held by parents, advisers, and friends, and also the cold fact that women who do win science degrees still find fewer attractive jobs waiting for them.[2]

Given that women are underrepresented in fields that are congenial to traditional science fiction, do they in fact differ in their attitudes toward subjects related to science fiction? Table 16 compares the responses of women students at the University of Washington (48 percent) and men (52 percent) to a number of questions about technology, spaceflight, and the sciences. The third column gives the correlation between being female and having the indicated attitude, measured by gamma, a coefficient appropriate for this format of the questions.

The first six items on the questionnaire were taken from a survey of public

Table 16. Students' opinions about technology, by sex ($N = 1,439$)

Statement	Agree (percent)		Correlation (gamma) with female
	Females	Males	
ANTITECHNOLOGY			
Machines have thrown too many people out of work.	26.0	13.1	.41
It would be nice if we would stop building so many factories and go back to nature.	50.4	32.7	.31
Technology has made life too complicated.	28.6	20.6	.24
PROTECHNOLOGY			
The potential dangers of nuclear energy are out-weighed by its potential benefits.	48.0	50.2	−.01
Technology does more good than harm.	64.8	72.7	−.23
In the long run, discoveries made in our space program will have a big payoff for the average person.	55.0	69.2	−.32
MISCELLANEOUS			
We should attempt to communicate with intelligent beings on other planets, perhaps using radio.	47.3	64.1	−.29
The United States is spending too much money on space, so appropriations for the space program should be reduced.	38.2	27.7	.31
Intelligent life probably does not exist on any planet but our own.	22.4	11.4	.34
ATTITUDES TOWARD SCIENCES			
Likes physical sciences	49.7	67.4	−.26
Likes social sciences	70.8	64.4	.16

Source: Survey of undergraduates at the University of Washington, Seattle, 1979.

attitudes toward technology carried out in 1972 by Irene Taviss.[3] The table shows that women are much more likely than men to express antitechnology attitudes and less likely to express protechnology attitudes. The one exception is the nuclear power item, on which there are no differences by sex. The questionnaire was administered just after the highly publicized Three Mile Island nuclear accident, and students may have considered this issue separately. Perhaps for this reason, responses to the nuclear question tend not to correlate with other items in the questionnaire. But five out of the six questions show men, on average, far more favorably disposed than women toward technological development.

The three miscellaneous statements evaluate attitudes toward spaceflight and contact with intelligent extraterrestrials, topics dear to the hearts of SF fans. Here again women are much less enthusiastic than men. The questionnaire included two preference questions that used the same seven-point scale employed in the Iguanacon survey. Students who gave a 4, 5, or 6 rating to the physical or the social sciences were recorded as liking those sciences. Women showed a small, but statistically significant, tendency to like the social sciences more than men, and a strong tendency to like the physical sciences less well. The student questionnaire, like students' choices of a college major, shows that men have a more positive orientation toward traditional science-fiction topics.

National polls of large random samples of the population often ask for respondents' opinion of the space program, a topic very dear to science fiction. In its annual General Social Survey, the National Opinion Research Center at the University of Chicago lists eleven government programs, among them "the space exploration program," and asks respondents whether appropriations for each are "too little," "about right (or not sure)," or "too much."[4] Table 17 summarizes responses from the 1978 survey, from interviews with 643 men and 889 women.

The first two columns in the table simply give the percentage of women and of men who said that too little was being spent on the particular program or social problem, who thought appropriations in that area should be increased. The third column gives the ratio of column one to column two, an indicator of any tendency for women to favor a program more than men do. The fourth column gives a more comprehensive measure, gamma, the association between female gender and the three answer categories for each item.

Most lines in the table show significant differences between men and women, but the last one reveals that the greatest disagreement is about support for the space program. Only 5 percent of the women wanted expenditures

Table 17. Comparison of support by men and by women of certain government programs, General Social Survey (NORC), 1978

Program	Appropriations should be increased (percent)		Tendency for women to favor program more than men	
	Women	Men	Ratio[a]	Gamma
Solving the problems of the big cities	47.4	40.5	1.17	.19
Improving and protecting the environment	58.2	51.5	1.13	.17
Welfare	15.1	11.3	1.34	.11
Dealing with drug addiction	59.9	55.8	1.07	.10
Halting the rising crime rate	68.8	65.1	1.06	.09
Improving the nation's education system	54.6	52.4	1.04	.08
Foreign aid	4.5	3.5	1.29	.08
Improving and protecting the nation's health	58.3	56.9	1.02	.05
Improving the conditions of blacks	25.6	26.9	.95	.05
The military, armaments, and defense	26.3	33.1	.79	−.08
The space exploration program	5.0	22.0	.23	−.50

a. Ratio of figure in column 1 to figure in column 2.

for space increased, compared to 22 percent of the men. Among the women, only foreign aid had less support; the men also rated welfare lower than space. The correlation between support for space and the respondent being female is strongly negative (gamma = −.50), by far the most powerful association in the table. The first seven programs in the list are favored by women slightly more than by men, improving the nation's health and improving the conditions of blacks show no sex differences, and support for the military is slightly stronger among men than among women, but the space exploration program shows a much greater sex difference. Clearly, fewer women have interests and careers that predispose them to become dedicated fans of science fiction.

WOMEN IN SCIENCE FICTION

WOMEN AS FANS

Historians of science fiction agree that fans used to be almost exclusively male and that women have become progressively more involved with every decade. Lester del Rey commented that the literature was originally intended for boys.[5] Harry Warner wrote: "Women were gradually emerging as genuine fans as the forties went along. Around 1940, it was possible to claim that there was no such thing as an independent, honest-to-goodness girl-type fan, because virtually all the females in fandom had a fannish boy friend, brother, husband, or some other masculine link. But by 1948, a Tucker survey showed that eleven per cent of all fandom now was feminine."[6]

Astounding Science Fiction polled its readership in 1949 and discovered that only 6.7 percent were female.[7] In 1958 the magazine found that the proportion of women among its readers had risen to 11.9 percent.[8] In the same year women constituted 10 percent of the readership of the British magazine *New Worlds*.[9] An unpublished 1978 poll of 1,000 subscribers to the new American magazine *Galileo* found that 26 percent were women.

One subcategory of SF fandom that was particularly open and attractive to women was the *Star Trek* segment. Fans of this television show of the 1960s, known as Trekkies or Trekkers, produced their own fanzines and conventions and are not fully integrated into the more traditional SF fandom. Bjo Trimble, the woman who did the most to organize *Star Trek* fans and maintain this subsubculture in the decade after the program was canceled, asked the readers of her column in *Starlog* why women played such a large role in Trek fandom:

> For those unaware of this interesting situation, back in ancient fannish times, before *Star Trek*, the ratio of women to men in active science-fiction fandom was about one female for every 22 males (not bad for us gals!); by the time *Star Trek* appeared on your TV set, the fannish ratio was something like one female for every 12 or 14 males. Soon after *Star Trek* caught on, the ratio was about one to five! What caused this? What was there about *Trek*—or the weather or the new awareness or the world situation—which allowed intelligent women to "come out of the closet" and admit they enjoyed science fiction; and even better to *participate* in fandom? For surely we had female science-fiction *readers* (but passive non-fans) long before *Star Trek*. They simply were not showing up at conventions or writing fanfiction or becoming involved in fan movements.[10]

The high ratio of women to men in the *Star Trek* subculture is easy to document. In 1977 Roberta Rogow published *Trexindex*, a book listing all

Trek fanzines.[11] It was a simple matter to count the number of feminine names of editors. Fifty people helped assemble *Trexindex*; thirty-five were women, fourteen were men, and one name was given only with initials. Of the 165 fanzine titles listed in this guide, 108, or 65 percent, clearly were edited by women and 40 by men. If we consider just the fanzines where the sex of the editor could be determined, 73 percent were edited by women.

I suggest three hypotheses for the high ratio of women among *Star Trek* fans. First, for years women have been especially interested in movie and television fandom, as evidenced by the female-oriented movie magazines and soap opera digests. *Star Trek* presented a consistent group of characters, predominantly male, with whom the viewer could develop a vicarious relationship, as some women have done with screen stars and soap opera characters. Second, the *Star Trek* subculture developed separately from traditional SF fandom, permitting women to develop their own social network without being rejected by male fans. Third, as a rather simple and limited kind of fandom, *Star Trek* may have provided an easy step toward the more demanding SF literature fandom, easier for a new group to take.

The student survey allows one to compare female and male college students' attitudes toward science fiction, using several measures. Table 18 analyzes

Table 18. Preferences of college students for various types of literature, movies, and TV programs by sex of respondent (N = 1,439; 48 percent female)

Preference	Mean preference score		Percent giving high score (5–6)		Correlation (r) with female
	Females	Males	Females	Males	
POPULAR LITERATURE					
Best-selling novels	4.12	3.14	44.2	20.2	.42
Stories of love and romance	4.06	2.20	45.4	6.7	.51
Spy and detective novels	3.08	3.27	24.2	25.1	−.06
Science fiction novels	1.42	3.58	6.8	35.6	−.26
MOTION PICTURES					
Star Wars	4.68	4.98	63.7	71.3	−.11
Close Encounters	4.11	4.40	49.6	55.2	−.09
TELEVISION PROGRAMS					
Star Trek	3.73	4.55	42.2	60.2	−.23
Battlestar Galactica	3.00	3.45	25.8	32.6	−.11

Source: Survey of undergraduates at the University of Washington, Seattle, 1979.

responses by women and men to eight questionnaire items, using the seven-point preference scale. It shows that women are much more positive than men about best-selling novels and about stories of love and romance. They differ little from men in appreciation of spy and detective novels and are somewhat less favorable toward science fiction. By comparing attitudes toward four different kinds of popular fiction, we can see that men and women do have powerfully different patterns of preference.

The sexes differ very little in appreciation of the two movies, but the difference is statistically significant. Because of the large number of respondents, coefficients greater than .10 in this table have less than one chance in ten thousand of really representing zero, inflated by random fluctuations in the data. Even the − .09 correlation between *Close Encounters* and the sex of the respondent does represent a real if very weak relationship. *Star Trek* is better liked by men, although most of the die-hard fans of this television show are female.

The most important row in the table is the one for science fiction novels. The negative correlation ($r = -.26$) with being female probably underestimates the sex factor. Pearson's r has the advantage of expressing all the responses, every shade of difference in people's preferences. But here the usual advantage may be a disadvantage. If we want to find just those respondents who like SF very much—the real fans—we may not be interested in the degrees of dislike or indifference among those who are not fans. Counting respondents who gave a 5 or 6 response as SF lovers, fans in at least a weak sense of the term, indicates a vast difference between men and women. Only 6.8 percent of the women, but 35.6 percent of the men, are SF lovers, a ratio of more than five to one in favor of the men.

WOMEN AS AUTHORS

Like the readers of science fiction, authors have been overwhelmingly male until quite recently. If the data presented above were not a sufficient clue to sex imbalance, one could predict a low percentage of women SF writers merely by looking at census statistics on female involvement in occupational categories related to SF writing. Traditional science fiction stories were often set in outer space and were based on facts and speculations in the physical sciences. According to the 1970 U.S. Census, only 1.5 percent of the nation's 71,587 aeronautical and astronautical engineers were women. The proportion female among the 22,071 physicists and astronomers was 4.3 percent.[12]

Few SF writers are scientists, of course. As Groff Conklin noted in his anthology *Great Science Fiction by Scientists*:

Scientists, on the whole, are far too enthralled with their scientific work to want to go off on side-trails that involve plot, characterization, and all that. Fiction writing is a wholly different skill. Scientists like to *read* science fiction, many of them, but just as much to escape from the humdrum, nuts-and-bolts aspect of scientific research and application as do nonscientists who need it to escape from the often tedious and dull practicalities of their own daily occupations.[13]

However, the better hard science authors often have had some training in engineering or the physical sciences, where women have found fewer opportunities. But of all the high-skill professions and arts, writing has probably been the most open to women over the past century. Many women have studied literature in college, and basic writing skills have been taught to girls and boys equally. Therefore professional writers should include a relatively high proportion of women. The 1970 census found that 30.5 percent of the 26,004 professional authors were women.[14]

Among popular women authors who published stories in science fiction magazines up to 1950 were Leigh Brackett, Judith Merril, C. L. Moore, Katherine MacLean, Margaret St. Clair, and Wilmar Shiras.[15] When *Analog* magazine polled readers in 1966 about their favorite authors, only one woman, Andre Norton, was listed among the eighteen most popular; a second, C. L. Moore, was indirectly represented through her collaborations with her husband, Henry Kuttner.[16]

A number of the earlier women SF authors used masculine or androgynous pen names. In the list of authors in my main questionnaire were two women's names with first initials: C. J. Cherryh and C. L. Moore. Some male authors have used only initials, notably A. E. van Vogt and E. E. Smith, but until recently women authors had reason to believe that science fiction did not welcome them. The list also contained some masculine pseudonyms. Andre Norton is actually Alice Mary Norton, and much of Alice (Raccoona) Sheldon's fiction was published under the name James Tiptree, Jr., although she has recently revealed her true identity.

A few early women authors actually kept their gender secret from readers. According to Sam Moskowitz, "The fact that C. L. Moore was a woman was carefully kept from the readers of *Weird Tales*."[17] Andre Norton, who specialized in science fiction for juveniles, commented, "When I entered the field I was writing for boys, and since women were not welcomed, I chose a pen name which could be either masculine or feminine. This is not true today, of course. But I still find vestiges of disparagement—mainly, oddly enough, among other writers. I find more prejudice against me as the writer of 'young people's' stories now than against the fact that I am a woman."[18]

One woman, Leslie F. Stone, who published a good deal in the magazines around 1930, was frequently identified as a female, and a picture of her accompanied a short biography.[19] When it was Leigh Brackett's turn to be featured in the author biography column of *Amazing Stories*, her photograph was printed, just as all the men's pictures were.[20] Brackett has reported her own experiences as a woman writer, including unpleasant incidents with women who wanted to make an issue of gender:

> I have never been discriminated against because of my sex, that I know of. Editors aren't buying sex, they're buying stories . . . The jealousy and spite I've encountered, oddly enough, has been almost entirely from women, most of them non-professionals . . . the cat-toothed smile and the sweet "My, how I wish I was smart like you and could write all those books . . . dumb me, I just had five kids," sort of thing, but occasionally from pros: one militant feminist actress with whom I found myself, to my dismay, on a panel, who said sneeringly that the men allow a few women to *write* for them, and an equally militant writer who said that *some* women write like *men*, and therefore can get employment in the male-dominated industry. I stay as far as I can from that lot, which I'm sure has not made me more popular with the women's group in the [Writers'] Guild. I despise the term "woman writer." I am not a woman writer. I am a writer, period. That I happen to be a woman is beside the point.[21]

It appears that in the early days there may have been a complex pattern of discrimination against women who wished to write SF, aggravated by factors like the targeted group of readers, the author's style and message, and the personalities of writer and editor. But prejudice against women authors has lessened considerably. One of the most active letter-writing fans of the 1940s, who is now a leading author, Marion Zimmer Bradley, feels that the contemporary situation is quite free. "If any woman believes that science fiction and fantasy publishers are closed to women, she is either gravely misinformed, or she is making excuses for her own incompetence by attributing her failure to editorial prejudice. The prejudice simply is no longer there, in this year of 1977."[22]

An index of the progress of women can be found in the Hugo awards for best fiction of the year, determined by popular vote of fans and authors attending the annual World Science Fiction Convention. Although Hugos were first awarded in 1953, no women won a Hugo for fiction until 1968. Since 1959 a two-stage procedure has been used for the Hugo voting. Months before the convention, ballots are mailed to hundreds of fans and authors, who nominate stories published in the previous year. Those stories with the most votes are listed on the final ballot, which is mailed to everyone who purchases early membership in the convention. I tabulated data on Hugo nominees, counting only categories for professional fiction and giving half credit for coauthorship. From 1959 through 1979, 339 works reached the finals. Only 6 percent of the 128 nominated from 1959 to 1968 were written by women. But 14 percent of the 87 works nominated between 1969 and 1973, and 18 percent of the 99 nominated from 1974 to 1978 were by women. This rising trend is dramatized (and perhaps exaggerated) by the figures for 1979, when 34 percent of the 25 nominees were works by women, including four of the five candidates for best novel.[23]

RESULTS OF THE CONVENTION SURVEY

Three of the 595 persons who completed the main Iguanacon survey failed to identify their sex. Of the remaining 592, 245 (41.5 percent) were women. This proportion seems high, considering the traditional male bias in science fiction, so it is important to begin by evaluating how fully these women participate in the subculture of fans and authors. Perhaps many of them are wives, daughters, or girl friends of men attending the convention.

One piece of evidence against this hypothesis is that women constituted essentially as great a fraction of the 409 good respondents as of the total 595, 39.2 percent compared with 41.5 percent. According to the data from the survey, women respondents tend to be somewhat older than men, with a mean age of 28.5 years compared with a mean of 26.4 years for men. The mean age when female respondents began reading science fiction was 11.8 years, while for men it was 10.4 years. Women began reading the literature later than men, started attending conventions more recently, and are now slightly older. Men and women claim to have read the same number of SF books in the past year, to have the same proportion of fellow fans among their friends, and to be equally active in clubs.

For the analysis that forms the heart of this chapter, I derived a list of sixteen well-known women authors who were included in the questionnaire. Women and men were equally familiar with these sixteen, although one might have predicted either that women readers would be more alert to women writers or that they would be less familiar with SF writers in general. There was no difference between the sexes in familiarity with a list of science-fiction magazines included in the questionnaire. Thus the female fans are just as good, active, and knowledgeable as the men, and one can analyze the structure of women's science fiction from both male and female perspectives.

Although they are just as involved as men in the subculture, women tend

Table 19. Correlation between preferences for various types of literature and being female (N = 592)

Literature type	Correlation (r) with being female
Feminist literature	.25
Stories in which the main character is warm and loving	.23
Stories in which the main character is sensitive and introspective	.20
Sword-and-sorcery	.01
New wave SF	.01
Hard science SF	−.19
Stories in which the main character is erotic and beautiful	−.27
Stories about war	−.31

to have somewhat different tastes in science fiction. Table 19 lists eight literature types and the correlations between preferences for them and the sex of respondent. Not surprisingly, women tend to like feminist literature better than men do. They also prefer fictional protagonists who seem to represent traditional feminine values: characters who are warm and loving and those who are sensitive and introspective. The table shows that women and men respond equally to both sword-and-sorcery and new wave science fiction. But women have a slight tendency (r = −.19) to like hard science less well than men do.

The table concludes with two descriptions of fiction preferred by men. Stories in which the main character is erotic and beautiful may provide male readers with attractive heroines to fill their fantasies. War as a background for space adventures is preferred by men more than by women. It is worth reporting that there is no association between gender and general political orientation, as measured by the NORC political question.

Table 19 shows that male and female fans differ somewhat in their preferences for styles and topics, but do they differ in their appreciation of specific authors? Table 20 lists the sixteen best-known women authors from the questionnaire, giving their mean popularity ratings as judged by 245 female respondents and 347 male respondents. While women readers prefer women authors to some extent, in six cases the differences in preference by women and men achieve statistical significance, with only one chance in a thousand

THE POWER OF IMAGINATION

Table 20. Popularity of sixteen women science fiction authors

Author	Women (N = 245)		Men (N = 347)	
	Average rating	Rank among 138 authors	Average rating	Rank among 138 authors
Anne McCaffrey	5.26	1	4.56	16
Zenna Henderson	5.08	3	4.18	40
Raccoona Sheldon	5.07	4	4.21	37
Ursula K. LeGuin	4.87	8	4.67	10
Marion Zimmer Bradley	4.67	13	4.27	31
C. J. Cherryh	4.66	14	4.19	39
C. L. Moore	4.63	16	4.18	41
Kate Wilhelm	4.43	27	4.01	57
Andre Norton	4.34	36	4.00	58
Joan D. Vinge	4.30	39	3.85	75
Vonda N. McIntyre	4.26	43	3.61	95
Katherine MacLean	4.05	62	3.58	101
Lisa Tuttle	3.87	78	3.42	108
Judith Merril	3.49	104	3.27	115
Joanna Russ	3.46	106	2.71	126
Ayn Rand	2.90	125	2.88	123

of being an accidental error. These six, correlated with respondent being female, are: Henderson ($r = .30$), Sheldon ($r = .27$), McCaffrey ($r = .25$), McIntyre ($r = .22$), Russ ($r = .20$), and Moore ($r = .18$).

Only one of the 117 male authors, C. S. Lewis, in the questionnaire is significantly better received by women readers than by men ($r = .17$). That weak association may reflect the religious character of Lewis's works. Among the most frequently reported findings in the sociology of religion is a disproportionate involvement by women in religious activities and supernatural beliefs.[24] In the Iguanacon questionnaire, women on average expressed a very slightly greater preference than men for the Bible ($r = .18$). Of course, many women reject supernatural beliefs.

In earlier chapters I demonstrated that correlations between reader preference scores can be used to identify the main kinds of fiction written by each author. Table 21 gives the coefficients linking preferences for each woman author with preferences for four types of literature: sword-and-sorcery, new wave, hard science, and feminist literature. The first six authors are clearly identified as writers of sword-and-sorcery or closely associated brands of fantasy. The following seven are identified as members of the new wave. Some of the sword-and-sorcery authors, and all of those in the new wave, are preferred by readers who also like feminist literature, so we can assume that their fiction contains more or less overt feminist messages. Two authors, Tuttle and MacLean, are associated only with feminist literature and not with any of the three other types.

The new wave is of particular interest in connection with the women's movement because it seeks to promulgate new ideas and values through science fiction. Although Table 19 shows that women are *not* more likely than men to favor new wave, in Chapter 4 I showed that there is a significant correlation between preferences for this style and for feminist literature. This

Table 21. Correlations of women authors and four types of literature ($N = 595$)

| Author | Correlation (r) with | | | |
	Sword-and-sorcery	New wave	Hard science	Feminist literature
Bradley	.37	.00	.06	.13
Norton	.35	−.08	.05	.06
McCaffrey	.24	.05	.05	.08
Henderson	.23	−.04	.07	.14
Cherryh	.22	.08	−.04	.23
Moore	.19	.06	.04	.17
Wilhelm	−.01	.41	−.10	.32
Russ	−.06	.36	−.07	.54
McIntyre	.05	.36	−.11	.36
Sheldon	−.06	.32	−.25	.35
Merril	.16	.31	−.03	.32
Vinge	.07	.25	−.04	.31
LeGuin	.02	.22	−.02	.20
Tuttle	.04	.15	−.08	.26
MacLean	.10	.09	.02	.25
Rand	.05	.08	.12	−.05

apparent contradiction may be explained by the fact that new wave is a diverse collection of new styles and attitudes rather than a cohesive school of literature. The strongest correlate of new wave is avant-garde fiction which experiments with new styles, a matter of pure literary technique.

To gain some perspective on the internal structure of the new wave, in Chapter 4 I performed a factor analysis of preferences for twenty-seven well-known authors that correlated with it. The analysis produced seven factors, not all of them important. Five of the six women in that list clustered together in Factor I: McIntyre, Merril, Russ, Sheldon, and Wilhelm. This factor as a unit correlated most highly with preference for feminist literature ($r = .46$), and this type was favored by women respondents ($r = .23$). The concentration of women authors in Factor I implies that attitudes toward feminism constitute one of the most powerful sources of disagreement within the new wave.

In addition to the five women authors, Factor I includes one man, Harlan Ellison, who has been the leading spokesman for the new wave movement and has the highest correlation with preference for new wave science fiction ($r = .49$). Ellison does not correlate significantly with respondent being female ($r = .06$), but he is associated with feminist literature ($r = .24$). His support for the Equal Rights Amendment, well known throughout the science fiction subculture, was dramatically publicized before the Iguanacon convention. Ellison had agreed to be guest of honor, an important role at these annual gatherings, but then discovered that the host state, Arizona, had not ratified the ERA. Women's organizations had started a national boycott of states that had failed to ratify ERA. In statements printed in various magazines and newsletters, Ellison announced he had consulted several friends about resigning from the convention in protest over Arizona's anti-ERA position. Among Ellison's advisers were four authors on my list of sixteen women: LeGuin, Russ, McIntyre, and Bradley. They decided that Ellison should appear in Phoenix and speak on behalf of the ERA but should live in a camper parked next to the hotel to avoid spending money in Arizona.[25]

If these public acts and proclamations rendered feminism very salient to readers' attitudes toward Ellison, they did so much more for men than for women. Preference for Ellison correlated with feminist literature more highly among men ($r = .30$) than among women ($r = .17$). A similar pattern held for some other new wave authors. Apparently, Ellison and other male writers do not get special credit for being sympathetic to feminism from female readers.

The most striking fact about Table 21 is that it does not identify a single woman author as a writer of hard science SF, the traditional core of the field.

The list of sixteen women authors includes all those who had won a standard award within SF and does not exclude any influential woman who would be more likely to be in the hard science tradition. The table reveals that women authors avoid the traditional heartland of SF, are divided roughly between the sword-and-sorcery and new wave styles, and are likely to write fiction oriented toward feminist concerns.

FACTOR ANALYSIS OF WOMEN AUTHORS

I have repeatedly employed factor analysis to verify hypotheses about the ideological structure of science fiction. Now I shall use this powerful technique to see if women authors do indeed fall into two main groups, one practicing sword-and-sorcery, the other affiliated with the new wave. For this analysis I focused on the 166 respondents who avoided rating either fake author and who rated twelve or more of the sixteen well-known women authors. I hypothesize only two factors, because hard science is absent and because the participation of women in science fiction is such a recent development that the dimension of time is greatly compressed. However, a two-factor analysis does not allow other clusters a chance to emerge, so I let the computer generate as many factors as it wanted.[26]

Five supposed factors emerged in the analysis, but only two are real groups of authors. With a cut-off point of .350, below which I ignored factor loadings—a rather permissive standard—I found six authors in Factor I, seven in Factor II, two in Factor III, and one each in IV and V. Factor I of the women authors is led by Bradley, with a factor loading of .705, and Norton is second at .675. McCaffrey and Henderson follow close behind with almost identical loadings of .647 and .646. Then there is a gap until Cherryh at .439 and Moore at .351. These are writers of sword-and-sorcery and similar varieties of fantasy.

Factor II contains McIntyre (.603), Wilhelm (.576), Russ (.548), Vinge (.509), LeGuin (.393), Merril (.382), and Sheldon (.367), the women's contingent of the new wave. Factor III is really just Lisa Tuttle, loaded at .857, although Vinge reappears far below at .381. Factor IV is dominated by Judith Merril (.864), who already appeared in the new wave factor; Raccoona Sheldon, similarly, is listed again in Factor V (.711). MacLean and Rand do not load highly on any factor. Figure 10, where the sixteen women authors are distributed according to their loadings on the first two factors, shows the pattern graphically. All but three of the authors are distributed very close to a diagonal line running from upper left to lower right, roughly from McCaffrey to Russ. The greatest departure is Ayn Rand, an author who did not personally

THE POWER OF IMAGINATION

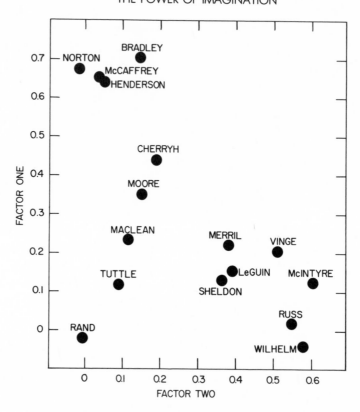

Figure 10. Factor analysis of women authors

participate in the SF subculture. However, she did launch her own political movement, the Objectivists, a libertarian atheist organization.[27]

Through its factor scores, Factor I is most strongly correlated with sword-and-sorcery (r = .49), science-fantasy (r = .42), stories about barbarians (r = .42), stories about magic (r = .36), and fantasy (r = .35). Factor II is new wave science fiction (r = .51) and feminist literature (r = .45). Interestingly, the two factors of women authors have exactly opposite correlations—.31 and −.30—with action-adventure fiction.

Factor I correlates with several items in the realm of the supernatural and paranormal powers, including occult literature (r = .34) and tales of the supernatural (r = .25). The miscellaneous items in the questionnaire included one about belief in ESP and, as reported in the previous chapter, women were far more likely than men to express a belief in the reality of ESP. The ESP question correlated positively with preference for the authors in Factor

I ($r = .29$). I interpret this to mean that women's tastes in science fiction are partly conditioned by their higher levels of belief in the supernatural and in parapsychology and greater acceptance of fiction incorporating such ideas.

Factor II, the other group of female writers (LeGuin, McIntyre, Merril, Russ, Sheldon, Vinge, and Wilhelm), correlates with new wave science fiction and with other types associated with it. The .45 correlation with feminist literature is both vigorous and revealing. These are women authors who write about social problems and social change. Their stories explore or imply issues concerning women today, often from an explicitly feminist perspective. This factor is preferred by respondents with a liberal political orientation, as measured by the question from the NORC General Social Survey ($r = .24$).

REPRESENTATIVE FICTION BY WOMEN AUTHORS

Brief descriptions of typical works by several female writers will show their exploration and advocacy of cultural change concerning sex roles. In general, stories by sword-and-sorcery writers are set in stratified societies with rigid systems of status ascription, but the women characters customarily assume great responsibilities and social power. New wave writers harshly criticize contemporary society and argue for radical changes in sex roles.

Criticism of traditional sex roles is hardly an invention of the 1960s. The 1930 story "Women with Wings" by Leslie F. Stone, a woman, describes a future male-dominated Earth where all humans have functioning wings growing from their bodies. A genetic alteration invented by a scientist decades earlier, the wings have greatly improved the quality of life and have led to the development of a benevolent world government, but they have also brought an unacceptably high level of mortality for women in childbirth. The male rulers of the world temporarily sterilize all the women until a solution is found. One research group looks into the dismal possibility of abandoning wings, while another prepares a spaceship to kidnap women from other planets to make up the terrestrial deficit.

Unexpectedly, an alien ship arrives from the planet Venus and battles the Earth defenses to a standstill, then kidnaps 15,000 men. A quickly organized Earth expeditionary force then defeats the Venusians on their own planet. To the surprise of everyone but the reader, it is revealed that the Venusians are a female-dominant winged species capable of interbreeding with Earth men. With their peoples joined, male Earth and female Venus set about to solve their common problems and extend the empire of personkind to the entire universe.

Contemporary women's science fiction frequently deals with sex-role questions. Marion Zimmer Bradley's sword-and-sorcery novel *The Forbidden Tower* tells of the struggle to free Callista, a young bride, from sexual frigidity. However, this is no mere soap opera. Callista is a tower keeper on far Darkover, who has taken a sacred oath of virginity and is shielded against sex by a magical force that will castrate her husband or kill her if they try to mate. Much of the action takes place on a supernatural plane where magician friends and a compassionate husband bring Callista to full erotic maturity and defend the family lineage against a challenge by a bastard pretender to the lordship of their clan. In the end, Callista consummates her marriage not only with her husband but also with her sister and her sister's husband.

Zenna Henderson's fantasy stories collected in *Pilgrimage* and *The People: No Different Flesh* postulate that an interstellar spaceship has disintegrated over the United States in the 1890s, scattering lifeboats containing The People. Afraid to reveal themselves to the backward Americans, The People establish little farming settlements and live according to a traditional, biblical way of life similar to that of Amish or Hutterite colonies. They gradually collect all the lost members of their tribe. The stories focus on women and their children. A frequent theme is learning, often under the guidance of a rural lady schoolteacher. Sex roles and age-based status are sources of stability rather than of conflict, and the stories idealize the extended family. Each member of The People has a magical gift, such as psychic healing, and most are able to levitate and communicate through telepathy. Since the most important source of individual power is magic, distributed evenly throughout the population, the status differentials implied by the family structure are not oppressive. Henderson's clear message is that conventional life becomes glorious and beautiful if ennobled by religious faith and by a sense of wonder.

Conflict between rigid traditional social roles and the powers of love and friendship is the theme of several works by C. J. Cherryh. Her *Faded Sun* trilogy concerns a warrior species, the Mri, driven to the brink of extinction by their inability to compromise with other cultures. The story would be over in a few chapters except for the heroic, altruistic efforts of a human friend to save the Mri. At the end of the first novel the Mri seem to be reduced to just two survivors, a brother and sister, who are forbidden to mate by laws of incest and by the roles assigned them in the complex Mri social structure. The continued existence of the species requires abandoning the old ways, which the Mri refuse to do, or the discovery of other Mri somewhere across the galaxy, which becomes the theme of the second book. In the conclusion a group of Mri become mercenaries of the humans, with all compromise coming from the human side. Although the trilogy focuses on the stern and inflexible Mri, it is really written in praise of human virtues—tolerance, understanding, adaptability, and love. Another novel by Cherryh, *Brothers of Earth*, concerns the tragic interplay of rigid cultures in the midst of war, where kinship obligations and tribal feuds can be transcended only by the power of friendship.

The Female Man, a new wave novel by Joanna Russ, is told in fragments of consciousness by four women who come from alternate Earths. In Jeannine's world women are docile and dominated by men. In Joanna's world, our own society, women have just begun to explore new possibilities for independent action. Note that the author uses her own name for the character living in our world. Janet's world is a happy Utopia inhabited by superior women who have gotten along supremely well ever since all the men died hundreds of years earlier. In Jael's world rages a brutal war to the death against men. This book triggered great controversy. *Analog*, the leading traditional SF magazine, carried an extremely negative review by Lester del Rey that called *The Female Man* "ultramilitant Feminism carried to the limit for propaganda purposes" and "a wish dream of vengeance, a vendetta against all the male half of mankind."[28]

In the "matriarchal" literary magazine *Windhaven*, Cheryl Cline wrote that each of the four women "represents a different stage of women's struggle for self-realization."[29] She considered *The Female Man* a book of analysis and exploration rather than a simplistic proclamation in favor of abolishing men. Russ has complained that other female science fiction writers have been too timid in expressing the challenges faced by contemporary women.[30]

Vonda McIntyre's novella "Aztecs" begins when a woman surgeon cuts the heart out of a spacewoman so she can become an interstellar pilot. The high-status characters are all women, and the story concerns the pilot's romance with a dependent, lower-status man, who finally leaves her in disgrace when his own application to become a space pilot is rejected. McIntyre's award-winning novel *Dreamsnake* follows a female hero trekking across a barren desert and mountains, practicing her rare skill as a snakehealer, who cures disease with the venom of serpents, despite dangers and the social fragmentation of an Earth ravaged by atomic war. Like other feminist science fiction authors, McIntyre writes of powerful, competent, courageous female characters who never wait for a man to rescue them nor let a man be the one to accomplish great deeds.

Ursula K. LeGuin's highly acclaimed novel *The Left Hand of Darkness* is an imaginative analysis of the meanings of sexuality and gender. On Gethen, a planet with human inhabitants of unusual biology, the inhabitants are androgynous and asexual for most of each month. Periodically they enter *kemmer*, a sexually active condition in which individuals pair off to mate. Until their kemmer is far advanced, the members of the pair do not know which is to be the male and which the female, which is to be the father and which the mother of any child that results. After a temporary mother has given birth, "she" returns to androgyny and may well be the father of the next child. LeGuin speculates that without stable gender, Gethenian society would differ from that of Earth in three main ways. There is no war and little class stratification; the technology is more natural and less exploitative; and social structures based on gender are absent.[31]

Several of Lisa Tuttle's stories are surreal allegories of sex-role conflict, alternating between raw reality and ecstatic madness. "Stone Circle" describes a woman who is forced to prostitute herself for every necessity of life in a future dystopia where rape and betrayal ruin every hope of love. In another story, "The Birds of the Moon," strange creatures fly off with a woman who is alienated from her astronaut husband and autistic daughter. In a third, "Mrs. T.," an old woman explains that when women take the role of men their breasts disappear because in our culture women are becoming males and men are becoming females.

Although she stands outside of the sword-and-sorcery and new wave styles, indeed outside of the SF subculture, Ayn Rand has written prophetic and science-related fiction, such as her short novel of the future, *Anthem*. Her two most popular novels, both strongly favorable toward technological creativity, are *The Fountainhead* and *Atlas Shrugged*. Both contain love stories in which a superior woman competes and cooperates with an even more powerful man. They discover a new form of love that does not bind, love based on admiration of genius and dedication to self-fulfillment stripped of self-sacrifice and blind duty to spouse or children. Ayn Rand is generally considered an intellectual of the radical right—she formed the Objectivist political movement partly to combat liberal sentiments like those expressed in the new wave—but she, too, rejects traditional female roles and proposes new values for a world in which women will no longer be bound by cultural norms.[32]

CONCLUSION

Women authors have made science fiction a medium for analysis of current sex roles and for advocacy of change, infusing their sword-and-sorcery and new wave stories with a concern for the disadvantages of contemporary sex roles. Although the worlds of sword-and-sorcery are fantastic ones, the analysis of alternate sex roles and family structures may contribute indirectly to creative innovation in our own society. New wave science fiction attacks traditional sex roles directly, demanding sweeping changes.

When science fiction began, it promoted positive attitudes toward scientific and technological progress. The men most responsible for the development of modern space rocketry were inspired in adolescence by reading science fiction stories about spaceflight. But women tend to like hard science SF less well than men do, and not a single one of the women authors studied correlates significantly with this variety. Therefore the continuing influx of women into science fiction may not promote engineering and the physical sciences among women, because the female authors express very different values in their fiction, urging social activism rather than technical competence.

There is no reason to think that women cannot write hard science stories, and one might predict that they will begin to write more knowledgeably and enthusiastically about physical science and technology. Several famous stories by women come very close to hard science, but miss because they fail to develop a major premise based on speculations in the physical sciences. The protagonist of Anne McCaffrey's novel *The Ship Who Sang* is a woman born terribly deformed, whose wretched body is built into the mechanism of a spaceship so she can take it on missions to the stars. A little attention is given to the technology of her encapsulation, and at the end of the book she takes on a difficult assignment in order to have her engines spectacularly upgraded, but the central theme is the emotional attachments she develops with her normal human passengers, a traditionally feminine topic.

Up the Walls of the World, by the pseudonymously masculine woman writer James Tiptree, concerns Tyree, a planet radically different from Earth, a huge Jupiterlike world where the intelligent species floats and soars through a thick atmosphere abundant with life. Hal Clement would have crafted a tale filled with discoveries in the physical sciences, as he did with the vast world Mesklin in *Mission of Gravity*, but Tiptree ignores questions of gas density and temperature inversions in favor of speculations on alien personality and sex life. Not spaceships, built according to the engineering creed of hard science, but new wave empathy and fantasy transmigration of souls carry travelers between Tyree and Earth.

In the time since the convention at which I administered the questionnaire, two arguably hard science novels by women have won Hugo awards: *Down-below Station*, by C. J. Cherryh, and *The Snow Queen*, by Joan Vinge. *Downbelow Station* has a very strong interpersonal theme, the struggle to find friendship and understanding across the boundaries of alien cultures. But the setting, events, and minutiae of props and behavior are very much in the hard science tradition. The primary location is a huge space station, orbiting a planet of Pell's Star, light years from Earth. The book contains engineering drawings of both the station and a typical spaceship. The station and its technology are carefully described, and nothing in the book would offend a hard science fan's sense of what is physically possible. The social and technical background is the first human interstellar war, in which the outer worlds of a string of Earth's colonies rebel. The geometry of linear colonization across many star systems places Pell's Star right at the boundary between the two warring superpowers. This military story could have been written by one of the more macho male writers, such as Heinlein, and the hard science aspects place the novel right at the center of the fiction traditionally produced by men of the old school.

The Snow Queen of Vinge's title is the ruler of Tiamat, a planet in a double star system that is itself revolving around a black hole. Ages ago a great interstellar empire fell, leaving many colonized worlds completely isolated because the technical means for unlimited faster-than-light travel were lost. Tiamat, however, is subject to a more limited interstellar Hegemony that is linked by instantaneous travel via black holes. Vinge describes in some detail the difficulties of aiming a specially designed spaceship into a black hole connected by space-time wormholes to other black holes strewn across the galaxy. The one near Tiamat becomes unstable whenever the planet's twin suns approach it on their long elliptical orbit, and thus periodically the Snow Queen's world is cut off from commerce with and dominance by the Hegemony.

Tiamat is divided into two regions and two peoples, Winter and Summer. Neither has indigenous advanced technology, but during periods of contact with the Hegemony, Winter, ruled by a queen, becomes the instrument of hegemonic dominance and the point of importation of technology so advanced that the people of Tiamat can only use it, not copy it. In return Tiamat gives the ruling class of the Hegemony a serum obtained by slaughtering mers, peaceful sea creatures, a serum that extends human life indefinitely. The Snow Queen uses the serum to remain young throughout a century-long reign in vice-ridden Winter, but when the black-hole gate closes, she must be sacrificed to the sea. Summer's virtuous, technophobic folk will rule until the gate opens again.

Vinge's hard science premise permits a drama about the conflict between technology and humanism, symbolized by Winter and Summer. But although Summer seems morally better than Winter, it is weak, and the lack of indigenous high technology prevents both peoples of Tiamat from defending themselves against the Hegemony and charting their own destiny. In the story the current Snow Queen plots to sustain her rule after the closing of the gate, by hoarding technology and by murdering thousands of Summers with an intentionally unleashed plague. In an alternative plan, she has produced a clone of herself, named Moon, and arranges to have this duplicate daughter become Summer Queen.

Moon, to the Snow Queen's disgust, has not inherited her clone mother's malevolent personality, and she seeks to become a sibyl, one of Summer's benevolent priests who can answer questions posed by suppliants through divine intervention by the mother goddess of the sea. At this point, the story seems to be located in the fantasy cluster, but Moon discovers that the sibyls gain their oracular powers not from the supernatural but from a vast computer hidden on Tiamat long ago by the declining empire in an effort to preserve civilization, rather like the hidden cabal of scientists working to revive the galactic empire in Asimov's *Foundation* series. Breaking interstellar law, Moon visits a high-technology planet, gaining a realistic understanding of the Hegemony. She also unravels the mystery of the peaceful mers, learning that they are intelligent creatures created by the dying empire to develop life extension and tend the oracular computer. Thus the slaughter of mers is heinous murder; the very highest technology, far above the brutal machines of the Hegemony, can be the positive source of humanist values rather than their heartless opponent.

Most of the strong characters in the novel are women, and there are occasional, brief speeches against the male chauvinism that pervades the Hegemony. *The Snow Queen* can be interpreted as a mythic examination of the relation of human-centered women toward cold male technology. Like the Summers, women traditionally are completely alienated from advanced technology, and when some rare women accept it they may do so in the insensitive, half-ignorant, exploitative manner of Winter's Snow Queen. Yet love and friendship can triumph over this tragic division of the world into female and male, Summer and Winter, mystic and tech. And the result may be a transcending synthesis of the formerly warring opposites into a higher unity, far better for humanity than either half alone.

Understood in this way, *The Snow Queen* is an important statement in the development of women's science fiction, expressing the traditional gender dilemma and promising that women writers—and women living in today's world of all-pervasive technology—can leap over the old barriers. If they do, they and the men they touch will become a higher form of being than either sex was capable of being before. But despite this optimistic ending, the novel warns that the division of our species into rigid roles of female and male, humanist and technocrat, is a false and unhealthy schizophrenia, productive of nothing good. With such themes and insights, science fiction by women informs our consciousness of vital current issues of science, technology, and sex roles. It may contribute to our evolution toward a happier and more comprehensive culture.

8

ENLIGHTENMENT

AND

TRANSCENDENCE

Science fiction is a literature of persuasion and debate, and it may teach scientific facts and encourage young people to enter technical careers. But its chief power may flow from the ideas it promotes—possibilities rather than certainties. Traditionally, SF has urged spaceflight and a freethinking attitude toward religion and politics. More recently, it has become a medium for discussion of the limitations of conventional sex roles and the advantages of alternatives. But the common message of all SF is one of questioning and exploring. Thus we must consider the extent to which science fiction aims to expand consciousness rather than dogmatically to inculcate particular facts and attitudes.

THE EDUCATIONAL VALUE OF SCIENCE FICTION

Whatever their propaganda impact, many of the classic hard science stories had educational value. A good example is the short novel "Around the Universe," by Ray Cummings. When this tale was published in a 1927 issue of *Amazing Stories*, the editor commented, "If you are attracted by astronomy, and like to take your lessons in sugar-coated pills, here is a story that you will not soon forget."[1] "Around the Universe" instructs the reader in the sizes, orbits, and rotation periods of all the known planets and shows the solar system in relationship to some of the better-known stars. A lad named Tubby meets the great inventor Sir Isaac Swift DeFoe Wells-Verne. Sir Isaac is the author of all science fiction stories written to date, including those of Ray Cummings, and thus is the ideal guide for Tubby's tour of the universe. An imminent attack on Earth by the bellicose Martians provides an excuse for the voyage as the heroes visit each planet in turn, seeking aid against the armies of the Red Planet. The author's more fanciful ideas are clearly labeled as such, so the young reader may come away with an accurate picture of our astronomical environment, complete with all the numbers necessary to establish the scale.

In the same issue, editor Hugo Gernsback estimated that 10 percent of *Amazing's* readers were youth. He was pleased that so many were reading and criticizing science fiction, because SF "is an education in itself."[2] In 1939 author John Taine said SF magazines gave science valuable public exposure beyond the limited readership of technical journals. "For even the wildest story contains at least one grain of fact, and this fact may remain in the reader's consciousness, almost unknown to himself, long after the plot of the story and all its characters are forgotten."[3]

Twenty years later H. L. Gold, founding editor of *Galaxy* magazine, commented that SF could be an especially effective medium of science education because it could place scientific discoveries in a meaningful context for persons without scientific training. "And science-fiction writers are the logical pipeline between the scientist and the public, as far as the *interpretation* (not the mere reporting) of new ideas is concerned. It is the imagination in depth of a first-rate science fiction writer that can flesh out a dry technical report and show us in human terms what these gifts of the laboratory will mean."[4]

The chief objection to the thesis that SF is educational is that its science is often *wrong*—whether fanciful, incompetent, or out of date—and that the reader may not be able to distinguish fact from wild speculation. Although the stories communicate a sense of wonder concerning science, and thus promote favorable attitudes toward science, they may instill tenacious misconceptions in the minds of many readers.

One charming series of stories with educational intent was the continuing saga of Posi and Nega, written by Joseph W. Skidmore in the 1930s. Posi is a male proton and very impressed with himself; Nega is a very feminine electron. The tales tell of their romance and of their adventures—a prodigious series of chemical reactions, atomic transmutations, and events of classical physics. The tales were meant to amuse, but Skidmore frequently expressed sincere wonder at the marvels of the universe. "Again, this impotent pen pauses uncertainly; estopped in reverent wonder; amazed at the vastness of things—and the smallness; pondering meekly on the astounding, numerical certainty of atoms—and the intricate, but timed movements of the stars; solemnly conscious of the Mighty intelligence directing all motion and matter."[5]

Lester del Rey complained that "The Romance of Posi and Nega" did a disservice to any students who tried to learn physics from it. "Skidmore's science was long out of date, since no scientist really believed in the simple solar-system type of atom. The neutron had been discovered in 1931, but this was completely overlooked."[6] But Alexei Panshin considered it a misconception that SF should teach science:

> Science fiction, as a literary form, cannot be scientific. If science fiction is reportage of science, it is debatable. If science fiction is accurate prediction of science, it is an ingenious triviality. If science fiction is inaccurate prediction of science, it is silly. In trying to live by Gernsback, science fiction has been as ingenious and silly as *Ralph 124C41 +* —written in 1911 [this Gernsback novel] told of a world of 2660 in which people explain television, juke boxes, liquid fertilizer, night baseball and vending machines to each other.
>
> The science in science fiction is at best a metaphor of science's hopes for itself, an expression of love for those who think quantitatively.[7]

As I have noted often, science fiction contains much pseudoscience and mysticism amid its speculations about physical science and technology. James Blish commented, " 'Science-fact' in our field has become a synonym for fraud and saucerism."[8] Several authors have looked back on the history of SF and concluded that the early pronouncements about its scientific educational value are now ridiculous. In 1978, Spider Robinson commented:

> I've always been surprised by how vanishingly little science fiction turns out to be fiction *about science*. (Even the Asimovs, Bovas, Nivens, and Clarkes most often write fictions involving science, rather than fictions concerning science.) And of the stories that *are* about science, half of them are actually bitterly *anti*-science (virtually all "sci fi" movies, and a shocking percentage of SF books and stories) and most of the rest are as dreadfully written as the stuff Uncle Hugo used to call "scientifiction."[9]

The hard science writers still try to follow norms of scientific accuracy. But they no longer punctuate their fables with long technical, explanatory passages, as was common in Gernsback's day, telling the reader how the scenes and events illustrate correct science. As Paul Walker noted in 1979, "SF writers long ago gave up educating their readers. There is more science behind the average sf story than in it. Once the writer has worked out the scientific problems behind his or her story, he spends only a minimal amount of space on details."[10]

A further difficulty for readers who want to learn about physical science is that many of the best-loved tales are out of date. In the thirtieth-anniversary issue of *Fantasy and Science Fiction*, Isaac Asimov contemplated his early fiction about the solar system, which was carefully based upon correct scientific knowledge of the time. "But how quickly science advances! How quickly statements made in science fiction, in good faith and after careful research, are outmoded and converted from science fiction into fantasy."[11] So much that was described in the old stories, especially the environments of outer space, is now known to be incorrect.

Despite all these problems, I think SF does have an educational function. In a limited sense, it may teach facts through the consensus of many stories rather than in the assertions of single works. But beyond that, it teaches something that may be more important: ideas. School courses can inform young people about the latest, "truest" findings of real science. What SF distinctively offers is an astonishing number and variety of hypotheses. It speculates on all aspects of life and all branches of science. Perhaps the naive reader has trouble telling the good ideas from the bad, but the sheer quantity of concepts gives the reader a rich background of thought, providing a context of discovery in which facts can later be placed.

In Chapter 3 I noted that hard science SF was often written as a puzzle and read as a game. The author solves interesting problems in terms of known science, and the reader tries both to spot technical errors and to anticipate the outcome, as readers do with detective stories. Especially for young readers, one of the rewards of SF is the sense of accomplishment in being able to analyze and understand the stories. I think this factor plays a role in committing young people to technical careers that grow out of their reading. Mastering the ideas in the stories can boost one's self-esteem, especially if one is the only kid on the block who can do so. Thus young people who lack social status with their immediate peers may derive compensatory social rewards in the mental world of SF.

Examples of physical-science puzzle stories are "Jupiter Five," by Arthur C. Clarke, and "Operation: Gravity," by Jack Williamson, both of which let readers exercise their understanding of orbital mechanics. Among other tidbits of celestial mechanics, Clarke's story says, "It's nearly as difficult to travel between Jupiter's satellites as it is to go between the planets, although the distances are so much smaller. This is because Jupiter's got such a terrific gravitational field and his moons are traveling so quickly. The innermost moon's moving almost as fast as Earth and the journey to it from Ganymede costs almost as much fuel as the trip from Earth to Venus, even though it takes only a day and a half."[12]

On Jupiter's innermost moon, Jupiter Five, the gravity is so weak that when the heroes want to punish the villain, they simply put him in a spacesuit and throw him at the planet. The poor man believes he will fall to his death in the giant planet's atmosphere, but the heroes know that the relatively slight change in velocity they gave him in throwing him off the moon placed him in an infinitesimally different orbit, from which he is easily retrieved.

Williamson's story involves an expedition to a collapsed star, in a stripped-down spaceship with exactly enough fuel for the round trip. Though only eight miles in diameter, the star is more massive than all the sun's planets combined. On the first pass, the ship drops in parabolic trajectory to within 400 miles of the star, where the gravitational force is 50,000 times that at the surface of Earth. The crew is not crushed flat because they are in free fall, and thus they experience no weight despite their rapid acceleration and the astoundingly strong gravity field. Unfortunately, at the last moment they discover that the star has a ring, which they strike twice, dropping and rising again in a split second. The ring is so tenuous it does not damage the ship, but it costs them precious velocity, and they are trapped in orbit. A second close pass, at 40 miles and 1,000,000 gravities, seems to doom them. But they test a new antigravity drive, which sends them home along a straight line from the star.

A story such as this challenges the reader with scientific interests twice. First the reader must think through the author's astounding conclusions to see how they follow from physical laws. Second, he or she may contemplate the factors the author fails to consider thoroughly. Even if a spaceship crew could survive the gravity of a collapsed star, its radiation belts would be lethal. For even a tenuous ring to slow the ship significantly in a split second, the required deceleration would kill the crew, because the force would be applied only to the ship's hull rather than evenly to all its atoms, as is the case with gravity. At its closest approach to the star, the ship would be in a substantial gravity gradient, with more force on one side of the ship than on the other, which might spin the ship to pieces. Finally, in a field of 1,000,000 gravities there should also be a substantial time dilation effect, and one might wonder if the time gradient would be steep enough to make time run appreciably slower on the near side of the ship than on the far side, perhaps causing the timing-sensitive computers to go crazy. Intellectual mastery of such questions may prepare a young mind for a technical career and instill commitment to such a life's course.

INVENTION AND TECHNICAL CAREERS

In the first year of *Amazing Stories*, Gernsback frequently argued that the ideas in SF, once they were absorbed by talented readers, could be the basis of new inventions and discoveries. In a 1928 editorial, "The Lure of Sci-entifiction," he commented that authors may not even realize the practical potential of the ideas in some of their more fantastic tales. "But the seriously-minded scientifiction reader absorbs the knowledge gained in such stories with avidity, with the result that such stories prove an incentive in starting some one to work on a device or invention suggested by some author of scientifiction."[13]

In his October 1926 editorial, "Imagination and Reality," Gernsback said that science fiction authors should be entitled to a patent on an idea if it was a workable device described in sufficient detail.[14] He asserted that several examples could be readily found in the pages of SF stories. As I described in *The Spaceflight Revolution*, I found that SF popularized good ideas developed elsewhere rather than that it actually invented them. But Gernsback may be right about some ideas in SF stories. Looking back from the perspective of 1953, he reiterated, "If you were an engineer, or an industrialist and had imagination, Science-Fiction often gave you valuable hints or stimulated your imagination sufficiently so you could derive material benefit from it. A num-ber of inventions, processes, machines thus came to life thanks to Science-Fiction."[15]

Editors of lesser magazines sometimes echoed this faith, even when their own magazines gave little evidence of its truth. In 1946 Ray Palmer was editor of *Amazing Stories* and rapidly making it the epicenter of pseudo-scientific fads, yet he was bold enough to claim, "Imaginative things in this magazine are a stimulus to the scientific mind. Who knows just what a power it is toward world progress? Our writers imagine the future, scientists make it come true!"[16] About the same time, Samuel Merwin, the editor of some low-quality magazines, announced, "It is the job of THRILLING WONDER STO-RIES and its companion magazines STARTLING STORIES and CAPTAIN FUTURE, to present their readers the shape of things to come as envisioned by our most imaginative writers today. Somewhere, some reader will derive from their fancies the facts of tomorrow and bring that tomorrow within our grasp."[17]

Whether or not SF provides inventions and discoveries for technological civilization, it may provide personnel. From the start, Gernsback hoped SF would draw young people into scientific or technical careers. Two guest editorials published in *Amazing Stories Quarterly* in 1929 reflected this hope. Joe Abrams said SF could influence the younger generation "to follow the path of science and invention."[18] J. Roy Chapman was convinced that SF stories helped its readers enjoy the life of the mind and seek further knowledge. "In truth, so captivating is this type of literature that readers are sometimes impelled to adopt various branches of science as lifetime professions. The stories become potential benefactors of mankind."[19]

Some information on this point has already been discussed, but the results of the 1979 student survey will focus the issue. Among the preference items were the physical sciences and the social sciences. There was a respectable association between liking SF novels and liking the physical sciences ($r = .30$), but SF was not significantly tied to the social sciences ($r = .05$). Indeed, there was only the weakest evidence that people felt there was any connection between the two kinds of science ($r = .17$). Perhaps they agree with John Campbell that no true social science yet exists. Dedicated SF fans place these two kinds of science in separate ideological factions, hard science and new wave. For college students, the science of science fiction appears to be physical science. Among the students who gave SF novels a top rating of six points, 36.9 percent also gave a top rating to the physical sciences. Of those who gave the lowest rating to SF, only 8.8 percent gave the top rating to the physical sciences. The equivalent percentages for the social sciences are 27.3 and 22.8. Does reading SF make people favor the physical sciences, or does involvement in the physical sciences make people favor SF? In the absence of better data, it is safest to conclude that both interpretations are correct.

In shaping the adult careers of young readers, science fiction may sometimes deceive and even damage its audience. For example, a twelve-year-old may decide to become a physicist without having any real idea what the day-to-day work of physicists involves. This may be a tragic error if the child's talents or personality are wrong for such a career, and lifelong frustration or a catastrophic breakdown may be the result. Hardly any SF stories are really about scientific research, and the subtype that most frequently has an inventor as protagonist is space opera, the overblown heroic fiction that most completely distorts reality.

Alfred Coppel's story "The Hills of Home" is a poignant psychological examination of a life shaped by science fiction. As a boy, the hero lives a fantasy life in the Martian novels of Edgar Rice Burroughs. For him, Mars is the ravishingly exciting world of Barsoom, populated by Tharks and Thoats and Therns. Even as an adult he strives to get to the Mars of his imagination. Indeed, he may be quite mad, concealing schizophrenic Martian hallucinations in order to become the first astronaut to reach the Red Planet. When he lands on Mars, to his mind it is Burroughs's Barsoom, and he wanders off to die in the hills, drawn by the siren songs of science fiction.

"The Hills of Home" was published in two versions in two competing magazines, *Future* in 1956 and *Galaxy* in 1960. The first version implied that the hero's madness was essential to the space program, which needed an astronaut willing to undertake a one-way suicide mission to Mars before round-trip commerce could be opened up. The second version left open the possibility that the hero's psychosis ruined the mission. Thus the story criticized the way science fiction shapes the lives of young people, suggesting that tragedy may sometimes be the result, but letting the reader be the final judge.

As well as drawing young people into specific careers, SF may give them the faith that they can make a better future. Harry Harrison said of science fiction, "It's fun, it's good literature, but basically what keeps the whole thing thundering along and what provides the prime motivation behind science fiction is the awareness of being able to *change* change! Science has changed every aspect of our lives and you've got to be aware of that."[20] Algis Budrys said the slogan of Golden Age science fiction was, "Knowledge had damn well better be Power."[21]

In 1943 John Campbell told the readers of *Astounding-Analog*, "One thing Astounding would very seriously like to do is to help more people retain the realization that the future must be different—but it can be made better."[22] His successor as editor of the magazine, Ben Bova, reported that Campbell urged people to be optimistic about the power of the human spirit to control its destiny. "Many years ago, John Campbell typed a letter in response to a writer who had sent in a hopelessly downbeat story, with an unresolved, blackly pessimistic ending. Campbell finished his rejection letter with this line: 'State your problem—but solve it!' "[23]

TO PROPOSE AND TO PROVOKE

The new wave reminds us that not all problems have effective solutions, but SF of all kinds proposes the widest range of conceivable solutions and provokes us to see problems we have not even considered. Most important, many stories disseminate the proposals and critiques of obscure intellectual movements. In some cases, as with the spaceflight and feminist movements, many authors are conscious proponents of these doctrines. Sometimes the stories extrapolate from a past social movement to make interesting comments on current social conditions. For example, in "The Shaker Revival," Gerald Jonas imagines how the nearly extinct Shaker religious sect might be reborn in the counterculture of the late 1960s. Often authors are caught up briefly in a movement, popularize and extend its ideology through their writing, then go on to a new enthusiasm.

SF stories based on intellectual movements, deviant or conventional, do not always explicitly acknowledge their sources. For example, psychologist James McConnell wrote the classic tale of a man who is made to run through rat mazes by extraterrestrial psychologists and titled it after the psychological school it represents—"Learning Theory." But many readers may have enjoyed his story "The Game of White" without realizing that it came straight from Freudian psychoanalysis, because it does not use the technical terminology although it is drenched in the symbolism.

Still other important stories examine, critique, or express the ideology of a profession that has a definite set of norms, beliefs, and ideals but has not produced a radical movement. The novel *Gravy Planet* (also called *The Space Merchants*) by Frederik Pohl and C. M. Kornbluth is a satire about the utopia American advertising executives would create if given the chance. Other stories use ideas that conceivably might be the doctrine of a social movement to shock the reader into an awareness of issues in the real world.

In "Four in One," Damon Knight assaults two inhibitions, the compulsive desire for autonomy and the obsessive fear of contamination by physical proximity with other human bodies. Four space explorers, two men and two women—two of whom are loyal servants of the totalitarian state and two potential defectors—are swallowed by a huge, amoeboid creature. It digests or eliminates every bit of the four except their nervous systems, but they do not die. Their brains and nets of nerves, tangled inside the gelatinous form, continue to feel and think. Gradually, the four learn how to live through the amoeba, how to make it hunt for food by projecting commands along their nerves. They discover they can grow new eyes and arms by sheer power of will. The two rebels, woman and man, grow toward love, closer together than any lovers have ever been, and they fall into a duel to the death against the pair of loyalists. Few SF readers would be disgusted by this clever, entertaining tale, but the shocks are frequent and intense.

Many stories remind us of intellectual, political, or religious issues that our culture has repressed from consciousness. The idea of eugenics, selective breeding of human beings, was popular decades ago, but it had lost persuasiveness even before the genocides of World War II. Today there seems to be an iron rule against discussing the fact that birth rates in some sectors of the population, including the intellectual elite, have dropped below the replacement level. C. M. Kornbluth's story, "The Marching Morons," thus shocks because it dares to speak openly of this unmentionable but critical problem.

In this story, the real estate wheeler-dealer Honest John Barlow is accidentally put into suspended animation in 1988. Generations later when he awakes, the average IQ has dropped from 100 to 45 because intelligent people have failed to produce children, while the stupid have multiplied. The favorite quiz show of the future, "Take It and Stick It," gives contestants a big cutout shape (triangle, circle, or square) and asks them to fit it into the right slot on the wall. They usually fail. Airplanes and automobiles are gussied up to look like hot, flaming rockets that are extremely fast. In fact, they crawl, but few people are able to compute their speeds. The world is sinking into cultural as well as mental retardation. A tiny cabal of superbright conspirators enlists Barlow to apply his unlimited huckster skills to selling the dolts on their own destruction. Conned into believing that the planet Venus is a paradise, all the dimwit majority of the world flies off in simulated spaceships that are actually designed to execute them cleanly.

Occasional studies and popular essays warn that our society has placed too great an emphasis on higher education as a route of upward mobility, because the high-status positions are limited. But intellectuals, especially professors, do not want to hear that they are too numerous and overfunded. David H. Keller's 1928 story "White Collars" imagines a not-too-distant future when there are five college-educated persons for every suitable job, and thus education has become devalued except among the proud but impoverished White Collars. Degrees are a dime a dozen, and blue-collar trades such as plumbing have become much more highly rewarded in power, prestige, and money than the learned professions. When the White Collars riot, they are summarily discarded by a nation that has neither use nor respect for them.

The *Eleventh Commandment*, by Lester del Rey, attacks the question of Catholic opposition to birth control. In the year 2190 Boyd Jensen is exiled from his home planet, Mars, to the vastly overpopulated, impoverished Earth. America is home to four billion diseased, starving, wretched people, ruled by the American Catholic Eclectic Church, which demands of its children, "Be Fruitful and Multiply." Roman Catholic readers may escape the accusation that their church is working for the horrible future foreseen in this novel, because the A.C.E.C. is identified as an unorthodox offshoot of Roman Catholicism; the tiny surviving minority of traditional Roman Catholics has been restricted to "Romish" ghettoes. Jensen discovers humane kindness as well as excruciating suffering in this future dystopia; the Catholic Eclectic priests who cause misery through enforcement of their Eleventh Commandment are surprisingly wise and helpful. In the end Jensen discovers an absolutely compelling scientific reason for the Eleventh Commandment, and he willingly converts to the American Catholic Eclectic Church.

Del Rey's novel exemplifies the best tendencies of science fiction. First it causes us to confront difficult questions that we usually keep just beyond our awareness. Then it makes us think twice about our instinctive responses. The message is awareness and imagination, not rigid ideological commitment. The real future depends on collective decisions about the social issues that are compellingly raised in such stories. SF may give us both the flexibility of mind and the range of possible solutions to meet these challenges. Science fiction seldom offers dogmatic, prepackaged answers to social problems. When it does, however, it tends to promote the extreme views of radical social movements, as the next section illustrates.

TECHNOCRACY AND GENERAL SEMANTICS

In 1933 Hugo Gernsback became involved in the Technocracy movement, briefly editing a magazine called *Technocracy Review*. Inspired by Thorstein Veblen (especially by his 1921 book *The Engineers and the Price System*), Technocracy became an organization of perhaps 10,000 members under the autocratic leadership of Howard Scott. Its utopian aim was the creation of the Technate States of North America, which were to be ruled by rational engineering rather than what the group considered the customary inefficiency, injustice, and insanity of the capitalist system. In his editorials in *Wonder Stories*, Gernsback wrote that the ideas of Technocracy had been developed long before by science fiction writers, mentioning a chapter of his novel *Ralph 124C 41+*, which proposed abandoning money in favor of a more scientific system of resource allocation. Gernsback praised the foresight of science fiction and argued that its readers had little allegiance to the primitive society around them:

We all know that the system under which we live is wrong. We are just muddling around, trusting to luck that something will happen that will put us on the right track again. The present order of civilization is highly unscientific, and when we contemplate our cycles of prosperity, followed by cycles of abject depression, every thinking individual must come to the conclusion that we have failed somewhere. When people are starving in the midst of plenty, when for the first time in the history of the human race it becomes possible for humanity to labor but a short fraction of its time and have leisure for a larger percentage of its time, then, indeed, we know that something must be done about it.

As I have pointed out many times before, the machine is beneficial, and it will be the machine which, in the end, will completely emancipate man. The thing that is wrong is our economic system, and our present money system. No doubt, as Technocrats put it, these are worn out and need a new control to gear them up to our machine age.[24]

In his analysis of Technocracy, Henry Elsner pointed out that the movement was in many ways an alternative to Marxism that was disguised and made more appealing to politically moderate Americans by being dressed up as an engineering solution to social problems.[25] Scientists and engineers, rather than politicians and plutocrats, would rule the future Technate society. But, as in the Marxist ideal of communism, prosperity would be shared equally by all citizens. Instead of traditional currency based on gold or the machinations of the financial system, there would be energy certificates. As a Technocracy booklet about this idea explained, "Every adult above 25 years of age will receive as his share of purchasing power an equal part of the total net consumed energy, and from birth to the twenty-fifth year every individual will receive a maintenance allowance."[26] These nontransferable and noninvestable certificates would not be money, and they would give the Technate states the appearance of a classless society.

One of the movement's books, *Technocracy: Technological Social Design*, asserted that society would be run by rationality and science rather than by a self-interested class of technocrats. Indeed, one of the main occupations of Technocracy members was to carry out elaborate surveys of world resources and industrial development, generating statistics to give the impression that technocrats have special expertise and can justly preside over an age of plenty. The movement stumbled at the outset of World War II, when its members rejoiced publicly at the spreading Armageddon; they believed that the war was the final collapse of the old order, and they prepared to take charge when the distraught people of the world called upon them to do so.

The 1963 story "Speakeasy," by Mack Reynolds, imagines what the North American Technate might have been like. The society is highly stratified, almost a caste system, headed by a Supreme Technician and an elite class of Technos and Technas. The language includes such interjections as, "Good Howard!" "Great Scott!" and "Heavens to Veblen!" Not only has the dream of a classless society been dashed, but the culture has fallen into complete stagnation, and scientific progress has stalled. Protagonist Rex Morris, a member of the elite, comments, "We've been in a rut for generations. Whatever happened to such ambitions as the conquest of space, as the improvement of the race by controlled genetics, as the eventual attainment of . . . the Godhead? At first the Technate seemed to be a step in advance, but it bogged down into a rut like that the Egyptians were in for millennia."[27]

To save the Technate, Morris stages near-assassinations to get the elite thinking and to stir things up. He finds that the entire leadership of the Technate is privately deliberating how they might start a gentle revolution, changing the society without endangering themselves. The "speakeasy" of the title refers to gathering places they have established where people feel free to discuss and criticize the system. Morris learns that the technocrats are incapable of carrying out their gentle revolution, but an ambitious security man from the lower classes launches his own revolution, violent and oppressive.

Another pseudoscientific movement that was promoted through SF was Count Alfred Korzybski's General Semantics. Today the word *semantics* refers to the study of word meanings in language, but in Korzybski's lexicon it was a total approach to understanding and solving all social and psychological problems. In his first book Korzybski joined the chorus of intellectuals bemoaning World War I and hoping that a science of humanity could be developed to avoid such scourges. His tome *Science and Sanity* offers such a science in a rush of neologisms, rash psychological assumptions, and platitudes. His disciple S. I. Hayakawa, an academic who later became a U.S. senator, provided a diluted and more reasonable presentation of General Semantics in his popular book *Language in Thought and Action*.

Korzybski believed that humans wander in the territory between sanity and insanity as members of the unsane, primarily because of certain bad mental habits encouraged by the primitiveness of our language. If we could train our minds properly, we would become vastly superior beings. Progress could be achieved through liberation from the naive concretizing of words and thoughts. If we could realize that the word is not the thing, that the map is not the territory, we would be able to transcend our archaic thought patterns. General Semantics teaches doctrines of supposedly non-Aristotelian, non-Euclidean, and non-Newtonian intelligence (called "null-A," "null-E," and "null-N"). Korzybski claimed his philosophical system was solidly grounded in physiology and mathematics.

General Semanticists postulate a mental technique, the "semantic pause" or "cortical-thalamic pause," that allows one to act rationally and effectively in times of stress when animal emotions and the debilitating contradictions of traditional language would lead to disaster. This maneuver supposedly disconnects the lower centers of the brain, thus permitting the higher centers to operate coolly according to the principles of General Semantics.

In his study of pseudoscientific cults, Martin Gardner acknowledged that General Semantics may have popularized some legitimate, liberating insights, but he denied that any of these insights were original with Korzybski. Gardner noted further that conventional philosophy and psychiatry learned nothing from the movement, although many educated people were for a time caught up in the fad. Some of the semantic exercises for teaching good thinking habits may have had some pedagogic use, Gardner felt, but "Korzybski and his followers magnified their therapeutic value out of all sane proportions.

At conventions, general semanticists have testified to semantic cures of alcoholism, homosexuality, kleptomania, bad reading habits, stuttering, migraine, nymphomania, impotence, and innumerable varieties of other neurotic and psychotic ailments."[28]

A. E. van Vogt's novel, *The World of Null-A*, depicts a society dominated by General Semantics. Around the year 2560 an elite, angelic, prepotent corps of General Semanticists rules Earth. Venus is inhabited solely by 240 million of these superhumans. To become a member of this class, a person must study the philosophy of null-A and related subjects, then submit to a month-long examination by a huge computer called the Games Machine. The book's chapter epigraphs quote Korzybski, and the Semantic Institute is located on Korzybski Square. John Campbell, the editor who first published the novel, is also quoted in an epigraph, and the book is dedicated to him.

The novel's hero is Gilbert Gosseyn—"go sane" being the opposite of "go crazy"—and the essential metaphor is a chess game. Gosseyn fights madness to find his true identity and to establish himself in the system of Semanticists. To do this, he must win a meta-game of which the Games Machine is but one component. He and the other characters never find out the nature of the essential struggle or the rules of the ultimate game. Gosseyn is a pawn or somebody's puppet. But on close inspection, it turns out that each puppeteer has string tied to his wrists and is operated by a puppet master from above. Even the players are pawns in a game played by men from the stars.

When Gosseyn finds the player who has used him as a pawn, the man seems to be a duplicate of Gosseyn. This discovery not only devastates Gosseyn's sense of unique identity, but it violates "the underlying credo of null-A, that no two objects of the universe can be identical."[29] Although Aristotle might have believed, as an axiom of logic, that A equals A, Korzybski rather grandly asserted that A generally does not equal A and that A certainly never equals B.

The World of Null-A is a wish-fulfillment fantasy. The notion that one can become a powerful member of the societal elite by practicing an arcane mental technique appeals to an under-rewarded subculture of intellectuals like SF fans. The novel hinted that the reader might already, unconsciously, be a member of a vast conspiracy that soon would establish a higher civilization ruled by the first representatives of a species evolutionarily above *homo sapiens*.

As reshaped in van Vogt's novel, General Semantics was one of the influences behind the Dianetics and Scientology cult, founded in the 1950s by L. Ron Hubbard. Both van Vogt and Hubbard were members of John Campbell's stable of writers. Hubbard, who spent three decades creating a worldwide religious financial empire, returned to writing SF with the huge 1982 novel

Battlefield Earth. Dianetics, which was first announced in the pages of *Astounding Science Fiction* in 1950, the year of Korzybski's death, claimed to be able to raise therapy clients to an exalted mental state called "clear," which sounded remarkably like the Semanticists' cortical-thalamic pause.

For a while van Vogt was very active in a movement to create a Church of General Semantics. After Dianetics was announced (but before it became the Church of Scientology), he became the leader of its California branch and editor of the *Journal of the Dianetic Sciences*. Hubbard's first Dianetics book named Korzybski as one of his chief precursors, an honor Korzybski had earlier bestowed on Aristotle; a tape recording of an early lecture by Hubbard was called "General Dianetics." John Campbell was the key social link in this evolution, in his role as editor and as a contributor to Hubbard's book, *Dianetics: The Modern Science of Mental Health*.

Many science fiction readers swarmed to Dianetics in 1950, including some who had earlier dabbled in General Semantics. The December 1950 issue of *Fantasy and Science Fiction* carried a thoroughly damning review of *Dianetics* by the psychologist C. Daly King, and the May 1951 issue of *Marvel Science Stories* contained essays by Theodore Sturgeon, Lester del Rey, and L. Ron Hubbard, debating the new movement.[30] Several stories based on Dianetics appeared, for example, "I'm a Stranger Here Myself," by Eric Frank Russell. But today, despite the worldly success of Scientology, the science fiction subculture bristles with hostility toward what it sees as Hubbard's perversion of SF's fantasies. In my Iguanacon survey, Hubbard achieved an average popularity score of only 2.15, lower than every other author except Richard S. Shaver, with 1.68. Shaver, like Hubbard, discredited himself by offering fiction-derived pseudoscience as fact.

PROPHECY AND SIMULATION OF THE FUTURE

From the beginning of the genre, many SF authors aspired to predict the future. *Amazing's* slogan on the first issue was "Extravagant Fiction Today . . . Cold Fact Tomorrow."[31] The idea was sustained in the slogan of *Science Wonder Stories*, "Prophetic Fiction is the Mother of Scientific Fact."[32] In a famous dictum known as Clarke's Law, Arthur C. Clarke asserted that real scientists have limited power as prophets: "When a distinguished but elderly scientist states that something is possible, he is almost certainly right. When he states that something is impossible, he is very probably wrong."[33] Bertrand Russell was once quoted in *Analog* as saying, "The prophecies of our science-fiction writers have proven more accurate than the expectations of our scientists and statesmen."[34]

An *Analog* advertisement of 1961 began, "Science fiction is the barometer of things to come!"[35] An editorial in *Amazing* at about the same time contended that we must "recognize that the science of today is the science fiction of yesterday; and that the science fiction of today is the science of tomorrow."[36] Practically every magazine in the field has used such a slogan at one time or another. In 1940 Charles D. Hornig wrote in *Future Fiction*, "So many things forecasted in science-fiction stories have come to pass that it is only reasonable to suppose that science-fiction will continue to be the soothsayer of coming events."[37] In 1956 Ray Palmer listed the virtues of SF in his magazine *Other Worlds*. "Not just entertainment and escapism, but *imagination, vision, foresight, progress, anticipation of a future and improved civilization to come!* Today's dream; tomorrow's fact!"[38] Ten years earlier, as editor of *Amazing*, Palmer wrote that SF was already a *respected* prophet.[39]

In their pioneering anthology *Adventures in Space and Time*, published in the aftermath of World War II, Raymond Healy and J. Francis McComas considered the prophetic role of SF in our society:

> Science-Fiction concerns itself with the world of the future, a world whose political, social and economic life has been shaped by the expansion of scientific knowledge. In depicting this world, science-fiction very nearly falls between two stools. Is it literature? Or is it prophecy?
>
> We contend that it is both. Literature should certainly reflect the conditions of its time. Our time is both conditioned and challenged by the quiet men in the laboratories. The war demonstrated that God is no longer on the side of the heaviest battalions, but on that of the heaviest thinkers. The atomic explosions have destroyed more than Japanese cities; they have broken the chains that have held man earthbound since his beginning. The universe is ours. Over and above all problems of imperialism, racism, economic and political instability, is the question: what shall we do with the universe? For once in history, the most average of men is concerned with more than his immediate future. The world of tomorrow is the problem of today, and writing that reflects this factor of our life reflects a most fascinating and complex condition of our time.[40]

Apart from its power to make technical prophecies, science fiction may succeed in exploring the human consequences of technical developments. According to Frederik Pohl, "Somebody once said that a good science-fiction story should be able to predict not the automobile but the traffic jam."[41] Isaac Asimov has argued that predicting social consequences is the most important task science fiction can perform: "Do you see, then, that the important prediction is not the automobile, but the parking problem; not radio, but the soap-opera; not the income tax but the expense account; not the Bomb but the nuclear stalemate? Not the action, in short, but the reaction."[42]

Prediction of social consequences, like the less subtle prediction of future inventions themselves, is a very uncertain business. SF frequently fails, and claims about its past successes often are exaggerated.[43] Social consequences may be harder to predict accurately than mere inventions, because the responses to change involve many factors, including counterinventions. On the issue of prophecy, Lester del Rey wrote: "It has never been the job of science fiction to foretell the future accurately, though we've had a few lucky hits from all our mining of the worlds and times of possibility. I began a book once, in the early fifties with: 'When Major Armstrong was the first man to set foot on the Moon . . .' I got the date wrong by five years and most other details wholly wrong. No matter, if the readers enjoyed the tale and found it somehow conveyed the *feeling* of a future."[44]

Perhaps SF has more value as simulation study of the future than as prophecy. An author designs a plausible future, then the reader explores and evaluates it. If it feels bad, the readers can work to prevent it. If it feels good, perhaps they can bring it about. As John Campbell said, "The greatest service science-fiction can render, it seems to me, is to point out the probable results of present trends—and then let the reader decide whether that's what he wants!"[45] Frederik Pohl also extolled the virtues of SF as a way of looking at the future. "For one thing, it's cheap. If you want to see what an atomic war is going to do, it is cheaper to write a story about it than it is to start a war. Also it is a sort of diluted reality; people can confront realities in a science-fiction story that they don't want to hear about in real life."[46] For *Galaxy* editor H. L. Gold, SF was conjecture rather than prediction, and anyone who did not realize that science fiction was devoted to "having fun with ideas" was "like an engineer trying to harness the energy of noisemakers at a New Year's party."[47]

But perhaps science fiction does prepare people for the future, not through prophecy but simply by accustoming people to think about the future and to realize that it may be very different from the past. Alexei Panshin once commented, "My idea of what makes science fiction worth reading is that it prepares people to accept change, to think in terms of change being both natural and inevitable, and that it allows us to look at familiar things from new angles."[48] This is really another assertion that SF has the power to expand consciousness, to give readers a richer imagination and a more profound capacity to view life creatively. In this connection, the new wave becomes not an alternative to hard science but an extension, increasing the already great scope of SF's speculation without necessarily undercutting the old traditions.

TRANSCENDENCE AND EXPANDED CONSCIOUSNESS

Whatever science fiction teaches or persuades readers to believe, it may help them achieve a higher level of awareness, an expanded consciousness transcending mundane concerns. This may be in the form of wisdom that guides an individual through the practical problems of life in a changing world. Or it may be a purely aesthetic understanding, subjectively valuable to the individual but lacking observable behavioral consequences. In this, SF may serve as a substitute for religion. Some say that the vicarious peak experience provided by science fiction is manifested in heightened creativity, less parochialism, and a deeper comprehension of man's place in the universe. Philip K. Dick, a leading contemporary writer, described the liberating sense of wonder he felt upon first reading SF in the early 1940s: "Here were ideas, vital and imaginative. Men moving across the universe, down into subatomic particles, into time; there was no limit. One society, one given environment was transcended. Stf was Faustian; it carried a person up and beyond."[49]

In 1964 Frederik Pohl wrote, "One of the advantages of reading science fiction is that it accustoms one to the long view."[50] From the eon-spanning perspective of SF, current social problems take on radically different meanings. As Pohl noted, people fear that spreading automation will cause chronic unemployment, but he argued that SF helps us see that technological advance will provide more jobs in the long run, even if it temporarily puts people out of work. This mundane example hints that the often ecstatic experience of SF may let us see current events in the vastly larger context of universal history. Ten years after Pohl's essay, Ben Bova made a similar point. "Science fiction requires a mind-set that encompasses millennia and parsecs, not merely weeks and nose-lengths."[51]

In 1932 author Clark Ashton Smith, in a rebuttal to a letter from Julian Gray, extolled the transcendent virtues of science fiction. Like many recent critics, Gray had argued that the standards of good conventional literature should be applied to science fiction. Smith felt that SF transcended conventional artistic criteria, just as it helped readers transcend the limitations of the human experience:

> The real thrill comes from the description of ultrahuman events, forces and scenes, which properly dwarf the terrene actors to comparative insignificance. For many people—probably more than Mr. Gray realizes—imaginative stories

offer a welcome and salutary release from the somewhat oppressive tyranny of the homocentric, and help to correct the deeply introverted, ingrowing values that are fostered by present-day "humanism" and realistic literature with its unhealthy materialism and earth-bound trend. Science fiction, at its best, is akin to sublime and exalted poetry, in its evocation of tremendous, non-anthropomorphic imageries. To demand in such tales the intensive earthly observation of a Hardy is idle and beside the point; and one who approaches them from this angle will miss the true value and beauty.[52]

Some say that fictional exploration of the future helps people cope with change in their own lives. As Theodore Sturgeon asserted, "Science fiction is the only possible pill against future shock."[53] But Poul Anderson observed, "Actually when very startling developments happen, science fiction people tend to be caught as flatfooted as everybody else."[54] Historian of the subculture Harry Warner supported Anderson's view, reporting that the subculture responded with anything but wisdom and rationality to the first atomic bombs.[55]

SF may be on safer ground in claiming philosophical benefits. As Rog Phillips wrote, "The true aim of science fiction is to create an interest in speculating on the possibilities of the future, and of the unknown past."[56] For P. Schuyler Miller, the elevated perspective afforded by SF permits one "to stand off, so to speak, and look at the universe as a whole, from 'outside,' making its vastness and complexity seemingly understandable."[57]

For John J. Pierce, this cosmic perspective places us in a necessary larger context: "In science fiction, we ask ourselves who we are and where we are and why we are in relation to a universe seemingly without limits."[58] Elsewhere Pierce wrote that the philosophical insights of science fiction may fill the gap left by the retreat of religion from its traditional role of interpreting mankind's relation to the cosmos: "At its best, science fiction realized that life and intelligence could still be meaningful in the universe, despite the demise of the churchman's eschatology—that while Man might not matter to the universe, the universe could still matter to Man."[59]

Lester del Rey believed that every good writer must become engaged with the ancient problems of philosophy, such as the meaning of the good, the nature of causality, and the question of teleology. "Is there a purpose and design to the universe and to man? It may not matter. If so, must we follow it blindly? If blind chance rules, can we not shape our own purpose, suitable to our ultimate possibilities?"[60]

No variety of literature except science fiction wonders about the long-term future of the human species, and none suggests such a wide range of alternative fates. Covers from the old magazines provide many examples. Ed Emshwiller's painting, "Relics of an Extinct Race," the cover of the June 1951 issue of *Galaxy Science Fiction*, shows reptilian astronauts examining an exposed cliff of sedimentary rock on a desolate, airless planet. In the lowest stratum is a stone axe. Above it are arrow heads and a human bone. Still higher, the astronauts see a complete human skeleton, a sword, and a steel battle axe. Then comes a layer containing a pistol, a rifle, and a hand grenade. The top layer, radioactive glass produced by a nuclear explosion, glows. The blasted planet is our Earth; the progress of military technology has led to doom.

Mel Hunter's cover for the November 1955 issue of *Fantastic Universe* depicts the monument of the presidents at Mount Rushmore in South Dakota. Before it, a family of naked savages struggles to climb a burned hillside strewn with twisted metal. The titanic sculpture includes six monumental heads rather than the familiar four. Washington, Jefferson, Roosevelt, and Lincoln, somewhat damaged, remain in dark, weathered stone. In more recently cut stone is the harsh face of a military dictator, who was succeeded, according to the evidence of the rubble, by a wizened old man, perhaps the scientist-dictator of many SF dystopias. Not extinct, but reduced to the level of animals, our species has fallen far from the civilization that carved noble faces on that mountain.

Many stories, such as S. Fowler Wright's novels *The Amphibians* and *The World Below*, tell of futures after human extinction, when the dominant race is a species derived from ours or alien creatures. In Fritz Leiber's short story "Later Than You Think," an archeologist of the distant future reports the results of his excavations. A member of an aquatic species that has inherited Earth, he finds a time capsule left by the mammalian civilization that once ruled the land. The myths of these long-dead mammals tell of an even earlier extinct species that gave the mammals their name before vanishing. The time capsule was left by the rats.

Another Leiber story, "When the Last Gods Die," consists of an argument between the last humans and one of their faithful machines. Having explored the universe and done all there is to do, the people find life purposeless, so they prepare to die. The machine begs them to live on, but in vain. The human species flickers briefly in the memory of the machine and is gone.

Exhaustion of the species through excessive development of the intellect is the theme of Harry Bates's tale "Alas, All Thinking!" A man from the present falls in love with a woman of a future age in which the human population is reduced to three dozen living mummies that meditate upon questions beyond the comprehension of the twentieth century. Wrapped in bloodless thoughts, these few inheritors of Earth dry to corpselike husks, dessicated by their absolute dedication to intellect. At the end the woman can offer her ancient lover only a weak wink before she joins the others in dusty death.

In his 1931 story "The Jameson Satellite," Neil R. Jones told of a genius scientist who arranges to have his body preserved indefinitely by being placed in orbit in the supposed cold of outer space. Legend has it that this story was the inspiration for Robert Ettinger's real-life cryogenics movement, which offered dying people the chance to have their bodies frozen until some future time when medical science would know how to cure their illness and could thaw them back to life and health. Ettinger has acknowledged his debt to SF by writing in a science fiction magazine on suspended animation as a means for interstellar travel.[61] But poor Professor Jameson, frozen in 1958 and revived 40 million years later, discovers that his will to live leaves just as he achieves immortality. The human species is long extinct, and everything that has been meaningful to him has vanished. The choice he faces is whether to remain on desolate Earth or to join a species of mechanical beings in a voyage of discovery across the universe.

None of these scenarios may prove to be good predictions, and many cannot be evaluated for eons to come. But all of them carry the reader's imagination beyond the immediate concerns of everyday existence. In wondering what the distant future may bring, the reader must confront questions of the greatest scope. Stories of the distant past, of alien cultures, and of the depths of the human personality may also stimulate the awe and the rush of ideas created by tales of the far future. James P. Hogan's series of novels, *Inherit the Stars*, *The Gentle Giants of Ganymede*, and *Giant's Star*, tell of a vast detective project to uncover the truth about humanity's past. The unraveling of the astonishing answer takes the reader's mind through puzzles of cosmic scope.

All of this fiction raises the three great intertwined mysteries: Where have we come from? Who are we? Where are we going? Perhaps the most intense debate over SF topics in our society today concerns our ability to extract the good from science and technology without being overwhelmed by the evil. The technological optimists hope we can manage progress successfully, while the pessimists doubt that we have the wisdom. But behind this debate is a more quiet and more subtle one concerning the natural limits of scientific discovery. There may in fact be no way of maintaining our present high use of energy without catastrophic environmental damage and ultimate economic collapse. The social sciences may never be able to solve the difficulties of living in peace with each other except by imposing a tyranny so heavy that it crushes our humanness.

Some of the most effective science fiction links issues of the present with these questions. The tetralogy *Cities in Flight*, by James Blish, outlines the future history of interstellar human culture. At the beginning, scientific and technological progress has been slowed by the stifling bureaucracy and by the escalating scale and cost of research. In the last spasm of Western civilization two secret, astronomically expensive projects are searching for the means to achieve interstellar flight. One project tests thousands upon thousands of biological samples to find a drug that will extend the human lifespan to permit crews to survive galactic voyages. The other project builds a vast ice bridge on Jupiter to get the data for designing engines for starships. Conquest of death, conquest of gravity—two dreams not just of science fiction fans but of all humanity. In this story of our future starflight is just barely possible, but it may never be achieved without the right conjunction of material resources and personal courage. Blish's answer is problematic rather than optimistic, revealing the issue rather than dismissing it. We cannot be sure whether conditions in the future will prove favorable to progress or will lead us into a hopelessly static culture, incapable of further achievement. This is the greatest, if not the most familiar issue of our age.

At the end of the first book of the tetralogy, the two secret projects are successful, and the Galactic Age of Man begins. The second and third books recount many wonderful adventures in space. But the final book returns to the themes of death and gravity, as dislocations in space-time bring about the premature collapse of the universe. Characters that the reader has grown to love struggle to cope with ordinary problems and gradually learn that their entire universe is about to end. Among the comforts we have against death is the hope that life will continue through our children and other people we have touched in our brief span of personal existence. But in this story the entire universe will die, science can do nothing to forestall the end, and there is no comfort.

In the fullest sense, this is not merely a sad story but a tragic one, in which the real issue is human awareness and responsibility. Science was able to give humanity a few grand centuries of galactic experiences, but now gives foreknowledge of doom. Had we never left Earth, had we never expanded our consciousness to include the whole cosmos, then species death would have come without warning and with little pain, as it did to the dinosaurs. But by becoming aware, we have accepted a special responsibility for our fate, even if we can do nothing to change it.

In the final chapters of the tetralogy, the characters we love find an exalted means for transcending their doom in the moment it crushes them. Mathematical calculations show that one particular point in space and time will be the focus of the collapsing universe and the epicenter of the explosion that will create new universes. Against opposition and despite great difficulties, a small group of people arranges to be at this point. The power of hard science has brought them to the cosmic absurdity postulated by the new wave. "At this hour, everything had meaning; or nothing had; it depended on what had been worth investing with meaning over a lifetime of several thousand years."[62] And there remained a fantasy. Although none of them could go into the universes of the future, if each were positioned just *so* at the moment of annihilation, each would become a universe, providing the dimensionless stuff for a separate Big Bang. Perhaps something in each person's character could determine in unexpected ways the nature of the universe born from him or her; a galaxy would grow from each cell in their bodies. Although memories would vanish, everything these people had been would live again.

Thus death and gravity are conquered twice in *Cities in Flight*, first by finding physical means to overcome them, and second by finding spiritual means to transcend them. At its best, science fiction deals with the problems of our age on all levels, from the most practical to the most philosophical, creating awareness that rises above mere optimism and pessimism.

CONCLUSION

Science fiction may be understood as a universe of three ideological dimensions, evolving through the fourth dimension of time. In a way, each of the three ideological factions represents one kind of intensification or unfolding of a shared overarching SF ideology. All science fiction loves space travel, wonders about the possibility of ESP, and considers radical political alternatives. All science fiction prefers other worlds to the society and century in which we live. In part, this explains why the three ideologies, quite separate in conceptual principles and statistical correlations, are not mutually exclusive. Fans may favor one, any pair of them, or all three.

However, my quantitative analysis of the ideological structure of science fiction did reveal distinct factions of authors. Although many fans may love all three types, the authors tend to specialize. Casual readers who are not members of the freethinking subculture may respond more dogmatically to different authors than do the sophisticated convention-goers who are familiar with the full sweep of SF. Thus the ideologies may operate more antagonistically outside fandom.

Reduced to their essential critiques of modern society, the three ideologies point in three different directions. Hard science urges the creation of a galactic utopia through progress in technology and the physical sciences. The new wave cautions against such optimism and demands the transformation of the contemporary dystopia through revolutions in psychological sensibility and social awareness. The fantasy cluster despairs of changing our world for the better and retreats into dreams about worlds which never can be achieved.

The questions posed by science fiction and the answers it suggests are of crucial importance for contemporary society. Shall we develop technology and the physical sciences aggressively? Shall we gain more profound aesthetic, psychological, and sociological understanding of the human condition? Shall we supplement an inevitably drab reality with whimsy, thrills, chills, and romance? Stated in this way, the ideological premises of hard science, new wave, and fantasy are compatible. We can answer "Yes!" to each question, without contradiction.

Yet our options are not wide open, and we may be forced to choose among ideologies, especially if lack of vision and archaic political structures cramp the process of collective decision. Perhaps it would be no disaster if the hard science ideology prevailed and sent our species roaring across the galaxy. Perhaps it would be no disaster if we devoted ourselves to cultivating poetic sensitivity, personality probing, and social activism, as the new wave urges. And the aesthetic pleasure and stimulation of imagination provided by fantasy will be valuable in any future society. But science fiction is greater than any of its three main ideologies, and our species deserves a grander future than any one of them advises.

The starships of the future will need crews and colonists thoroughly trained in the physical sciences. Yet they also will need deep human understanding based on artistic insight as much as on social science to create a way of life worth spreading across the cosmos. And, since the real world will always fall short of the ideal, humans need wild dreams and fantastic imagination. Together the three ideologies of science fiction point toward a utopian, cosmopolitan future.

"A man's reach should exceed his grasp," the poet Robert Browning said, "or what's a heaven for?" The utopians dream of grasping heaven, yet many authors named in this book reach farther. Not content with eternal answers, they raise new questions. They hunt for signs of rot in the ideal futures postulated by more complacent minds, and they see past the horizon of ordinary assumptions to bold new alternatives. As technological progress increases the scope for human action, our consciousness must expand faster still. Whatever utopia our descendants build, science fiction imagines greater worlds beyond.

The three main ideologies of science fiction are really three general dimensions of transcendence. Each tells the reader how to rise above the mundane problems of material existence. From the astronomical perspective, all directions are "up," and in SF there are three orthogonal directions that may be considered "above." Each of these is a valid alternative for all individuals and all societies, not just for readers and writers in the small world of the science fiction subculture. By exploring these dimensions in ships of the imagination, SF authors are truly pilgrims and pioneers in space and time.

The hard science dimension reaches toward perfect rationality, control, understanding of existence in terms of mechanisms and predictable forces. It is oriented toward the external world, toward mastery of the physical environment. Critics may see the hard science approach as heartless, soulless, and reductionist, yet its proponents write with great optimism and spirit. They find hope and transcendence in the human capacity to think clearly and to create by shaping material things. All varieties of science fiction are human-centered, and hard science does not turn away from humanity as it turns toward the physical universe. Rather, it teaches that the universe is ours.

The new wave represents a dimension of inner space, psychological and literary sensitivity, communication with the hidden self, and interaction between personalities. In one direction, this is a dimension of extreme intimacy. But many authors have explored the opposite direction of estrangement, alienation, opposition, and radical political contradiction. Critics find the new wave pessimistic and pathological. But even in its darkest stories, the new wave exalts the human spirit, because the author becomes a hunter in the forests of the night, bagging the biggest wild game of all, the monsters of the id and of cultural repression. If the new wave protagonist often goes down in defeat, it is in sacrifice to the reader, who, though sharing the protagonist's annihilation, lives on, the wiser for the experience.

A cluster of various impossible worlds, fantasy is also the dimension of aesthetics and free imagination. Although its fictional worlds cannot be attained and its characters cannot be emulated, it is not wholly escapist. The magic by which fantasy lives is, after all, magic created by the author. Of all the types, fantasy is most emphatically art for art's sake. The best paintings in SF convention art exhibitions usually depict fiction from the fantasy cluster, and the modest but significant correlations linking the cluster with poetry and science fiction art suggest that a future study should investigate the ways in which this ideology represents the aesthetic dimension in science fiction. Like religion, which also rests upon supernatural assumptions, fantasy is born in the human capacity to postulate ideal worlds, gods, and demigods. In spinning beautiful tales for each other, we decorate our cultural habitat and embellish lives that otherwise would be excruciatingly dull.

Over the years, science fiction has expanded at varying rates along these three dimensions, like a tentacled nebula exploding irregularly from a supernova. The questionnaire for this study, administered on two days in late summer 1978, thus is a snapshot of an important stage in the evolution of SF. The questionnaire's inclusion of many older authors and the items about earlier literary periods added the dimension of past time, but since the survey we have moved a short distance into the future. The three ideologies are permanent dimensions that will always serve well in analyzing new fiction, even if authors of the future combine them in novel ways.

Future debates undoubtedly will divide the subculture, and not all of the divisions will be perfectly mapped along these three dimensions. At the time of this writing, the real-world question causing the greatest disagreements among SF authors is the Reagan administration's Strategic Defense Initiative, a set of largely space-based defenses against intercontinental missiles, popularly called by the science-fiction catch phrase Star Wars. The *New York Times* recently reported that SF authors Jerry Pournelle and Robert A. Heinlein had taken public stands in favor of S.D.I., while Arthur C. Clarke, Isaac Asimov, and Frederik Pohl were against it, and Ray Bradbury could not decide.[63] These authors are well informed about the technical questions, and they have thought deeply about space-based missile defense. Some readers may validly form their opinions on the basis of what their favorite authors say. But science fiction is not designed to resolve the serious issues of the mundane world. It is greatest when it expands our consciousness of the possibilities for thought and action.

In a century or two or ten, when Mars is colonized and a hundred million households are plugged into an electronic public library, will people still read the classic, twentieth-century tales that foresaw the first human expeditions to that planet? They will, and I think they will not find these stories outdated by the march of history. "A Martian Odyssey" by Stanley G. Weinbaum and "In the Hall of the Martian Kings" by John Varley will still teach them that alien life forms can be friendly and amusing rather than hostile and deadly. Robert A. Heinlein's novel *Red Planet* will remind them of the many rites of passage experienced by a person growing to adulthood and suggest that still higher plateaus of wisdom await the maturation of our species. *The Gods of Mars*, by Edgar Rice Burroughs, will convince them that even a society's most widely held truth may turn out to be a lie designed to serve the interests of the few. Although shaped by three ideological dimensions, science fiction breaks through the walls of ideology, opening eternal doors of transcendence through which the human spirit may fly, out into the vast universe.

APPENDIX

NOTES

BIBLIOGRAPHY

INDEX

APPENDIX:

QUESTIONNAIRE

RESPONSES

The following four tables report questionnaire responses from 595 dedicated members of the science fiction subculture. The survey was administered at the 1978 world science fiction convention, held in Phoenix, Arizona. The respondents rated each of the items on a preference scale from zero (do not like) to six (like very much), and they were instructed to skip any items with which they were unfamiliar.

Table A1. Popularity of science fiction authors

Author	Mean rating	Percentage giving author top rating	Percentage of 595 fans responding
1. Brian W. Aldiss	3.80	8.0	68.9
2. Poul Anderson	4.87	38.0	87.1
3. Piers Anthony	3.89	16.0	62.0
4. Isaac Asimov	5.08	48.2	97.3
5. Gregory Benford	3.89	11.0	35.3
6. Alfred Bester	4.51	27.1	66.9
7. Eando Binder	3.05	7.4	29.6
8. James Blish	4.37	16.2	86.1
9. Robert Bloch	4.24	19.1	72.3
10. Anthony Boucher	4.07	14.6	52.8
11. Ben Bova	3.72	6.1	79.8
12. Ray Bradbury	4.21	29.3	95.3
13. Marion Zimmer Bradley	4.44	33.3	67.2

Table A1 (*continued*)

Author	Mean rating	Percentage giving author top rating	Percentage of 595 fans responding
14. Fredric Brown	4.43	22.9	58.0
15. John Brunner	4.19	18.5	74.5
16. Algis Budrys	3.89	11.0	53.6
17. Anthony Burgess	3.68	10.2	44.4
18. Edgar Rice Burroughs	3.54	18.0	83.2
19. John W. Campbell, Jr.	3.97	12.5	67.2
20. Orson Scott Card	4.16	21.4	24.4
21. Lin Carter	2.74	6.3	71.8
22. Jack Chalker	3.54	10.3	34.1
23. A. Bertram Chandler	3.81	10.7	45.4
24. C. J. Cherryh	4.37	26.0	48.4
25. Arthur C. Clarke	4.93	38.9	93.3
26. Hal Clement	4.18	19.2	71.9
27. Mark Clifton	3.31	3.8	17.5
28. John Collier	3.75	16.1	19.8
29. Ray Cummings	2.93	1.4	23.2
30. Avram Davidson	3.82	9.1	51.9
31. L. Sprague de Camp	4.41	22.5	79.2
32. Lester del Rey	4.03	12.7	79.5
33. Samuel R. Delany	4.02	16.9	76.5
34. August W. Derleth	3.70	12.3	40.8
35. Philip K. Dick	3.83	13.1	70.6
36. Gordon R.Dickson	4.64	30.7	79.5
37. Stephen R. Donaldson	3.85	17.1	32.4
38. Arthur Conan Doyle	4.27	26.2	80.7
39. Gordon Eklund	3.26	1.7	39.2
40. Harlan Ellison	4.01	32.0	93.6
41. Philip Jose Farmer	4.43	27.6	83.5
42. Randall Garrett	4.03	15.8	40.5
43. Hugo Gernsback	2.55	6.7	42.7
44. H. Rider Haggard	3.47	14.9	40.5
45. Joe Haldeman	4.41	23.8	71.3
46. Edmond Hamilton	4.00	12.9	50.9
47. Harry Harrison	4.21	18.4	76.0

Table A1 (*continued*)

Author	Mean rating	Percentage giving author top rating	Percentage of 595 fans responding
48. Robert A. Heinlein	5.05	52.6	97.1
49. Zenna Henderson	4.58	38.0	59.3
50. Frank Herbert	4.42	26.3	87.6
51. Robert E. Howard	3.50	16.7	52.4
52. Fred Hoyle	3.37	4.7	60.7
53. L. Ron Hubbard	2.15	3.6	46.4
54. Aldous Huxley	3.68	10.2	74.5
55. Raymond F. Jones	3.15	2.6	25.7
56. Daniel Keyes	3.94	12.4	33.9
57. Stephen King	4.03	28.1	25.7
58. Otis Adelbert Kline	2.77	1.5	22.2
59. Damon Knight	3.97	9.8	74.1
60. C. M. Kornbluth	4.38	18.6	66.1
61. Henry Kuttner	4.47	26.2	57.8
62. R. A. Lafferty	4.04	17.1	59.8
63. Keith Laumer	4.31	26.5	69.1
64. Ursula K. LeGuin	4.76	41.4	85.7
65. Fritz Leiber	4.85	38.5	85.0
66. Murray Leinster	4.10	15.0	59.5
67. Stanislaw Lem	2.73	9.2	45.9
68. C. S. Lewis	3.85	19.9	71.9
69. H. P. Lovecraft	3.76	18.4	68.4
70. Elizabeth A. Lynn	3.50	13.5	12.4
71. Katherine MacLean	3.78	8.9	30.1
72. Barry Malzberg	2.64	4.4	53.9
73. George R. R. Martin	4.28	19.0	49.6
74. Richard Matheson	4.09	16.2	45.7
75. Anne McCaffrey	4.85	44.5	80.0
76. J. T. McIntosh	3.43	7.4	20.3
77. Vonda N. McIntyre	3.88	14.1	53.8
78. Richard McKenna	3.72	9.4	21.5
79. Robert Merle	2.62	5.7	14.6
80. Judith Merril	3.36	5.2	55.5
81. A. Merritt	3.58	16.3	43.4

Table A1 (*continued*)

Author	Mean rating	Percentage giving author top rating	Percentage of 595 fans responding
82. Walter M. Miller, Jr.	4.35	22.0	41.3
83. Michael Moorcock	3.77	17.1	70.8
84. C. L. Moore	4.35	22.6	57.1
85. Larry Niven	5.06	47.4	89.1
86. Andre Norton	4.14	24.9	84.4
87. George Orwell	3.65	12.5	86.2
88. Lewis Padgett	4.46	29.6	38.0
89. Raymond A. Palmer	2.33	2.4	14.1
90. Edgar Pangborn	3.96	16.5	41.8
91. Alexei Panshin	3.75	10.7	51.6
92. P. J. Plauger	3.28	5.2	16.3
93. Edgar Allan Poe	4.28	28.6	89.9
94. Frederik Pohl	4.56	21.9	85.4
95. Jerry Pournelle	3.96	18.7	76.3
96. Ayn Rand	2.90	13.4	53.8
97. Tom Reamy	3.92	18.1	27.9
98. Mack Reynolds	3.47	10.9	55.6
99. Frank Riley	3.12	1.5	10.9
100. Jeanne Robinson	3.97	20.2	33.3
101. Spider Robinson	4.45	29.7	69.1
102. Sax Rohmer	3.31	12.6	29.4
103. Joanna Russ	3.02	11.3	56.5
104. Eric Frank Russell	4.11	19.8	45.9
105. James H.Schmitz	4.43	31.1	43.2
106. Carter Scholz	3.02	5.4	9.4
107. Richard S. Shaver	1.68	1.1	15.1
108. Robert Sheckley	4.05	16.5	54.1
109. Raccoona Sheldon	4.56	36.5	37.3
110. Robert Silverberg	4.52	23.6	84.7
111. Clifford D. Simak	4.54	25.6	79.5
112. E. E. "Doc" Smith	3.48	18.1	68.7
113. Norman Spinrad	3.58	12.2	59.2
114. Olaf Stapledon	3.44	10.1	39.8
115. Bruce Sterling	3.27	12.5	10.8

Table A1 (*continued*)

Author	Mean rating	Percentage giving author top rating	Percentage of 595 fans responding
116. George R. Stewart	3.86	12.4	24.4
117. Theodore Sturgeon	4.69	31.8	86.6
118. James Tiptree, Jr.	4.52	33.9	62.5
119. J. R. R. Tolkien	4.73	48.4	90.9
120. Wilson Tucker	3.83	11.1	43.9
121. Lisa Tuttle	3.58	7.8	27.9
122. A. E. van Vogt	4.10	18.1	81.5
123. Jack Vance	4.37	20.5	63.2
124. John Varley	4.40	29.6	47.7
125. Jules Verne	3.75	13.9	88.6
126. Joan D. Vinge	4.03	11.5	38.0
127. Kurt Vonnegut, Jr.	3.36	17.1	84.5
128. Karl Edward Wagner	3.57	9.3	18.2
129. Stanley G. Weinbaum	4.00	17.5	47.9
130. H. G. Wells	4.06	18.7	92.4
131. Kate Wilhelm	4.19	19.2	63.0
132. Jack Williamson	4.13	13.8	64.5
133. Richard Wilson	3.24	4.2	20.0
134. Gene Wolfe	3.65	10.1	36.5
135. Donald A. Wollheim	3.52	5.9	53.9
136. Philip Wylie	3.81	11.9	47.9
137. John Wyndham	4.13	17.9	51.8
138. Roger Zelazny	4.72	34.4	85.4
Mean for 138 authors:	3.89	17.9	55.9

Table A2. Popularity of various types of literature

Type of literature	Mean rating	Percentage giving type top rating	Percentage of 595 fans responding
1. Stories that convey a sense of wonder	4.97	42.5	94.5

Table A2 (*continued*)

Type of literature	Mean rating	Percentage giving type top rating	Percentage of 595 fans responding
2. Stories which take current knowledge from one of the sciences and logically extrapolate what might be the next steps taken in that science	4.83	35.7	95.1
3. Science fiction art	4.80	38.8	95.6
4. Humor	4.75	33.2	97.3
5. Science-fantasy	4.71	35.2	95.0
6. Science fiction movies	4.66	34.7	96.5
7. Stories about new technology	4.60	23.6	95.3
8. Hard science fiction	4.53	31.5	97.0
9. Stories set in a universe where the laws of nature are very different from those found on our world	4.50	26.2	96.8
10. Fantasy	4.49	34.7	97.3
11. Fiction which deeply probes personal relationships and feelings	4.30	26.4	96.3
12. Factual reports on the space program and spaceflight	4.26	27.8	96.8
13. Fiction based on the physical sciences	4.26	19.3	94.8
14. Myths and legends	4.22	25.3	96.3
15. Action-adventure fiction	3.99	18.0	94.5
16. Sagas and epics	3.96	17.9	94.1
17. Factual science articles	3.92	15.2	96.5
18. Sword-and-sorcery	3.84	24.6	96.3
19. British science fiction	3.79	9.0	80.0
20. Fiction based on the social sciences	3.74	11.0	92.9
21. Golden Age science fiction	3.72	14.3	91.9
22. Fiction that is critical of our society	3.65	9.1	94.3
23. Stories in which there is a rational explanation for everything	3.57	12.3	94.6
24. Space opera	3.54	15.0	93.9
25. Classic science fiction from the early days of SF	3.45	9.8	94.6
26. Fanzines	3.43	15.7	85.4
27. New wave science fiction	3.32	13.4	87.9
28. Fiction concerned with harmful effects of scientific progress	3.19	7.0	95.8

Table A2 (*continued*)

Type of literature	Mean rating	Percentage giving type top rating	Percentage of 595 fans responding
29. Mainstream literature	3.18	6.8	93.8
30. Erotic literature	3.15	11.6	94.1
31. Avant-garde fiction which experiments with new styles	3.14	7.9	91.6
32. Tales of the supernatural	3.08	10.7	95.8
33. Poetry	3.01	11.4	95.5
34. Horror-and-weird	2.92	11.0	95.1
35. Comic books	2.84	12.1	94.8
36. Feminist literature	2.65	7.4	90.3
37. Ghost stories	2.58	7.4	95.6
38. Utopian political novels and essays	2.56	4.4	92.3
39. The Holy Bible	2.31	8.4	90.4
40. Occult literature	2.13	8.3	93.4
Mean for 40 literature types	3.71	18.4	94.0

Table A3. Popularity of various time periods and topics

Time period, subject matter	Mean rating	Percentage giving type top rating	Percentage of 595 fans responding
Science fiction of the 1920s and 1930s	2.81	6.0	88.9
Science fiction of the 1940s and 1950s	3.97	13.4	93.1
Science fiction of the 1960s and 1970s	4.92	32.7	95.0
Telepathy	4.27	22.8	93.6
Alien cultures	5.09	40.1	93.8
Magic	4.00	20.8	93.6
War	3.00	6.9	93.1
Sex	3.43	12.3	94.1
Robots	4.00	12.9	93.9
Barbarians	2.85	5.6	93.6

Table A4. Popularity of different kinds of protagonists

Stories in which main character is	Mean rating	Percentage giving type top rating	Percentage of 595 fans responding
Warm and loving	4.15	14.4	77.1
Strong and tough	3.89	11.7	77.8
Clever and intelligent	5.11	40.6	78.3
Sensitive and introspective	4.40	21.8	77.8
Brave and aggressive	3.91	12.1	77.6
Cool and unemotional	3.34	8.9	77.8
Erotic and beautiful	3.39	9.2	77.1
Helpful and cooperative	3.87	9.1	77.3
Strange and unusual	4.64	26.2	77.5
Independent and ambitious	4.65	25.7	77.3
Average person	3.63	13.2	77.6
Superior person	4.12	16.6	77.8

NOTES

1. AN APPROACH TO SCIENCE FICTION

1. Ray Bradbury, *The Martian Chronicles* (New York: Bantam, 1954), pp. 179–180.

2. Milton C. Albrecht, "The Relationship of Literature and Society," *American Journal of Sociology* 59 (1954): 425–436; "Does Literature Reflect Common Values?" *American Sociological Review* 21 (December 1956): 722–729.

3. Talcott Parsons, *The Social System* (Glencoe, Ill.: Free Press, 1951); William Sims Bainbridge, "Cultural Genetics," in *Religious Movements: Genesis, Exodus, and Numbers*, ed. Rodney Stark (New York: Rose of Sharon Press, 1985).

4. Claude Lévi-Strauss, *The Raw and the Cooked* (New York: Harper and Row, 1969), p. 13.

5. Robert K. Merton, *Social Theory and Social Structure* (New York: Free Press, 1968), p. 195.

6. Elihu Katz, "Communication Research and the Image of Society: The Convergence of Two Traditions," *American Journal of Sociology* 65 (1960): 435–440; Elihu Katz and Paul F. Lazarsfeld, *Personal Influence* (Glencoe, Ill.: Free Press, 1955); Everett M. Rogers, *Social Change in Rural Society* (New York: Appleton-Century-Crofts, 1960); Otto N. Larsen, "Innovators and Early Adopters of Television," *Sociological Inquiry* 32 (1962): 16–33.

7. Frank P. Manuel and Fritzie P. Manuel, *Utopian Thought in the Western World* (Cambridge: Harvard University Press, 1979).

8. Rodney Stark and William Sims Bainbridge, "Of Churches, Sects, and Cults," *Journal for the Scientific Study of Religion* 18 (1979): 117–131; William Sims Bainbridge and Rodney Stark, "The 'Consciousness Reformation' Revisited," *Journal for the Scientific Study of Religion* 20 (1981): 1–15.

9. Manuel and Manuel, *Utopian Thought*, p. 775.

10. Anthony West, *H. G. Wells: Aspects of a Life* (New York: Random House, 1984).

11. T. K. Penniman, *A Hundred Years of Anthropology* (London: Duckworth, 1965).

12. Miles J. Breuer, "The Future of Scientifiction," *Amazing Stories Quarterly* 2 (Summer 1929): 291.

13. Robert Bloch, "Fandora's Box," *Imagination* 7 (August 1956): 94.

14. Ted White, editorial, *Amazing Stories* 43 (July 1969): 127.

15. Ted White, editorial, *Amazing Stories* 47 (June 1973): 117.

16. P. Schuyler Miller, "A Trend to Integration," *Astounding Science Fiction* 64 (January 1960): 168–169.

17. John W. Campbell, Jr., "The Nature of Literature," *Analog* 76 (October 1965): 7.

18. Harry Harrison, "SF and the Establishment," *Amazing Stories* 42 (November 1968): 4.

19. Philip Jose Farmer, "White Whales, Raintrees, Flying Saucers . . . ," *Fantastic Universe* 2 (July 1954): inside front cover.

20. Theodore Sturgeon, book review, *Venture Science Fiction* 1 (September 1957): 49.

21. Theodore Sturgeon, book review, *Venture Science Fiction* 2 (March 1958): 66–67.

22. Lester del Rey, *The World of Science Fiction* (New York: Ballantine, 1979), p. 348.

23. Damon Knight, "Infinity's Choice," *Infinity* 3 (March 1958): 59.

24. John W. Campbell, Jr., reply to a letter, *Astounding Science Fiction* 66 (December 1960): 177.

25. C. P. Snow, *The Two Cultures* (London: Cambridge University Press, 1964).

26. Andrew Feenberg, "The Politics of Survival: Science Fiction in the Nuclear Age," *Alternative Futures* 1 (Summer 1978): 5–6.

27. P. Schuyler Miller, book review, *Astounding Science-Fiction* 39 (March 1947): 137.

28. Poul Anderson, editorial, *Amazing Stories* 39 (February 1965): 124.

29. Ibid., p. 130.

30. Isaac Asimov, quoted by Ben Bova, "The Reality Test," *Analog* 98 (September 1978): 9.

31. Robert A. Heinlein, "Science Fiction: Its Nature, Faults, and Virtues," in *The Science Fiction Novel*, ed. Basil Davenport (Chicago: Advent, 1969), p. 42.

32. Robert A. Heinlein, "Channel Markers," *Analog* 92 (January 1974): 170–171.

33. Barry N. Malzberg, "Robert Silverberg," *Fantasy and Science Fiction* 46 (April 1974): 69.

34. Jack Williamson, "Vanguard of Science," *Startling Stories* 2 (September 1939): 15.

35. Sam Moskowitz, *Explorers of the Infinite* (Cleveland: Meridian, 1963), p. 315.

36. Ray Cummings, "This Atom—Earth," *Startling Stories* 1 (May 1939): 13; Otis Adelbert Kline, letter to the editor, *Startling Stories* 1 (January 1939): 116.

37. Hugo Gernsback, "A New Sort of Magazine," *Amazing Stories* 1 (April 1926): 3.

38. Forrest J. Ackerman, letter to the editor, *Astounding Stories* 9 (January 1932): 134.

39. T. O'Conor Sloane, reply to a letter, *Amazing Stories* 8 (May 1933): 185.

40. Hugo Gernsback, "Science Wonder Stories," *Science Wonder Stories* 1 (June 1929): 5.

41. Ted White, editorial, *Amazing Stories* 43 (July 1969): 126; editorial, *Amazing Stories* 48 (May 1975): 119; Lester del Rey, "SF, Sci-Fi—and Whadat," *Analog* 95 (December 1975): 165.

42. Hugo Gernsback, "A New Sort of Magazine," *Amazing Stories* 1 (April 1926): 3.

43. Gernsback, "Science Wonder Stories," p. 5.

44. Isaac Asimov, editorial, *Isaac Asimov's Science Fiction Magazine* 2 (March–April 1978): 8.

45. Sol Cohen, editorial, *Amazing Stories* 40 (August 1965): 4.

46. Paul W. Fairman, "The Observatory," *Amazing Stories* 32 (February 1958): 3.

47. John W. Campbell, Jr., "Too Good at Guessing," *Astounding Science-Fiction* 29 (April 1942): 6.

48. H. J. Campbell, editorial, *Authentic Science Fiction* 1 (April 1953): 3.

49. John Litster, letter to the editor, *Astounding Science Fiction* 53 (April 1954): 150.

50. Irene E. Hollar, letter to the editor, *Astounding Science Fiction* 49 (August 1952): 132.

51. R. A. Bradley, letter to the editor, *Planet Stories* 4 (Spring 1950): 112.

52. Aloysius Cupay, letter to the editor, *Worlds of If* 20 (July–August 1971): 3.

53. Jack Leit and Lee Mortimer, "Mars Confidential," *Amazing Stories* 27 (April–May 1953): 19.

54. Lester del Rey, "Reading Room," *Worlds of If* 21 (July–August 1972): 136.

55. James Blish, "Science in Science Fiction: The Mathematical Story," *Science Fiction Quarterly* 1 (August 1951): 83.

56. Frederik Pohl, book review, *If* 9 (November 1959): 94.

57. Tom Clareson, "The Evolution of Science Fiction," *Science Fiction Quarterly* 2 (August 1953): 97.

58. James Gunn, *Alternate Worlds* (Englewood Cliffs, N.J.: Prentice-Hall, 1975), p. 32.

59. James Gunn, "On the Road to Science Fiction: From Wells to Heinlein," *Isaac Asimov's Science Fiction Magazine* 3 (January 1979): 67.

60. Theodore Sturgeon, book review, *Galaxy* 34 (December 1973): 73.

61. Ibid., p. 70.

62. Damon Knight, "The Dissecting Table," *Science Fiction Adventures* 1 (November 1952): 122.

63. Ibid.

64. Damon Knight, "In the Balance," *If* 8 (October 1958): 109.

65. Heinlein, "Science Fiction: Its Nature, Faults, and Virtues," p. 15; Judith Merril, "Fish out of Water, Man beside Himself," in *SF12*, ed. Judith Merril (New York: Dell, 1968), p. 11; Spider Robinson, book review, *Destinies* 1 (April–June 1979): 183.

66. Alexei Panshin and Cory Panshin, book review, *Fantasy and Science Fiction* 51 (July 1976): 32.

67. Joanna Russ, "The Image of Women in Science Fiction," *Vertex* 1 (February 1974): 54.

68. Andrew Queen Morton, *Literary Detection* (Epping, England: Bowker, 1978).

69. Milton Rokeach, Robert Homant, and Louis Penner, "A Value Analysis of the Disputed Federalist Papers," *Journal of Personality and Social Psychology* 16 (1970): 245–250.

70. Ranier C. Baum, "Values and Democracy in Imperial Germany," *Sociological Inquiry* 38 (Spring 1968): 179–196.

71. Karl Erik Rosengren, *Sociological Aspects of the Literary System* (Stockholm: Natur och Kultur, 1968).

72. Walter Hirsch, "The Image of the Scientist in Science Fiction: A Content Analysis," *American Journal of Sociology* 63 (1958): 506–512.

73. William Sims Bainbridge and Murray Dalziel, "New Maps of Science Fiction," in *Analog Yearbook*, ed. Ben Bova (New York: Baronet, 1978), pp. 277–299; and, by the same authors, "The Shape of Science Fiction," *Science-Fiction Studies* 5 (July 1978): 165–171.

74. Calculations based on all 595 respondents come out almost the same as calculations based on only the 409 good respondents. For example, Tables 5 and 7 report 53 correlations figured on both bases. The average difference in the coefficients is .024, and the coefficients based on 595 are, on average, .008 lower than those based on 409. I had decided to depend most heavily on data from good respondents, as defined in this study, before I began the computer analysis; thus a decision to use all 595 instead would be methodologically capricious. Despite the similarity in results, I think the original decision was sound. Persons not familiar with many authors should, logically, have less of a cultural framework in which to judge the authors they do know. The point of the survey was to get the knowledgable judgments of a set of experts, not to chart the opinions of a random sample of science fiction readers. The fact that some procedures, such as factor analysis, are especially unforgiving of missing data further supports the original plan to rely most heavily upon the good respondents.

75. Ted White, editorial, *Amazing Stories*, 52 (November 1978): 114.

76. Alva Rogers, *A Requiem for Astounding* (Chicago: Advent, 1964), p. 128.

77. William Sims Bainbridge, "In Search of Delusion," *Skeptical Inquirer* 4 (Fall 1979): 33–39.

2. THE STRUCTURE OF SCIENCE FICTION

1. Richard A. Lupoff, *Barsoom: Edgar Rice Burroughs and the Martian Vision* (Baltimore: Mirage Press, 1976), p. 39.

2. Richard A. Lupoff, "Science Fiction Hawks and Doves: Whose Future Will You Buy?" *Ramparts* 10 (February 1972): 25–30.

3. William Sims Bainbridge and Rodney Stark, "The 'Consciousness Reformation' Reconsidered," *Journal for the Scientific Study of Religion* 20 (1981): 1–15; see also William Sims Bainbridge and Richard Wyckoff, "American Enthusiasm for Spaceflight," *Analog* 99 (July 1979): 59–72; and William Sims Bainbridge and Robert

D. Crutchfield, "Sex Role Ideology and Delinquency," *Sociological Perspectives* 26 (1983): 253–274.

4. Poul Anderson, "Reality, Fiction, and Points Between," *Destinies* 1 (November–December 1978): 304.

5. William Sims Bainbridge and Murray Dalziel, "New Maps of Science Fiction," in *Analog Yearbook*, ed. Ben Bova (New York: Baronet, 1978), pp. 277–299; and, by the same authors, "The Shape of Science Fiction," *Science-Fiction Studies* 5 (July 1978): 165–171.

6. L. David Allen, *Science Fiction: An Introduction* (Lincoln, Neb.: Cliffs Notes, 1973), p. 5.

7. Bob Olsen, "Wanted: A Definition for Science Fiction," *Future Science Fiction*, no. 33 (Summer 1957): 102.

8. Judith Merril, ed., *England Swings SF* (New York: Ace, 1968) and *SF12* (New York: Dell, 1968).

9. Harlan Ellison, ed., *Dangerous Visions* (Garden City, N.Y.: Doubleday, 1967), p. xix.

10. James A. Davis, Tom W. Smith, and C. Bruce Stephenson, *General Social Surveys, 1972–1978: Cumulative Codebook* (Chicago: National Opinion Research Center, 1978).

3. THE HARD SCIENCE TRADITION

1. Jack Williamson, letter to the editor, *Science Wonder Stories* 1 (June 1929): 89.

2. B. S. Moore, letter to the editor, *Science Wonder Stories* 1 (June 1929): 89.

3. *Wonder Stories* 2 (August 1930): 235.

4. W. J. Luyten, "The Fallacy in 'Ten Million Miles Sunward,'" *Amazing Stories* 3 (April 1928): 25.

5. *Science Wonder Stories* 1 (October 1929): 435 and 1 (January 1930): 746.

6. Miles J. Breuer, M.D., letter to the editor, *Amazing Stories* 3 (January 1929): 957.

7. "What Is Your Knowledge of Science?" *Science Wonder Stories* 1 (April 1930): 985.

8. Hugo Gernsback, "Interplanetary Travel," *Amazing Stories* 1 (February 1927): 981.

9. *Wonder Stories* 2 (June 1930): 78; see also William Sims Bainbridge, *The Spaceflight Revolution* (New York: Wiley-Interscience, 1976), pp. 125–145.

10. Hugo Gernsback, "The Science Fiction League," *Wonder Stories* 5 (April 1934): 933.

11. "Good News for Members of the Science Fiction League," *Wonder Stories* 6 (June 1934): 127.

12. Hugo Gernsback, "Fiction versus Fact," *Amazing Stories* 1 (July 1926): 291.

13. Hugo Gernsback (or his assistant, T. O'Conor Sloane), reply to letter, *Amazing Stories* 2 (December 1927): 904.

14. T. O'Conor Sloane, replies to letters, *Amazing Stories* 8 (November 1933): 142; 9 (May 1934): 141; 12 (April 1938): 141.

15. T. O'Conor Sloane, "Interplanetary Flight," *Amazing Stories* 5 (July 1930): 291.

16. John W. Campbell, Jr., letter to the editor, *Amazing Stories* 4 (March 1930): 1200.

17. T. O'Conor Sloane, "Acceleration in Interplanetary Travel," *Amazing Stories* 4 (November 1929): 677.

18. Hugo Gernsback, quoted lecture, *Amazing Stories* 35 (February 1961): 5–6.

19. Poul Anderson, interviewed by Jeffrey Elliot, *Galileo*, combined nos. 11 and 12 (1979): 13.

20. John W. Campbell, Jr., "The Modern Black Arts," *Analog* 86 (December 1970): 5.

21. John W. Campbell, Jr., reply to letter, *Analog* 86 (September 1970): 173.

22. John W. Campbell, Jr., "Science to Come," *Astounding Science-Fiction* 35 (August 1945): 5.

23. Isaac Asimov, reply to letter, *Isaac Asimov's Science Fiction Magazine* 2 (September–October 1978): 186.

24. Isaac Asimov, reply to letter, *Isaac Asimov's Science Fiction Magazine* 3 (March 1979): 186.

25. Poul Anderson, "On Imaginary Science," *Destinies* 1 (April–June 1979): 305.

26. Robert A. Heinlein, "Waldo," *Astounding Science-Fiction* 29 (August 1942): 10.

27. Robert A. Heinlein, book review of *Rockets* by Willy Ley, *Astounding Science-Fiction* 33 (July 1944): 155.

28. Jack Williamson, "The Next Century of Science Fiction," *Analog* 98 (February 1978): 9–10.

29. Harry Harrison, interviewed by John Brosnan, *Vertex* 3:2 (1975): 20.

30. Jerry Pournelle and Larry Niven, "Building the Mote in God's Eye," *Galaxy* 37 (January 1976): 99.

31. Donald H. Tuck, *The Encyclopedia of Science Fiction and Fantasy* (Chicago: Advent, 1978), p. 412.

32. P. Schuyler Miller, "Quantitative Thought," *Analog* 83 (June 1969): 160.

33. Damon Knight, *In Search of Wonder* (Chicago: Advent, 1967), p. 177.

34. Hal Clement, "Iceworld," *Astounding Science-Fiction* 48 (October 1951): 17.

35. R. S. Richardson, "The World of 61 Cygni C," *Astounding Science-Fiction* 31 (July 1943): 67–86.

36. Hal Clement, "Whirligig World," *Astounding Science Fiction* 51 (June 1953): 102–114.

37. James Blish, "The Inhabited Universe, Part IV. The Iron Dwarf," *Thrilling Wonder Stories* 39 (December 1951): 64–69; Hal Clement and James Blish, letters to the editor, *Thrilling Wonder Stories* 40 (April 1952): 134–135.

38. Clement, "Whirligig World," p. 102.

39. Hal Clement, "Science for Fiction #7," *Unearth* 2 (Summer 1978): 66.

40. Hal Clement, "Science for Fiction #2," *Unearth* 1 (Spring 1977): 37.

41. Murray Leinster, quoted by Damon Knight, *In Search of Wonder* (Chicago: Advent, 1967), p. 137.

42. John Jewkes, David Sawers, and Richard Stillerman, *The Sources of Invention* (New York: Norton, 1969).

43. James Gunn, *Alternate Worlds: The Illustrated History of Science Fiction* (Englewood Cliffs, N.J.: Prentice-Hall, 1975), p. 155.

44. Isaac Asimov, editorial, *Isaac Asimov's Science Fiction Magazine* 3 (June 1979): 5.

45. Isaac Asimov, ed., *Before the Golden Age* (Greenwich, Conn.: Fawcett, 1974), p. 11.

46. John J. Pierce, "The Golden Age," *Galaxy* 38 (November 1977): 158.

47. Robert Randall, "Fanfare," *Infinity* 1 (October 1956): 86.

48. Terry Carr, letter to the editor, *Fantasy and Science Fiction* 54 (February 1978): 159–160; Avram Davidson, book review, *Fantasy and Science Fiction* 45 (October 1973): 40.

49. Oliver Saari, letter to the editor, *Amazing Stories* 10 (May 1935): 136.

50. Eando Binder, "I, Robot," *Amazing Stories* 13 (January 1939): 17.

51. Paul A. Carter, *The Creation of Tomorrow* (New York: Columbia University Press, 1977), pp. 203, 206.

52. Isaac Asimov, *I, Robot* (New York: Grosset and Dunlap, 1950), p. 7.

53. Isaac Asimov, "The Word I Invented," *Fantasy and Science Fiction* 59 (October 1980): 124.

54. Isaac Asimov, "Asimov's Guide to Asimov," in *Isaac Asimov*, ed. Joseph D. Olander and Martin Harry Greenberg (New York: Taplinger, 1977), p. 203.

55. Isaac Asimov, *The Robots of Dawn* (New York: Ballantine, 1983), p. 105.

56. Sam Moskowitz, *Seekers of Tomorrow* (Westport, Conn.: Hyperion, 1974), p. 258.

57. Isaac Asimov, *Foundation* (New York: Avon, 1966), p. 17.

58. Charles Elkins, "Asimov's *Foundation* Novels: Historical Materialism Distorted into Cyclical Psychohistory," in Olander and Greenberg, *Isaac Asimov*, p. 100.

59. Some social scientists, and I count myself among them, attempt to discover such laws: George C. Homans, *Social Behavior: Its Elementary Forms* (New York: Harcourt Brace Jovanovich, 1974); Rodney Stark and William Sims Bainbridge, "Towards a Theory of Religion: Religious Commitment," *Journal for the Scientific Study of Religion* 19 (1980): 114–128.

60. Isaac Asimov, "The Caves of Steel," *Galaxy* 7 (November 1953): 145.

61. Jerome Bixby, letter to the editor, *Starlog*, no. 41 (December 1980): 7.

62. Lester del Rey, "Instinct," in *Omnibus of Science Fiction*, ed. Groff Conklin (New York: Crown, 1952), p. 554.

63. Brian Aldiss, ed., *Space Opera* (New York: Berkley, 1977), p. xi.

64. Sam Moskowitz, *Seekers of Tomorrow* (Westport, Conn.: Hyperion, 1974), p. 9.

65. Edward Elmer Smith, "Author's Note," *Amazing Stories* 5 (August 1930): 389.

66. E. E. Smith, "The Skylark of Space," *Amazing Stories* 3 (September 1928): 531.

67. Ibid., p. 532.

68. John W. Campbell, Jr., letter to the editor, *Amazing Stories* 5 (September 1930): 566.

69. John W. Campbell, Jr., letter to the editor, *Amazing Stories* 5 (November 1930): 764.

70. P. Schuyler Miller, letter to the editor, *Amazing Stories* 6 (August 1931): 475, 477.

71. E. E. Smith, letter to the editor, *Amazing Stories* 5 (December 1930): 856, 858.

72. Jack Williamson, "The Legion of Space," *Astounding Stories* 13 (June 1934): 118.

73. Murray Leinster, "The Disciplinary Circuit," *Thrilling Wonder Stories* 28 (Winter 1946): 58.

74. Poul Anderson, letter to the editor, *Thrilling Wonder Stories* 31 (December 1947): 108; in fact Leinster had also said that overdrive increased the velocity of light.

75. Murray Leinster, "The Manless Worlds," *Thrilling Wonder Stories* 29 (February 1947): 18.

76. Asimov, *Foundation*, p. 8.

77. H. G. Wells, *The Discovery of the Future* (New York: Huebsch, 1913), pp. 42–43.

78. Arthur C. Clarke, "All the Time in the World," in *The Other Side of the Sky* (New York: Signet, 1959), p. 105.

79. L. Sprague de Camp, *Lest Darkness Fall* (New York: Ballantine, 1979), p. 2.

80. Groff Conklin, book review, *Galaxy* 5 (January 1953): 98.

81. Lester del Rey, "Reading Room," *Worlds of If* 22 (May–June 1974): 153; Clement, "Whirligig World," p. 102.

82. Robert W. Lowndes, reply to a letter, *Science Fiction Quarterly* 4 (February 1956): 94.

83. Raymond J. Healy and J. Francis McComas, eds., *Adventures in Space and Time* (New York: Ballantine, 1975), unpaginated introduction.

84. T. O'Conor Sloane, reply to a letter, *Amazing Stories* 10 (October 1935): 137.

4. THE NEW WAVE

1. Michael Moorcock, interview in Paul Walker, *Speaking of Science Fiction* (Oradell, N.J.: Luna, 1978), p. 216.

2. P. Schuyler Miller, book review, *Analog* 91 (July 1973): 167–168.

3. Damon Knight, interview in Walker, *Speaking of Science Fiction*, p. 163.

4. Ted White, editorial, *Amazing Stories* 43 (May 1969): 4–5.

5. Robert Silverberg, "Diversity in Science Fiction," *Fantastic* 18 (February 1969): 4.

6. Lester del Rey, quoted by Lin Carter, "Meanwhile, Back at the Worldcon . . . ," *Worlds of If* 18 (April 1968): 90.

7. Lester del Rey, *The World of Science Fiction* (New York: Ballantine, 1979), p. 253.

8. John J. Pierce, "The Devaluation of Values," *Algol*, no. 16 (December 1970): 10.

9. John J. Pierce, letter to the editor, *Amazing Stories* 43 (September 1969): 141.

10. John J. Pierce, untitled essay, *Fantastic* 19 (August 1970): 126.

11. C. M. Kornbluth, "The Failure of the Science Fiction Novel as Social Crit-

icism," in *The Science Fiction Novel*, ed. Basil Davenport (Chicago: Advent, 1969), p. 61.

12. William Atheling, Jr. (James Blish), *More Issues at Hand* (Chicago: Advent, 1970), p. 123.

13. Donald A. Wollheim, Introduction to *England Swings SF*, ed. Judith Merril (New York: Ace, 1968), p. 1.

14. Alexei Panshin and Cory Panshin, book review, *Fantasy and Science Fiction* 42 (March 1972): 65.

15. Barry N. Malzberg, "A Word from the Editor," *Amazing Stories* 42 (January 1969): 138–139.

16. Damon Knight, *In Search of Wonder* (Chicago: Advent, 1967), p. 32.

17. John J. Pierce, letter to the editor, *Amazing Stories* 44 (July 1970): 120.

18. Philip Jose Farmer, interview in Walker, *Speaking of Science Fiction*, p. 46.

19. Philip Jose Farmer, *Tarzan Alive* (New York: Popular Library, 1976) and "The Arms of Tarzan," *Burroughs Bulletin*, no. 22 (Summer 1971): 3–7.

20. Sidney Coleman, book review, *Fantasy and Science Fiction* 45 (November 1973): 23.

21. Richard Lupoff, "Man Swings SF," *Fantastic* 19 (October 1969): 45.

22. Alexei Panshin, "Science Fiction in Dimension," *Fantastic* 19 (June 1970): 126.

23. Robert J. Hughes, book review, *Fantasy and Science Fiction* 35 (October 1968): 23.

24. Judith Merril, book review, *Fantasy and Science Fiction* 33 (November 1967): 29.

25. Merril, *England Swings SF*, p. 10.

26. L. Sprague de Camp and Catherine Crook de Camp, *Science Fiction Handbook, Revised* (New York: McGraw-Hill, 1977), p. 49.

27. Samuel R. Delany, *Dhalgren* (New York: Bantam, 1975), pp. 528–529.

28. Ibid., p. 462.

29. Ibid., p. 1.

30. Ibid., p. 879.

31. Ibid., p. 770.

32. Ibid., p. 415.

33. Norman Spinrad, interview in Darrell Schweitzer, *SF Voices* (Baltimore: TK Graphics, 1976), p. 54.

34. Norman Spinrad, *The Iron Dream* (New York: Avon, 1972), p. 161.

35. Ursula K. LeGuin, interview in Walker, *Speaking of Science Fiction*, p. 27.

36. Roger Zelazny, "He Who Shapes," *Amazing Stories* 39 (January 1965): 84–85.

37. Hans J. Eysenck, "The Effects of Psychotherapy," *International Journal of Psychiatry* 1 (1965): 99–144; Stanley Rachman, *The Effects of Psychotherapy* (Oxford: Pergamon, 1971).

38. Albert Bandura, *Principles of Behavior Modification* (New York: Holt, Rinehart and Winston, 1969).

39. Anthony Burgess, *A Clockwork Orange* (New York: Ballantine, 1965), pp. 108–109.

40. Ibid., pp. 125–126.

41. Ibid., p. 128.

42. Ibid., p. 27.

43. Ibid., p. 156.

44. Ibid., pp. 153–154.

45. Ibid., p. 43.

46. Ursula K. LeGuin, interviewed by Gene Van Troyer, *Vertex* 2 (December 1974): 92.

47. Harlan Ellison, " 'Repent Harlequin!' said the Ticktockman," *Galaxy* 24 (December 1965): 92.

48. Ray Bradbury, "Carnival of Madness," *Thrilling Wonder Stories* 36 (April 1950): 98.

49. Stanislaw Lem, *Memoirs Found in a Bathtub* (New York: Avon, 1976), p. 173.

50. Barry N. Malzberg, *Beyond Apollo* (New York: Pocket Books, 1974), p. 117.

51. Ibid., p. 11.

52. Ibid., p. 29.

53. Ibid., pp. 29–30.

54. Ibid., p. 33.

55. Ibid., p. 43.

56. Ibid., p. 141.

57. Ibid., p. 37.

58. Barry N. Malzberg, *The Best of Barry N. Malzberg* (New York: Pocket Books, 1976), p. 322.

59. Poul Anderson, letter to the editor, *Analog* 92 (October 1973): 167.

60. Harry Harrison, letter to the editor, *Analog* 92 (October 1973): 169.

61. Kate Wilhelm, *Fault Lines* (New York: Pocket Books, 1977), p. 142.

62. Ibid., p. 13.

63. Ibid., p. 110.

64. Ibid., p. 147.

65. Ibid.

66. Ibid., p. 152.

67. Ibid., p. 161.

68. When the magazine of the British new wave, *New Worlds*, was in dire financial trouble, Aldiss campaigned successfully to get a grant from the Arts Council to keep the avant-garde periodical afloat. See Charles Platt, *Dream Makers* (New York: Berkley, 1980), p. 270.

69. Brian W. Aldiss, quoted in ibid., p. 275.

70. Brian W. Aldiss, quoted in Walker, *Speaking of Science Fiction*, p. 403.

71. Brian W. Aldiss, "Frankenstein Unbound," *Fantastic* 23 (March 1974): 10.

72. Ibid., pp. 11–12.

73. Ibid., p. 12.

74. Ibid., p. 38.

75. Brian W. Aldiss, quoted in James Gunn, *The Road to Science Fiction*, vol. 3 (New York: Mentor, 1979), p. 342.

76. William Sims Bainbridge, *The Spaceflight Revolution* (New York: Wiley-Interscience, 1976).

77. Brian W. Aldiss, "Frankenstein Unbound," *Fantastic* 23 (May 1974): 103.

78. Harlan Ellison, "Ellison on Ellison," in *The Book of Ellison*, ed. Andrew Porter (New York: Algol Press, 1978), p. 75.

79. Vonda N. McIntyre, "(Or She)," *Bulletin of the Science Fiction Writers of America* 14 (Winter 1979): 17–18.

80. Alexei Panshin, *Heinlein in Dimension* (Chicago: Advent, 1968); Richard Lupoff, "Science Fiction Hawks and Doves: Whose Future Will You Buy?" *Ramparts* 10 (February 1972): 25–30.

81. Robert A. Heinlein, *Expanded Universe* (New York: Ace, 1980).

82. Ted White, editorial, *Amazing Stories* 50 (December 1976): 4.

83. Varimax rotation of all factors with eigenvalues greater than one.

84. Varimax rotation of all factors with eigenvalues greater than one.

85. Harlan Ellison, book review, *Fantasy and Science Fiction* 46 (May 1974): 38.

86. Samuel R. Delany, "Science and 'Literature' or the Conscience of the King," *Analog* 99 (May 1979): 60.

87. Paul Walker, "Galaxy Bookshelf," *Galaxy* 39 (September 1978): 141.

88. Terry Carr, "A Modest Manifesto," *Fantastic* 19 (October 1969): 131.

89. Damon Knight, interview in Walker, *Speaking of Science Fiction*, p. 160.

90. Ben Bova, reply to a letter, *Analog* 96 (May 1976): 173.

5. THE FANTASY CLUSTER

1. Sam Moskowitz, *Explorers of the Infinite* (Cleveland: Meridian, 1963), p. 11.

2. Fletcher Pratt, quoted by Theodore Sturgeon, editorial, *Worlds of Fantasy* 1 (Winter 1970–1971): 2.

3. Anthony Boucher, quoted in Basil Davenport, book review, *Fantasy and Science Fiction* 28 (April 1965): 74.

4. Samuel Merwin, reply to a letter, *Startling Stories* 20 (January 1950): 150; this comment is unsigned, but Merwin was editor at the time; Samuel Mines did not take over the magazine's departments until the November 1951 issue.

5. Samuel Merwin, reply to a letter, *Startling Stories* 18 (September 1948): 131.

6. Samuel Merwin, reply to a letter, *Startling Stories* 16 (September 1947): 101.

7. Poul Anderson, "Reality, Fiction, and Points Between," *Destinies* 1 (November–December 1978): 305–306.

8. Ibid., p. 306.

9. Robert A. W. Lowndes, editorial, *Future Science Fiction*, no. 47 (February 1960): 130.

10. Lawrence E. Spivak, "Introduction," *Magazine of Fantasy* 1 (Fall 1949): 3.

11. Advertisement, *Rocket Stories* 1 (September 1953): 136.

12. Lester del Rey, comment, *Fantasy Fiction* 1 (June 1953): 77.

13. L. Sprague de Camp, letter to the editor, *Astounding Science Fiction* 49 (April 1952): 169.

14. Richard Kyle, letter to the editor, *Future Science Fiction*, no. 40 (December 1958): 126.

15. Hugo Gernsback, "The Impact of Science-Fiction on World Progress," *Science-Fiction Plus* 1 (March 1953): 2.

16. Samuel Mines, reply to a letter, *Startling Stories* 26 (May 1952): 135.

17. Joe Kennedy, letter to the editor, *Thrilling Wonder Stories* 24 (August 1943): 120.

18. The editors, book review, *Fantasy and Science Fiction* 2 (February 1951): 58.

19. L. Sprague de Camp and Catherine Crook de Camp, *Science Fiction Handbook, Revised* (New York: McGraw-Hill, 1977), pp. 5–6.

20. William Atheling, Jr. (James Blish), *More Issues at Hand* (Chicago: Advent, 1970), p. 107.

21. James Blish, letter to the editor, *Fantasy and Science Fiction* 25 (August 1963): 127.

22. Poul Anderson, "Star-Flights and Fantasies: Sagas Still to Come," in *The Craft of Science Fiction*, ed. Reginald Bretnor (New York: Barnes and Noble, 1977), p. 23.

23. One can compare the clarity of the myth-saga axis with that of the science-technology axis from Figure 5, using correlations of correlations. The unit of analysis is authors, and the two variables in the correlation formula are the x and y coordinates of the dots on the graph. For Figure 5 the correlation is $r = .85$, very near the theoretical maximum, indicating that new science and new technology, as expressed in the authors' fiction, are very highly correlated. For Figure 8, $r = .64$, expressing the correlation between myths and sagas as expressed in the authors' fiction. This also is high, but it might be best to compare the coefficients by squaring them to get proportion of variance explained. This gives .72 for science and technology and .41 for myths and sagas, which suggests that the former axis is 1.8 times as tight as the latter axis.

24. Leigh Brackett, interviewed by Darrell Schweitzer, *Amazing Stories* 51 (January 1978): 116.

25. Ted White, reply to a letter, *Amazing Stories* 47 (August 1973): 126.

26. The editors, book review, *Fantasy and Science Fiction* 2 (August 1951): 84.

27. William L. Hamling, reply to a letter, *Imagination* 5 (September 1954): 118.

28. Groff Conklin, book review, *Galaxy* 3 (March 1952): 83.

29. Leonard Isaacs, book review, *Fantasy and Science Fiction* 49 (December 1975): 34.

30. *Galaxy* 1 (October 1950): 162 (back cover).

31. Baird Searles, "On Books," *Isaac Asimov's Science Fiction Magazine* 3 (July 1979): 18.

32. P. Schuyler Miller, "The Reference Library," *Analog* 94 (January 1975): 173.

33. Mari Wolf, "Fandora's Box," *Imagination* 5 (December 1954): 111–112.

34. William L. Hamling, reply to a letter, *Imaginative Tales* 3 (September 1956): 127.

35. Tom Staicar, "The Interstellar Connection," *Amazing Stories* 27 [sic—the publisher confused the volume numbers with those of its companion magazine *Fantastic*] (November 1979): 11.

36. P. Schuyler Miller, book review, *Astounding Science-Fiction* 42 (October 1948): 141.

37. Sam Moskowitz, *Seekers of Tomorrow* (Westport, Conn.: Hyperion, 1974), p. 82.

38. Ron Ellik and Bill Evans, *The Universes of E. E. Smith* (Chicago: Advent, 1966).

39. Ibid., pp. 38–39.

40. Larry T. Shaw, editorial, *Science Fiction Adventures* 1 (December 1956): 50. This first issue was misnumbered 6, a fact that becomes especially confusing because this was the second magazine with this name.

41. Lester del Rey, "Adventure," *Analog* 96 (December 1976): 164.

42. Probably Charles D. Hornig, quoted by Derwin Lesser, "How to Write Science Fiction," *Future Fiction* 1 (November 1940): 77.

43. Samuel Mines, "Blast Off . . . ," *Space Stories* 1 (October 1952): 9.

44. Marion Zimmer Bradley, letter to the editor, *Planet Stories* 4 (Summer 1950): 103.

45. Announcement, *Planet Stories* 2 (Winter 1942): 97.

46. Irwin Porges, *Edgar Rice Burroughs* (New York: Ballantine, 1976), pp. 724–726.

47. Cartoon, *Vertex* 3 (1975): 15.

48. Edgar Rice Burroughs, *The Cave Girl* (New York: Ace, 1963), pp. 7–8.

49. Lin Carter, "Our Man in Fandom," *Worlds of If* 16 (April 1966): 79.

50. Lester del Rey, "What's in a Name?" *Analog* 97 (May 1977): 166.

51. L. Sprague de Camp, Introduction to Robert E. Howard, *Conan the Conqueror* (New York: Lancer, 1967), p. 9.

52. Damon Knight, *In Search of Wonder* (Chicago: Advent, 1967), p. 19.

53. Arthur C. Clarke, *Voices from the Sky* (New York: Harper, 1965), p. 175; William Sims Bainbridge, *The Spaceflight Revolution* (New York: Wiley-Interscience, 1976), pp. 152–154.

54. P. Schuyler Miller, "Is It SF?" *Astounding Science Fiction* 63 (June 1959): 149.

55. See the following by John W. Campbell, Jr.: "Psionic Machine—Type One," *Astounding Science Fiction* 57 (June 1956): 97–108; "Unprovable Speculation," *Astounding Science Fiction* 58 (February 1957): 54–70; "Addendum on the Symbolic Psionic Machine," *Astounding Science Fiction* 59 (June 1957): 125–127.

56. John W. Campbell, Jr., "Concerning Dianetics," *Astounding Science-Fiction* 45 (May 1950): 4–5; L. Ron Hubbard, "Dianetics—The Evolution of a Science," *Astounding Science-Fiction* 45 (May 1950): 43–87; and "The Analytical Mind," *Astounding Science-Fiction* 46 (October 1950): 139–162; John W. Campbell, Jr., "The Space-Drive Problem," *Astounding Science Fiction* 65 (June 1960): 83–106; see also the anonymously written *"Reactionless" Space Drive Handbook* (Kingston Springs, Tenn.: Cosmic Enterprises, 1977); A. V. Cleaver, "Interplanetary Flight: Is the Rocket the Only Answer?" *Journal of the British Interplanetary Society* 6 (June 1947): 127–148.

57. Judith Merril, book review, *Fantasy and Science Fiction* 36 (February 1969): 23.

58. P. Schuyler Miller, "Then and Now," *Analog* 71 (July 1963): 87.

59. Ibid.

60. Ibid., p. 88; P. Schuyler Miller, "Magic and Mechanism," *Analog* 73 (August 1964): 84.

61. Sam Moskowitz, *Seekers of Tomorrow* (Westport, Conn.: Hyperion, 1974), p. 284.

62. Fritz Leiber, Jr., "Gather Darkness!" *Astounding Science-Fiction* 31 (July 1943): 126.

63. L. Sprague de Camp and Fletcher Pratt, *The Incomplete Enchanter* (New York: Pyramid, 1960), p. 9.

64. Ibid., pp. 167–168.

65. Donald A. Wollheim, quoted in *Astonishing Stories* 3 (June 1942): 60. The original publication was in the April 1935 issue of *Fantasy Magazine*. For a longer but more awkward statement of the same idea see Donald A. Wollheim, "The Vortex," *Stirring Stories* 1 (February 1941): 67.

66. Robert W. Lowndes, "The Weird and the Fantastic," *Future Ficion* 1 (August 1941): 83.

67. H. P. Lovecraft, quoted by Paul A. Carter, *The Creation of Tomorrow* (New York: Columbia University Press, 1977), p. 7.

68. H. P. Lovecraft, quoted in J. Vernon Shea, "H. P. Lovecraft: The House and the Shadows," *Fantasy and Science Fiction* 30 (May 1966): 87.

69. H. P. Lovecraft, "The Colour out of Space," *Amazing Stories* 2 (September 1927): 559.

70. Ibid.

71. Fritz Leiber, "Fantasy Books," *Fantastic* 22 (October 1972): 113.

72. H. P. Lovecraft, "The Shadow out of Time," *Astounding Stories* 17 (June 1936): 110.

73. Ibid., p. 114.

74. Theodore Sturgeon, book review, *Galaxy* 33 (March–April 1973): 155.

75. Emile Durkheim, *The Elementary Forms of the Religious Life* (New York: Free Press, 1965), pp. 419–420; Bronislaw Malinowski, *Magic, Science, and Religion* (Garden City, N.Y.: Doubleday, 1948), p. 101.

6. THE EFFECTS OF SCIENCE FICTION

1. Lester del Rey, "Homesteads on Venus," *Amazing* 34 (October 1960): 107.

2. Rodney Stark and William Sims Bainbridge, *The Future of Religion* (Berkeley: University of California Press, 1985), and "Towards a Theory of Religion: Religious Commitment," *Journal for the Scientific Study of Religion* 19 (1980): 114–128.

3. Travis Hirschi and Rodney Stark, "Hellfire and Delinquency," *Social Problems* 17 (1969): 202–213; compare Victor B. Cline and James M. Richards, "A Factor-Analytic Study of Religious Belief and Behavior," *Journal of Personality and Social Psychology* 1 (1965): 569–578.

4. Paul C. Higgins and Gary L. Albrecht, "Hellfire and Delinquency Revisited," *Social Forces* 55 (1977): 952–958; compare Steven R. Burkett and Mervin White, "Hellfire and Delinquency: Another Look," *Journal for the Scientific Study of Religion* 13 (1974): 455–462.

5. Rodney Stark, Daniel P. Doyle, and Lori Kent, "Rediscovering Moral Communities: Church Membership and Crime," in *Understanding Crime*, ed. Travis Hirschi and Michael Gottfredson (Beverly Hills, Calif.: Sage, 1980), pp. 43–52; Rodney Stark, William Sims Bainbridge, Robert D. Crutchfield, Daniel P. Doyle, and Roger Finke, "Crime and Delinquency in the Roaring Twenties," *Journal of Research in Crime and Delinquency* 20 (1983): 4–23.

6. Rodney Stark, Lori Kent, and Daniel P. Doyle, "Religion and Delinquency:

The Ecology of a 'Lost' Relationship," *Journal of Research in Crime and Delinquency* 19 (1982): 4–24.

7. Travis Hirschi, *Causes of Delinquency* (Berkeley: University of California Press, 1969): 3.

8. Ronald L. Akers, *Deviant Behavior: A Social Learning Approach* (Belmont, Calif.: Wadsworth, 1977); George C. Homans, *The Human Group* (New York: Harcourt, Brace and World, 1950); and *Social Behavior: Its Elementary Forms* (New York: Harcourt Brace Jovanovich, 1974).

9. William Sims Bainbridge and Rodney Stark, "Suicide, Homicide, and Religion: Durkheim Reassessed," *Annual Review of the Social Sciences of Religion* 5 (1981): 33–56; Rodney Stark, Daniel P. Doyle, and Jesse Rushing, "Beyond Durkheim: Religion and Suicide," *Journal for the Scientific Study of Religion* 22 (1983): 120–131; Stark and Bainbridge, *The Future of Religion*.

10. Matina Horner, "Femininity and Successful Achievement: A Basic Inconsistency," in *Feminine Personality and Conflict*, ed. J. M. Bardwick et al. (Belmont, Calif.: Brooks/Cole, 1970), pp. 45–74; Adeline Levine and Janice Crumrine, "Women and the Fear of Success: A Problem in Replication," *American Journal of Sociology* 80 (1975): 964–974; John Condry and Sharon Dyer, "Fear of Success: Attribution of Cause to the Victim," *Journal of Social Issues* 32 (1976): 63–83.

11. William Sims Bainbridge and Robert D. Crutchfield, "Sex Role Ideology and Delinquency," *Sociological Perspectives* 26 (1983): 253–274; William Sims Bainbridge and Linda Davenport, "Love of Math: Ideological versus Utilitarian Explanations of Gender Differences" (working paper, University of Washington, 1982).

12. William Sims Bainbridge, "Collective Behavior and Social Movements," in Rodney Stark, *Sociology* (Belmont, Calif.: Wadsworth, 1985), pp. 493–523.

13. William Sheridan Allen, *The Nazi Seizure of Power* (Chicago: Quadrangle, 1965).

14. John Humphrey Noyes, *History of American Socialisms* (Philadelphia: Lippincott, 1870); Charles Nordhoff, *The Communistic Societies of the United States* (London: John Murray, 1875); Karen H. Stephan and G. Edward Stephan, "Religion and the Survival of Utopian Communities," *Journal for the Scientific Study of Religion* 12 (1973): 89–100.

15. William Sims Bainbridge, "Shaker Demographics: An Example of the Use of U.S. Census Enumeration Schedules," *Journal for the Scientific Study of Religion* 21 (1982): 352–365; "The Decline of the Shakers: Evidence from the United States Census," *Communal Societies* 4 (1984): 19–34; and "Utopian Communities: Theoretical Issues," in *The Sacred in a Secular Age*, ed. Phillip E. Hammond (Berkeley: University of California Press, 1985).

16. Bainbridge and Stark, "Suicide, Homicide, and Religion."

17. Burkett and White, "Hellfire and Delinquency: Another Look"; William Sims Bainbridge and Elise Lake, "Religion and Killing" (working paper, University of Washington, 1982).

18. Lester del Rey, *The World of Science Fiction* (New York: Ballantine, 1979), p. 328.

19. William Sims Bainbridge, *The Spaceflight Revolution* (New York: Wiley-Interscience, 1976), pp. 38, 42–44.

20. Carl Sagan, *The Cosmic Connection* (New York: Dell, 1973), p. 101.

21. Will Stewart (Jack Williamson), "Minus Sign," *Astounding Science-Fiction* 30 (November 1942): 47.

22. Robert A. Heinlein, "Shooting 'Destination Moon,' " *Astounding Science-Fiction* 45 (July 1950): 6–18.

23. Transcribed from the soundtrack of the 1950 film *Destination Moon*, produced by George Pal.

24. Bainbridge, *Spaceflight Revolution*; John M. Logsdon, *The Decision to Go to the Moon* (Cambridge: M.I.T. Press, 1970); Vernon van Dyke, *Pride and Power: The Rationale of the Space Program* (Urbana: University of Illinois Press, 1964).

25. Albert I. Berger, "Science Fiction Critiques of the American Space Program, 1945–1958," *Science-Fiction Studies* 5 (July 1978): 101–102.

26. Arthur C. Clarke, *Prelude to Space* (New York: World, 1951), p. 91.

27. Ibid., p. 125.

28. Bainbridge, *Spaceflight Revolution*, p. 233.

29. William Sims Bainbridge, "The Impact of Science Fiction on Attitudes toward Technology," in *Science Fiction and Space Futures*, ed. Eugene M. Emme (San Diego: American Astronautical Society, 1982), pp. 121–135.

30. Irene Taviss, "A Survey of Popular Attitudes toward Technology," *Technology and Culture* 13 (1972): 617.

31. J. B. Rhine, *Extra-Sensory Perception* (Boston: Bruce Humphries, 1964); Gertrude Schmeidler, ed., *Extrasensory Perception* (New York: Atherton, 1969); cf. C. E. M. Hansel, *ESP: A Scientific Evaluation* (New York: Scribner's, 1966).

32. Brian Ash, ed., *The Visual Encyclopedia of Science Fiction* (New York: Harmony, 1977), pp. 204–211.

33. See the following articles by L. Ron Hubbard: "Dianetics: The Evolution of a Science," *Astounding Science-Fiction* 45 (May 1950): 43–87; "The Analytical Mind," *Astounding Science-Fiction* 46 (October 1950): 139–162; and "Dianometry," *Astounding Science-Fiction* 46 (January 1951): 76–100. See also William Sims Bainbridge, *Satan's Power: Ethnography of a Deviant Psychotherapy Cult* (Berkeley: University of California Press, 1978); William Sims Bainbridge and Rodney Stark, "Cult Formation: Three Compatible Models," *Sociological Analysis* 40 (Winter 1979): 283–295; and William Sims Bainbridge and Rodney Stark, "Scientology: To Be Perfectly Clear," *Sociological Analysis* 41 (Summer 1980): 128–136.

34. Robert Silverberg, interviewed by Darrell Schweitzer, *Amazing Stories* 49 (January 1976): 62.

35. Gardner Dozois, "Living the Future: You Are What You Eat," in *Writing and Selling Science Fiction*, ed. C. L. Grant (Cincinnati: Writer's Digest, 1976), p. 115.

36. Algis Budrys, "Galaxy Bookshelf," *Galaxy* 32 (September–October 1971): 144.

37. Alfred Bester, book review, *Fantasy and Science Fiction* 20 (February 1961): 106–107.

38. Lester del Rey, "Reading Room," *Worlds of If* 20 (September–October 1970): 63.

39. Forrest J. Ackerman, "Brave Nude World," *Fantastic* 17 (May 1968): 134.

40. Bainbridge, *The Spaceflight Revolution*, p. 210.

41. *Gallup Opinion Index* (December 1973): 17–25.

42. James A. Davis, Tom W. Smith, and Bruce C. Stephenson, *General Social*

Surveys, 1972–1978: Cumulative Codebook (Chicago: National Opinion Research Center, 1978), p. 44.

43. Ted Robert Gurr, *Why Men Rebel* (Princeton: Princeton University Press, 1970).

44. James O'Meara, "I.Q. Testing Session," in *The Proceedings: Chicon III*, ed. Earl Kemp (Chicago: Advent, 1963), pp. 66–69.

45. Davis, Smith, and Stephenson, *General Social Surveys, 1972–1978*, p. 27.

46. *Locus*, April 20, 1974, p. 3.

47. William Sims Bainbridge, "Public Support for the Space Program," *Astronautics and Aeronautics* 16 (1978): 60–61, 76; William Sims Bainbridge and Richard Wyckoff, "American Enthusiasm for Spaceflight," *Analog* 99 (July 1979): 59–72.

48. William Sims Bainbridge, "Attitudes toward Interstellar Communication: An Empirical Study," *Journal of the British Interplanetary Society* 36 (1983): 298–304.

49. Davis, Smith, and Stephenson, *General Social Surveys, 1972–1978*.

50. Rodney Stark and William Sims Bainbridge, "Secularization, Revival, and Cult Formation," *Annual Review of the Social Sciences of Religion* 4 (1980): 85–119; and, by the same authors, *The Future of Religion*.

51. Mark Wynn, "Who Are the Futurists?" *Futurist* 6 (April 1972): 73–77.

52. Bainbridge, *The Spaceflight Revolution*, pp. 158–197.

53. Seymour Martin Lipset, *Rebellion in the University* (Boston: Little, Brown, 1971).

54. Davis, Smith, and Stephenson, *General Social Surveys, 1972–1978*, p. 64.

55. Norman Spinrad, "The Future of Science Fiction," in *Nebula Winners Fourteen*, ed. Frederik Pohl (New York: Bantam, 1982), p. 115.

7. WOMEN IN SCIENCE FICTION

1. William Sims Bainbridge and Rodney Stark, "The 'Consciousness Reformation' Reconsidered," *Journal for the Scientific Study of Religion* 20 (1981): 1–15; and "Friendship, Religion, and the Occult," *Review of Religious Research* 22 (1981): 313–327.

2. Lynn H. Fox, Linda Brody, and Dianne Tobin, eds., *Women and the Mathematical Mystique* (Baltimore: Johns Hopkins University Press, 1980); Dorothy Zinberg, "The Past Decade for Women Scientists," *Trends in Biochemical Sciences* 2 (1977): N123–N126.

3. Irene Taviss, "A Survey of Popular Attitudes toward Technology," *Technology and Culture* 13 (October 1972): 606–621.

4. James A. Davis, Tom W. Smith, and C. Bruce Stephenson, *General Social Surveys, 1972–1978: Cumulative Codebook* (Chicago: National Opinion Research Center, 1978).

5. Lester del Rey, eulogy for John W. Campbell, Jr., Hugo Awards Banquet, Noreascon World Science Fiction Convention, Boston, 1971.

6. Harry Warner, *All Our Yesterdays* (Chicago: Advent, 1969), p. 26.

7. *Astounding Science-Fiction* 43 (July 1949): 161.

8. *Astounding Science Fiction* 61 (May 1958): 136.

9. *New Worlds*, no. 83 (May 1959): 2.

10. Bjo Trimble, "Ideas about Ideas," *Starlog*, no. 40 (November 1980): 21.

11. Roberta Rogow, ed., *Trexindex* (Patterson, N.J.: April Publications, 1977).

12. U.S. Bureau of the Census, *Census of Population: 1970—Occupational Characteristics* (Washington, D.C.: Government Printing Office, 1973), pp. 1–2.

13. Groff Conklin, ed., *Great Science Fiction by Scientists* (New York: Collier, 1962), p. 9.

14. Bureau of the Census, *Census: 1970 Occupational Characteristics*.

15. Donald B. Day, *Index to the Science-Fiction Magazines, 1926–1950* (Portland, Ore.: Perri Press, 1952).

16. P. Schuyler Miller, "So Say You All," *Analog* 78 (November 1966): 166–169.

17. Sam Moskowitz, *Seekers of Tomorrow* (Westport, Conn.: Hyperion, 1974), p. 305.

18. Andre Norton, interview in Paul Walker, *Speaking of Science Fiction* (Oradell, N.J.: Luna, 1978), p. 269.

19. Leslie F. Stone, "Women with Wings," *Air Wonder Stories* 1 (May 1930): 985.

20. Leigh Brackett, "Meet the Authors," *Amazing Stories* 15 (July 1941): 136.

21. Leigh Brackett, interview in Walker, *Speaking of Science Fiction*, pp. 382–383.

22. Marion Zimmer Bradley, "An Evolution of Consciousness," *Science Fiction Review* 6 (August 1977): 45.

23. Donald Franson and Howard DeVore, *A History of the Hugo, Nebula, and International Fantasy Awards* (Dearborn, Mich.: Misfit Press, 1978); 1977–1979 issues of *Locus*.

24. Gallup Opinion Index, "Religion in America, 1977–1978," no. 145 (Princeton: American Institute of Public Opinion, 1977).

25. Harlan Ellison, "A Statement of Ethical Position," *Galaxy* 39 (May 1978): 6–8.

26. That is, all factors with eigenvalues greater than one; varimax rotation.

27. Nathaniel Branden and Barbara Branden, *Who Is Ayn Rand?* (New York: Random House, 1962).

28. Lester del Rey, "War of the Sexes," *Analog* 96 (June 1975): 168.

29. Cheryl Cline, "Feminist Perspective: The Female Man," *Windhaven* 1 (1977): 7.

30. Joanna Russ, "The Image of Women in Science Fiction," *Vertex* 1 (February 1974): 53–57.

31. Ursula K. LeGuin, "Is Gender Necessary?" in *Aurora: Beyond Equality*, ed. Susan Janice Anderson and Vonda N. McIntyre (Greenwich, Conn.: Fawcett, 1976), pp. 130–139.

32. Ayn Rand, *The Virtue of Selfishness* (New York: Signet, 1964).

8. ENLIGHTENMENT AND TRANSCENDENCE

1. *Amazing Stories* 2 (October 1927): 627.

2. Hugo Gernsback, "Amazing Youth," *Amazing Stories* 2 (October 1927): 625; for one example, see the letter to the editor from Harvard student Dick Clarkson, *Fantastic Story Magazine* 5 (May 1953): 140.

3. John Taine, "Why Science Fiction?" *Startling Stories* 1 (March 1939): 15.

4. H. L. Gold, "What Kind of Fiction?" *Galaxy* 18 (February 1960): 7.

5. Joseph W. Skidmore, "A Saga of Posi and Nega," *Amazing Stories* 10 (May 1935): 98.

6. Lester del Rey, *The World of Science Fiction* (New York: Ballantine, 1979), p. 62.

7. Alexei Panshin, "The Nature of Science Fiction," *Fantastic* 19 (August 1970): 120.

8. William Atheling, Jr. (James Blish), *The Issue at Hand* (Chicago: Advent, 1964), p. 98.

9. Spider Robinson, "The Reference Library," *Analog* 98 (September 1978): 168.

10. Paul Walker, "Galaxy Bookshelf," *Galaxy* 39 (March–April 1979): 140.

11. Isaac Asimov, "Just Thirty Years," *Fantasy and Science Fiction* 57 (October 1979): 273.

12. Arthur C. Clarke, "Jupiter Five," *If* 2 (May 1953): 7.

13. Hugo Gernsback, "The Lure of Scientifiction," *Amazing Stories* 1 (June 1926): 195.

14. Hugo Gernsback, "Imagination and Reality," *Amazing Stories* 1 (October 1926): 579.

15. Hugo Gernsback, "The Impact of Science-Fiction on World Progress," *Science-Fiction Plus* 1 (March 1953): 2.

16. Raymond A. Palmer, reply to a letter, *Amazing Stories* 20 (December 1946): 165.

17. Samuel Merwin, "Looking Forward," *Thrilling Wonder Stories* 24 (April 1943): 8.

18. Joe Abrams, "The Younger Generation and Future Science," *Amazing Stories Quarterly* 2 (Fall 1929): 435.

19. J. Roy Chapman, "The Amazing Value of Scientifiction," *Amazing Stories Quarterly* 2 (Spring 1929): 147.

20. Harry Harrison, interviewed by John Brosnan, *Vertex* 3 (1975): 20.

21. Algis Budrys, "Foundation and Asimov," *Analog* 95 (July 1975): 166.

22. John W. Campbell, reply to a letter, *Astounding Science-Fiction* 31 (August 1943): 155.

23. Ben Bova, "Problem Grokking," *Analog* 97 (September 1977): 5.

24. Hugo Gernsback, "Wonders of Technocracy," *Wonder Stories* 4 (March 1933): 741.

25. Henry Elsner, *The Technocrats* (Syracuse, N.Y.: Syracuse University Press, 1967).

26. Technocracy, Inc., *The Energy Certificate* (Savannah, Ohio, 1938), p. 13.

27. Mack Reynolds, "Speakeasy," *Fantasy and Science Fiction* 24 (January 1963): 110.

28. Martin Gardner, *Fads and Fallacies in the Name of Science* (New York: Dover, 1957), p. 285.

29. A. E. van Vogt, *The World of Null-A* (New York: Ace, 1948), p. 57.

30. C. Daly King, "Dianetics: A Book Review," *Fantasy and Science Fiction* 1

(December 1950): 99–103; L. Ron Hubbard, "Homo Superior, Here We Come," *Marvel Science Stories* 3 (May 1951): 111–114; Theodore Sturgeon, "How to Avoid a Hole in the Head," *Marvel Science Stories* 3 (May 1951): 114–116; Lester del Rey, "Superman—C.O.D.," *Marvel Science Stories* 3 (May 1951): 116–119.

31. *Amazing Stories* 1 (April 1926): 3.

32. *Science Wonder Stories* 1 (June 1929): 5.

33. Arthur C. Clarke, "Hazards of Prophecy," in *The Futurists*, ed. Alvin Toffler (New York: Random House, 1972), p. 144.

34. Bertrand Russell, quoted in an advertisement, *Analog* 69 (August 1962): 156.

35. Advertisement, *Analog* 68 (October 1961): 179.

36. Norman M. Lobsenz or Cele Goldsmith, editorial, *Amazing Stories* 36 (December 1962): 5.

37. Charles D. Hornig, "Future Facts," *Future Fiction* 1 (March 1940): 55.

38. Raymond A. Palmer, editorial, *Other Worlds Science Stories* (April 1956): 4.

39. Raymond A. Palmer, editorial, *Amazing Stories* 20 (February 1946): 3.

40. Raymond J. Healy and J. Francis McComas, *Adventures in Space and Time* (New York: Ballantine, 1975), unpaginated introduction.

41. Frederik Pohl, "The Great Inventions," *Galaxy* 27 (December 1968): 6.

42. Isaac Asimov, "Future? Tense!" *Fantasy and Science Fiction* 29 (June 1965): 107.

43. See, for example, the proud claims of success in predicting the jet plane, on the inside back cover of the December 1945 issue of *Amazing Stories*.

44. Lester del Rey, "Visions and Nightmares," *Worlds of Tomorrow* 5 (Spring 1971): 2.

45. John W. Campbell, reply to a letter, *Astounding Science Fiction* 51 (June 1953): 117.

46. Frederik Pohl, "A Short Term Solution," *Galaxy* 36 (April 1975): 10.

47. H. L. Gold, "Gueffef on Progreff," *Galaxy* 6 (May 1953): 3; see also "Step Outside," *Galaxy* 3 (November 1951): 2–3.

48. Alexei Panshin, *Heinlein in Dimension* (Chicago: Advent, 1968), p. 83.

49. Philip K. Dick, "Introducing the Author," *Imagination* 4 (February 1953): 2.

50. Frederik Pohl, "All We Unemployed," *Galaxy* 22 (June 1964): 4.

51. Ben Bova, editorial, *Analog* 94 (September 1974): 8.

52. Clark Ashton Smith, letter to the editor, *Amazing Stories* 7 (October 1932): 670.

53. Theodore Sturgeon, "Future Writers in a Future World," in *The Craft of Science Fiction*, ed. Reginald Bretnor (New York: Barnes and Noble, 1977), p. 92; Alvin Toffler, *Future Shock* (New York: Random House, 1970).

54. Poul Anderson, interviewed, *Science Fiction Review* 7 (May 1978): 37.

55. Harry Warner, *All Our Yesterdays* (Chicago: Advent, 1969), pp. 38–39.

56. Rog Phillips, "The Club House," *Amazing Stories* 22 (October 1948): 149.

57. P. Schuyler Miller, "The Universe Our Stage," *Analog* 72 (January 1964): 86.

58. John J. Pierce, "Imagination and Evolution," *Galaxy* 39 (February 1978): 5.

59. John J. Pierce, "The Devaluation of Values," *Algol*, no. 16 (December 1970): 11.

60. Lester del Rey, Afterword to "Evensong," in *Dangerous Visions*, ed. Harlan Ellison (Garden City, N.Y.: Doubleday, 1967), p. 8.

61. Robert C. W. Ettinger, "Interstellar Travel and Eternal Life," *If* 18 (January 1968): 109–114.

62. James Blish, *Cities in Flight* (New York: Avon, 1970), p. 592.

63. William J. Broad, "Science Fiction Authors Choose Sides in 'Star Wars,' " *New York Times*, 26 February 1985, pp. C1, C3.

BIBLIOGRAPHY

Akers, Ronald L. *Deviant Behavior: A Social Learning Approach*. Belmont, Calif.: Wadsworth, 1977.

Albrecht, Milton C. "Does Literature Reflect Common Values?" *American Sociological Review* 21 (December 1956): 722–729.

—— "The Relationship of Literature and Society." *American Journal of Sociology* 59 (March 1954): 425–436.

Aldiss, Brian W. *Billion Year Spree*. New York: Schocken, 1974.

—— "Frankenstein Unbound." *Fantastic* 23 (March 1974): 6–61, 108–110 and (May 1974): 38–103.

—— "The Gulf and the Forest: Contemporary SF in Britain." *Fantasy and Science Fiction* 54 (April 1978): 4–11.

——, ed. *Space Opera*. New York: Berkley, 1977.

Alexander, W. "The Ananias Gland." *Amazing Stories* 3 (November 1928): 707–709.

—— "The Fighting Heart." *Amazing Stories* 2 (February 1928): 1099–1102.

—— "New Stomachs for Old." *Amazing Stories* 1 (February 1927): 1039–1041, 1073.

Allen, L. David. *Science Fiction: An Introduction*. Lincoln, Neb.: Cliffs Notes, 1973.

Allen, William Sheridan. *The Nazi Seizure of Power*. Chicago: Quadrangle, 1965.

Anderson, Poul. "A Cyclical Theory of Science Fiction." *Galaxy* 35 (August 1974): 6–16.

—— "The Hardness of Hard Science Fiction." *Destinies* 1 (February–March 1979): 248–262.

—— "The High Crusade." *Astounding Science Fiction* 65 (July 1960): 8–46 and (August 1960): 126–164; 66 (September 1960): 56–82, 163–174.

—— "On Imaginary Science." *Destinies* 1 (April–June 1979): 304–320.

—— "Reality, Fiction, and Points Between." *Destinies* 1 (November–December 1978): 292–308.

Archer, Dirce. "Surveying British Science Fiction." *Astounding Science Fiction* 52 (September 1953): 135–146.

Ash, Brian. *Who's Who in Science Fiction.* New York: Taplinger, 1976.

———, ed. *The Visual Encyclopedia of Science Fiction.* New York: Harmony, 1977.

Ashley, Michael. *The History of the Science Fiction Magazine.* 3 vols. Chicago: Regnery, 1974–1976.

Asimov, Isaac. "The Caves of Steel." *Galaxy* 7 (October 1953): 4–66; (November 1953): 98–159; (December 1953): 108–159.

——— *Foundation.* New York: Avon, 1966.

——— *Foundation and Empire.* New York: Avon, 1966.

——— *Foundation's Edge.* Garden City, N.Y.: Doubleday, 1982.

——— "Future? Tense!" *Fantasy and Science Fiction* 29 (June 1965): 100–109.

——— *I, Robot.* New York: Grosset and Dunlap, 1950.

——— "Just Thirty Years." *Fantasy and Science Fiction* 57 (October 1979): 273–283.

——— "Nightfall." *Astounding Science-Fiction* 28 (September 1941): 9–34.

——— *The Robots of Dawn.* New York: Ballantine, 1983.

——— "Runaround." *Astounding Science-Fiction* 29 (March 1942): 94–103.

——— *Second Foundation.* New York: Avon, 1964.

——— "The Word I Invented." *Fantasy and Science Fiction* 59 (October 1980): 122–131.

Bainbridge, William Sims. "The Analytical Laboratory, 1938–1976." *Analog* 100 (January 1980): 121–134.

——— "Attitudes toward Interstellar Communication: An Empirical Study." *Journal of the British Interplanetary Society* 36 (1983): 298–304.

——— "Chariots of the Gullible." *Skeptical Inquirer* 3 (Winter 1978): 33–48.

——— "Collective Behavior and Social Movements." In *Sociology,* edited by Rodney Stark, pp. 493–523. Belmont, Calif.: Wadsworth, 1985.

——— "Cultural Genetics." In *Religious Movements: Genesis, Exodus, and Numbers,* edited by Rodney Stark. New York: Rose of Sharon Press, 1985.

——— "The Decline of the Shakers: Evidence from the United States Census," *Communal Societies* 4 (1984): 19–34.

——— "The Impact of Science Fiction on Attitudes toward Technology." In *Science Fiction and Space Futures,* edited by Eugene M. Emme, pp. 121–135. San Diego: American Astronautical Society, 1982.

——— "In Search of Delusion." *Skeptical Inquirer* 4 (Fall 1979): 33–39.

——— "Public Support for the Space Program." *Astronautics and Aeronautics* 16 (1978): 60–61, 76.

——— *Satan's Power: Ethnography of a Deviant Psychotherapy Cult.* Berkeley: University of California Press, 1978.

——— *The Spaceflight Revolution.* New York: Wiley-Interscience, 1976.

——— "Utopian Communities: Theoretical Issues." In *The Sacred in a Secular Age,* edited by Phillip E. Hammond, pp. 21–35. Berkeley: University of California Press, 1985.

Bainbridge, William Sims, and Robert D. Crutchfield. "Sex Role Ideology and Delinquency." *Sociological Perspectives* 26 (1983): 253–274.

Bainbridge, William Sims, and Murray Dalziel. "New Maps of Science Fiction." In *Analog Yearbook*, edited by Ben Bova, pp. 277–299. New York: Baronet, 1978.
—— "The Shape of Science Fiction." *Science-Fiction Studies* 5 (July 1978): 165–171.
Bainbridge, William Sims, and Richard Wyckoff. "American Enthusiasm for Spaceflight." *Analog* 99 (July 1979): 59–72.
Bainbridge, William Sims, and Rodney Stark. "Cult Formation: Three Compatible Models." *Sociological Analysis* 40 (Winter 1979): 283–295.
—— "The 'Consciousness Reformation' Reconsidered." *Journal for the Scientific Study of Religion* 20 (1981): 1–16.
—— "Friendship, Religion, and the Occult: A Network Study." *Review of Religious Research* 22 (1981): 313–327.
—— "Scientology: To Be Perfectly Clear." *Sociological Analysis* 41 (Summer 1980): 128–136.
—— "Suicide, Homicide, and Religion: Durkheim Reassessed." *Annual Review of the Social Sciences of Religion* 5 (1981): 33–56.
Bandura, Albert. *Principles of Behavior Modification.* New York: Holt, Rinehart and Winston, 1969.
Barron, Neil, ed. *Anatomy of Wonder: Science Fiction.* New York: Bowker, 1976.
Bates, Harry. "Alas, All Thinking!" In *Imagination Unlimited*, edited by Everett F. Bleiler and T. E. Dikty, pp. 201–247. New York: Farrar, Straus and Young, 1952.
—— "Farewell to the Master." *Astounding Science-Fiction* 26 (October 1940): 58–87.
Baum, Rainer C. "Values and Democracy in Imperial Germany." *Sociological Inquiry* 38 (Spring 1968): 179–196.
Benford, Gregory. "The Secret of SF Is Awe." *New Scientist* 72 (December 23/30, 1976): 765–767.
Berger, Albert I. "Science-Fiction Critiques of the American Space Program, 1945–1958." *Science-Fiction Studies* 5 (July 1978): 99–109.
Berger, Harold L. *Science Fiction and the New Dark Age.* Bowling Green, Ohio: Bowling Green University Popular Press, 1976.
Bergonzi, Bernard, ed. *H. G. Wells.* Englewood Cliffs, N.J.: Prentice-Hall, 1976.
Bester, Alfred. "The Demolished Man." *Galaxy* 3 (January 1952): 4–66; (February 1952): 101–158; (March 1952): 101–158.
—— "Fondly Fahrenheit." *Fantasy and Science Fiction* 7 (August 1954): 3–21.
—— "The Stars My Destination." *Galaxy* 12 (October 1956): 8–58 and 13 (November 1956): 88–143; (December 1956): 88–142; (January 1957): 98–142.
Binder, Eando. "Adam Link Fights a War." *Amazing Stories* 14 (December 1940): 10–41.
—— "Adam Link in Business." *Amazing Stories* 14 (January 1940): 44–61.
—— "Adam Link Saves the World." *Amazing Stories* 16 (April 1942): 10–46.
—— "Adam Link's Vengeance." *Amazing Stories* 14 (February 1940): 8–27, 128.
—— "I, Robot." *Amazing Stories* 13 (January 1939): 8–18.
—— "The Trial of Adam Link, Robot." *Amazing Stories* 13 (July 1939): 30–43.
Blish, James. *Cities in Flight.* New York: Avon, 1970.
—— *The Issue at Hand.* Chicago: Advent, 1964.

—— *More Issues at Hand*. Chicago: Advent, 1970.

—— "Poul Anderson: The Enduring Explosion." *Fantasy and Science Fiction* 40 (April 1971): 52–55.

—— "Science in Science Fiction: The Astronomical Story." *Science Fiction Quarterly* 1 (November 1951): 111–113.

—— "Science in Science Fiction: The Biological Story." *Science Fiction Quarterly* 1 (May 1951): 89–91.

—— "Science in Science Fiction: The Mathematical Story." *Science Fiction Quarterly* 1 (August 1951): 83–86.

Bova, Ben. *Notes to a Science Fiction Writer*. Boston: Houghton Mifflin, 1981.

Bradbury, Ray, "Carnival of Madness." *Thrilling Wonder Stories* 36 (April 1950): 95–104.

—— *The Martian Chronicles*. New York: Bantam, 1954.

Bradley, Marion Zimmer. "An Evolution of Consciousness." *Science Fiction Review* 6 (August 1977): 34–45.

—— *The Forbidden Tower*. New York: DAW, 1977.

—— "My Trip through Science Fiction." *Algol* 15 (Winter 1977–1978): 10–20.

Branden, Nathaniel, and Barbara Branden. *Who Is Ayn Rand?* New York: Random House, 1962.

Bretnor, Reginald, ed. *The Craft of Science Fiction*. New York: Barnes and Noble, 1977.

—— *Modern Science Fiction*. Chicago: Advent, 1979.

Breuer, Miles J. "Buried Treasure." *Amazing Stories* 4 (April 1929): 38–47.

—— "The Gostak and the Doshes." *Amazing Stories* 4 (March 1930): 1142–1149, 1185.

Briney, Robert E., and Edward Wood. *SF Bibliographies*. Chicago: Advent, 1972.

Brown, Fredric. "Pi in the Sky." *Thrilling Wonder Stories* 26 (Winter 1945): 46–59, 66.

Budrys, Algis. "Foundation and Asimov." *Analog* 95 (July 1975): 163–169.

Burgess, Anthony. *A Clockwork Orange*. New York: Ballantine, 1965.

Burkett, Steven R., and Mervin White. "Hellfire and Delinquency: Another Look." *Journal for the Scientific Study of Religion* 13 (1974): 455–462.

Burroughs, Edgar Rice. "Autobiographical Sketch." *Amazing Stories* 15 (June 1941): 138–139.

—— *The Cave Girl*. New York: Ace, 1963.

—— *The Chessmen of Mars*. New York: Ballantine, 1976.

—— *The Gods of Mars*. New York: Grosset and Dunlap, 1918.

—— *Pellucidar*. New York: Dover, 1963.

—— *A Princess of Mars*. New York: Ballantine, 1975.

—— *Tarzan and the Ant Man*. New York: Ballantine, 1976.

—— *Tarzan and the Lost Empire*. New York: Ballantine, 1963.

—— *Tarzan the Terrible*. New York: Ballantine, 1976.

—— *Thuvia, Maid of Mars*. New York: Ballantine, 1974.

Campbell, John W., Jr. "Addendum on the Symbolic Psionic Machine." *Astounding Science Fiction* 59 (June 1957): 125–127.

—— "Concerning Dianetics." *Astounding Science-Fiction* 45 (May 1950): 4–5.

—— "The Modern Black Arts." *Analog* 86 (December 1970): 4–7, 175–178.

———— "The Nature of Literature." *Analog* 76 (October 1965): 6–7, 159–162.

———— "Non-Escape Literature." *Astounding Science Fiction* 62 (February 1959): 5–7, 161–162.

———— "Psionic Machine—Type One." *Astounding Science Fiction* 57 (June 1956): 97–108.

———— "The Space-Drive Problem." *Astounding Science Fiction* 65 (June 1960): 83–106.

———— "Unprovable Speculation." *Astounding Science Fiction* 56 (February 1957): 54–70.

———— "When the Atoms Failed." *Amazing Stories* 4 (January 1930): 910–925.

———— "The Word and the Truth." *Astounding Science Fiction* 64 (February 1960): 4–7, 176–178.

Capek, Karel. *R.U.R.* Garden City, N.Y.: Doubleday, Page, 1923.

Carter, Paul A. *The Creation of Tomorrow.* New York: Columbia University Press, 1977.

Cherryh, C. J. *Brothers of Earth.* New York: DAW, 1976.

———— *Downbelow Station.* New York: DAW, 1981.

———— "The Faded Sun: Kesrith." *Galaxy* 39 (February 1978): 8–66; (March 1978): 82–128; (April 1978): 72–120; (May 1978): 76–117.

———— *The Faded Sun: Kutath.* New York: DAW, 1979.

———— *The Faded Sun: Shon'jir.* New York: DAW, 1978.

Clareson, Thomas D. "The Evolution of Science Fiction." *Science Fiction Quarterly* 2 (August 1953): 85–98.

———— "Robert Silverberg: The Compleat Writer." *Fantasy and Science Fiction* 46 (April 1974): 73–80.

———— "SF: The Academic Dimensions." *Fantasy and Science Fiction* 42 (May 1972): 116–123.

————, ed. *Many Futures, Many Worlds.* Kent, Ohio: Kent State University Press, 1977.

———— *SF: The Other Side of Realism.* Bowling Green, Ohio: Bowling Green University Popular Press, 1971.

Clarke, Arthur C. *Childhood's End.* New York: Ballantine, 1982 (1953).

———— "Jupiter Five." *If* 2 (May 1953): 4–28, 75.

———— *Prelude to Space.* New York: World, 1951.

———— *Profiles of the Future.* New York: Bantam, 1963.

———— *2001: A Space Odyssey.* New York: New American Library, 1968.

———— *Voices from the Sky.* New York: Harper, 1965.

Cleaver, A. V. "Interplanetary Flight: Is the Rocket the Only Answer?" *Journal of the British Interplanetary Society* 6 (June 1947): 127–148.

Clement, Hal. "Iceworld." *Astounding Science-Fiction* 48 (October 1951): 10–62, 151–158; (November 1951): 120–159; (December 1951): 99–156.

———— "Mission of Gravity." *Astounding Science Fiction* 51 (April 1953): 8–62; (May 1953): 90–139; (June 1953): 121–167; (July 1953): 101–151.

———— "Whirligig World." *Astounding Science Fiction* 51 (June 1953): 102–114.

Clifton, Mark, and Frank Riley. "They'd Rather Be Right." *Astounding Science Fiction* 53 (August 1954): 12–47 and 54 (September 1954): 108–146; (October 1954): 106–141; (November 1954): 96–133.

Cline, Cheryl. "Feminist Perspective: The Female Man." *Windhaven* 1 (1977): 6–9.

Cline, Victor B., and James M. Richards. "A Factor-Analytic Study of Religious Belief and Behavior." *Journal of Personality and Social Psychology* 1 (1965): 569–578.

Cochran, Russ, ed. *The Edgar Rice Burroughs Library of Illustration*, 3 vols. West Plains, Mo.: Cochran, 1976, 1977, 1984.

Condry, John, and Sharon Dyer. "Fear of Success: Attribution of Cause to the Victim." *Journal of Social Issues* 32 (1976): 63–83.

Conklin, Groff, ed. *Great Science Fiction by Scientists*. New York: Collier, 1962.

Coppel, Alfred. "The Hills of Home." *Future*, no. 30 (1956): 115–123. Alternate version, *Galaxy* 19 (October 1960): 43–52.

Cummings, Ray. "Around the Universe." *Amazing Stories* 2 (October 1927): 626–661, 675.

Davenport, Basil, ed. *The Science Fiction Novel*. Chicago: Advent, 1969.

Davis, James A.; Tom W. Smith; and C. Bruce Stephenson. *General Social Surveys, 1972–1978: Cumulative Codebook*. Chicago: National Opinion Research Center, 1978.

Day, Donald B. *Index to the Science-Fiction Magazines, 1926–1950*. Portland, Ore.: Perri Press, 1952.

de Camp, L. Sprague. *Lest Darkness Fall*. New York: Ballantine, 1979.

—— *Lovecraft: A Biography*. New York: Ballantine, 1976.

—— "The Stolen Dormouse." *Astounding Science-Fiction* 27 (April 1941): 9–32 and (May 1941): 130–161.

—— "Where Were We?" *Galaxy Science Fiction* 3 (February 1952): 4–12.

de Camp, L. Sprague, and Catherine Crook de Camp. *Science Fiction Handbook, Revised*. New York: McGraw-Hill, 1977.

de Camp, L. Sprague, and Fletcher Pratt. *The Incomplete Enchanter*. New York: Pyramid Books, 1960.

Delany, Samuel R. *Dhalgren*. New York: Bantam, 1975.

—— "Science Fiction and 'Literature.'" *Analog* 99 (May 1979): 59–78.

Delap, Richard. "Harlan Ellison: The Healing Art of Razorblade Fiction." *Fantasy and Science Fiction* 53 (July 1977): 71–79.

del Rey, Lester. *The Eleventh Commandment*. New York: Ballantine, 1970.

—— "Frederik Pohl: Frontiersman." *Fantasy and Science Fiction* 45 (September 1973): 55–64.

—— "The Hand at Issue." *Fantasy and Science Fiction* 42 (April 1972): 72–77.

—— "Helen O'Loy." *Astounding Science-Fiction* 22 (December 1938): 118–125.

—— "Homesteads on Venus." *Amazing Stories* 34 (October 1960): 107–117.

—— "Instinct." In *Omnibus of Science Fiction*, edited by Groff Conklin, pp. 551–561. New York: Crown, 1952.

—— "Nerves." *Astounding Science-Fiction* 30 (September 1942): 54–90.

—— "Superman—C.O.D." *Marvel Science Stories* 3 (May 1951): 116–119.

—— "Willy Ley—The First Citizen of the Moon." *Galaxy* 29 (September 1969): 151–157.

—— *The World of Science Fiction*. New York: Ballantine, 1979.

Dickson, Gordon R. "Profile: Poul Anderson." *Fantasy and Science Fiction* 40 (April 1971): 46–51.

———— *Time Storm*. New York: Bantam, 1979.

Durkheim, Emile. *The Elementary Forms of the Religious Life*. New York: Macmillan, 1965.

Ellik, Ron, and Bill Evans. *The Universes of E. E. Smith*. Chicago: Advent, 1966.

Ellison, Harlan. "Count the Clock That Tells the Time." *Omni* 1 (December 1978): 60–62, 126–131.

———— "I Have No Mouth and I Must Scream." *If* 17 (March 1967): 24–36.

———— " 'Repent Harlequin!' said the Ticktockman." *Galaxy* 24 (December 1965): 135–145.

———— "A Statement of Ethical Position." *Galaxy* 39 (May 1978): 6–8.

———— "A Statement of Ethical Position by the Worldcon Guest of Honor." *Unearth* 2 (Spring 1978): 3–5, 46.

————, ed. *Dangerous Visions*. Garden City, N.Y.: Doubleday, 1967.

Elsner, Henry. *The Technocrats*. Syracuse, N.Y.: Syracuse University Press, 1967.

Elwood, Roger. *The Book of Andre Norton*. New York: DAW, 1975.

Eney, Dick, ed. *The Proceedings: Discon*. Chicago: Advent, 1965.

Eshbach, Lloyd Arthur, ed. *Of Worlds Beyond*. Chicago: Advent, 1964.

Ettinger, Robert C. W. "Interstellar Travel and Eternal Life." *If* 18 (January 1968): 109–114.

Evans, I. O. *Jules Verne and His Work*. London: Arco, 1965.

Eysenck, Hans J. "The Effects of Psychotherapy." *International Journal of Psychiatry* 1 (1965): 99–144.

Farmer, Philip Jose. "The Arms of Tarzan." *Burroughs Bulletin*, no. 22 (Summer 1971): 3–7.

———— *Tarzan Alive*. New York: Popular Library, 1976.

Feenberg, Andrew. "The Politics of Survival: Science Fiction in the Nuclear Age." *Alternative Futures* 1 (Summer 1978): 3–23.

Fiedler, Leslie A. "Who Was William Olaf Stapledon?" *Galileo*, combined nos. 11 and 12 (1979): 34–36.

Finer, S. E. "A Profile of Science Fiction." *Sociological Review* 2 (December 1954): 239–256.

Fox, Lynn H.; Linda Brody; and Dianne Tobin, eds. *Women and the Mathematical Mystique*. Baltimore: Johns Hopkins University Press, 1980.

Franson, Donald, and Howard DeVore. *A History of the Hugo, Nebula, and International Fantasy Awards*. Dearborn, Mich.: Misfit Press, 1978.

Gardner, Martin. *Fads and Fallacies in the Name of Science*. New York: Dover, 1957.

Gernsback, Hugo. "Baron Muenchhausen's Scientific Adventures." *Amazing Stories* 2 (February 1928): 1060–1071 and (March 1928): 1150–1160; 3 (April 1928): 38–47, 84; (May 1928): 148–156; (June 1928): 242–251; (July 1928): 347–357.

———— "The Impact of Science-Fiction on World Progress." *Science-Fiction Plus* 1 (March 1953): 2, 67.

———— *Ralph 124C41 +*. Boston: Stratford, 1925.

Gerrold, David. *The World of Star Trek*. New York: Ballantine, 1973.

BIBLIOGRAPHY

Gibbon, Edward. *The History of the Decline and Fall of the Roman Empire.* London: Methuen, 1896.

Girsdansky, Michael. "Science and Science Fiction: Who Borrows What?" *Worlds of Tomorrow* 1 (December 1963): 59–65.

Gold, Horace L. *What Will They Think of Last?* Crestline, Calif. Institute for the Development of the Harmonious Human Being, 1976.

Goulart, Ron. *An Informal History of the Pulp Magazines.* New York: Ace, 1973.

—— "That Buck Rogers Stuff." *Fantasy and Science Fiction* 48 (June 1975): 30–40.

Grant, C. L., ed. *Writing and Selling Science Fiction.* Cincinnati: Writers Digest, 1976.

Gunn, James. *Alternate Worlds: The Illustrated History of Science Fiction.* Englewood Cliffs, N.J.: Prentice-Hall, 1975.

—— "On the Road to Science Fiction: From Wells to Heinlein." *Isaac Asimov's Science Fiction Magazine* 3 (January 1979): 64–81.

—— "On the Road to Science Fiction: From Heinlein to Here." *Isaac Asimov's Science Fiction Magazine* 3 (March 1979): 100–121.

—— "The Philosophy of Science Fiction." *Dynamic Science Fiction* 1 (March 1953): 104–113 and (June 1953): 83–91.

Gurr, Ted Robert. *Why Men Rebel.* Princeton: Princeton University Press, 1970.

Hamilton, Edmund. "The Universe Wreckers." *Amazing Stories* 5 (May 1930): 102–129; (June 1930): 254–279; (July 1930): 346–371.

Hansel, C. E. M. *ESP—A Scientific Evaluation.* New York: Scribner's, 1966.

Hayakawa, S. I. *Language in Thought and Action.* New York: Harcourt, Brace, 1949.

Healy, Raymond J., and J. Francis McComas, eds. *Adventures in Space and Time.* New York: Ballantine, 1975.

Heinlein, Robert A. "All You Zombies—," *Fantasy and Science Fiction* 16 (March 1959): 5–15.

—— "Beyond This Horizon." *Astounding Science-Fiction* 29 (April 1942): 9–50 and (May 1942): 55–97.

—— "Blowups Happen." *Astounding Science-Fiction* 26 (September 1940): 51–85.

—— "By His Bootstraps." *Astounding Science-Fiction* 28 (October 1941): 9–47.

—— "Channel Markers." *Analog* 92 (January 1974): 5–10, 166–178.

—— "Common Sense." *Astounding Science-Fiction* 28 (October 1941): 102–154.

—— *Expanded Universe.* New York: Ballantine, 1976.

—— *The Moon Is a Harsh Mistress.* New York: Putnam, 1966.

—— *Red Planet.* New York: Ballantine, 1976.

—— *Rocket Ship Galileo.* New York: Ballantine, 1977.

—— "Shooting 'Destination Moon.'" *Astounding Science-Fiction* 45 (July 1950): 6–18.

—— *Space Cadet.* New York: Ballantine, 1978.

—— "Universe." *Astounding Science-Fiction* 27 (May 1941): 9–42.

Henderson, Zenna. *The People: No Different Flesh.* Garden City, N.Y.: Doubleday, 1967.

—— *Pilgrimage.* Garden City, N.Y.: Doubleday, 1961.

Hewelcke, Geoffrey. "Ten Million Miles Sunward." *Amazing Stories* 2 (March 1928): 1126–1149.

Higgins, Paul C., and Gary L. Albrecht. "Hellfire and Delinquency Revisited." *Social Forces* 55 (1977): 952–958.

Hillegas, Mark R. "Dystopian Science Fiction: New Index to the Human Situation." *New Mexico Quarterly* 31 (Autumn 1961): 238–249.

Hirsch, Walter. "The Image of the Scientist in Science Fiction: A Content Analysis." *American Journal of Sociology* 63 (1958): 506–512.

Hirschi, Travis. *Causes of Delinquency*. Berkeley: University of California Press, 1969.

Hirschi, Travis, and Rodney Stark. "Hellfire and Delinquency." *Social Problems* 17 (1969): 202–213.

Hogan, James P. *The Gentle Giants of Ganymede*. New York: Ballantine, 1978.

——— *Giant's Star*. New York: Ballantine, 1981.

——— *Inherit the Stars*. New York: Ballantine, 1977.

——— *Voyage from Yesteryear*. New York: Ballantine, 1982.

Homans, George C. *The Human Group*. New York: Harcourt, Brace and World, 1950.

——— *Social Behavior: Its Elementary Forms*. New York: Harcourt Brace Jovanovich, 1974.

Horner, Matina. "Femininity and Successful Achievement: A Basic Inconsistency." In *Feminine Personality and Conflict*, edited by Judith M. Bardwick, Elizabeth Douvan, Matina S. Horner, and David Gutmann, pp. 45–74. Belmont, Calif.: Brooks/Cole, 1970.

Howard, Robert E. *Conan the Conqueror*. New York: Lancer, 1967.

Hoyle, Fred. *October the First Is Too Late*. Greenwich, Conn.: Fawcett, 1968.

Hubbard, L. Ron. "The Analytical Mind." *Astounding Science-Fiction* 46 (October 1950): 139–162.

——— *Battlefield Earth*. Los Angeles: Bridge, 1982.

——— *Dianetics: The Modern Science of Mental Health*. New York: Paperback Library, 1950.

——— "Dianometry." *Astounding Science-Fiction* 46 (January 1951): 76–100.

——— "The Evolution of a Science." *Astounding Science-Fiction* 45 (May 1950): 43–87.

——— "Homo Superior, Here We Come." *Marvel Science Stories* 3 (May 1951): 111–114.

Huxley, Aldous. *Brave New World*. New York: Bantam, 1968.

Jakubowski, Maxim, and Malcolm Edwards. *The SF Book of Lists*. New York: Berkley, 1983.

Jewkes, John; David Sawers; and Richard Stillerman. *The Sources of Invention*. New York: Norton, 1969.

Jonas, Gerald. "The Shaker Revival." *Galaxy* 29 (February 1970): 4–33.

Jones, Neil R. "The Jameson Satellite." *Amazing Stories* 30 (April 1956): 156–176. Reprinted from the July 1931 issue.

Jones, Raymond F. *The Alien*. New York: Belmont, 1966.

Keller, David H. "The Revolt of the Pedestrians." *Amazing Stories* 2 (February 1928): 1048–1059.

—— "White Collars." *Amazing Stories* 40 (April 1966): 98–113. Reprinted from the February 1928 issue.

Kemp, Earl, ed. *The Proceedings: Chicon III.* Chicago: Advent, 1963.

King, C. Daly. "Dianetics: A Book Review." *Fantasy and Science Fiction* 1 (December 1950): 99–103.

Knight, Damon. "Four in One." *Galaxy* 5 (February 1953): 4–36.

—— *The Futurians.* New York: John Day, 1977.

—— *In Search of Wonder.* Chicago: Advent, 1967.

Kornbluth, C. M. "The Marching Morons." *Galaxy* 2 (April 1951): 128–158.

Korzybski, Alfred. *Manhood of Humanity.* Lakeville, Conn.: International Non-Aristotelian Library, 1950.

—— *Science and Sanity.* Lakeville, Conn.: International Non-Artistotelian Library, 1948.

Kyle, David. *The Illustrated Book of Science Fiction Ideas and Dreams.* London: Hamlyn, 1977.

—— *A Pictorial History of Science Fiction.* London: Hamlyn, 1976.

Larson, Glen A., and Robert Thurston. *Battlestar Galactica.* New York: Berkley, 1978.

Lasswitz, Kurd. *Two Planets.* Carbondale: Southern Illinois University Press, 1971.

LeGuin, Ursula K. "Escape Routes." *Galaxy* 35 (December 1974): 40–44.

—— "Is Gender Necessary?" In *Aurora: Beyond Equality,* edited by Susan Janice Anderson and Vonda N. McIntyre, pp. 130–139. Greenwich, Conn.: Fawcett, 1976.

—— *The Lathe of Heaven.* New York: Avon, 1973.

—— *The Left Hand of Darkness.* New York: Ace, 1969.

Leiber, Fritz, Jr. "Gather, Darkness!" *Astounding Science-Fiction* 31 (May 1943): 9–59; (June 1943): 109–159; (July 1943): 118–162.

—— "Later than You Think." *Galaxy* 1 (October 1950): 108–113.

—— "When the Last Gods Die." *Fantasy and Science Fiction* 2 (December 1951): 3–7.

Leinster, Murray. "The Boomerang Circuit." *Thrilling Wonder Stories* 30 (June 1947): 11–37.

—— "The Disciplinary Circuit." *Thrilling Wonder Stories* 28 (Winter 1946): 44–63.

—— "The Manless Worlds." *Thrilling Wonder Stories* 29 (February 1947): 11–35.

—— "Proxima Centauri." *Astounding Stories* 15 (March 1935): 10–44.

—— "Sidewise in Time." *Astounding Stories* 13 (June 1934): 10–47.

Lem, Stanislaw. *Memoirs Found in a Bathtub.* New York: Avon, 1976.

Lester, Colin, ed. *The International Science Fiction Yearbook.* New York: Quick Fox, 1978.

Lévi-Strauss, Claude. *The Raw and the Cooked.* New York: Harper and Row, 1969.

Levine, Adeline, and Janice Crumrine. "Women and the Fear of Success: A Problem in Replication." *American Journal of Sociology* 80 (1975): 964–974.

Lewis, C. S. *That Hideous Strength.* New York: Macmillan, 1965.

—— *Out of the Silent Planet.* New York: Macmillan, 1965.

—— *Perelandra.* New York: Macmillan, 1965.

Ley, Willy. "Fifteen Years of Galaxy—Thirteen Years of F.Y.I." *Galaxy* 24 (October 1965): 84–94.

——— *Rockets, Missiles, and Men in Space.* New York: Signet, 1969.

Lipset, Seymour Martin. *Rebellion in the University.* Boston: Little, Brown, 1971.

Logsdon, John M. *The Decision to Go to the Moon.* Cambridge: M.I.T. Press, 1970.

Lovecraft, H. P. "The Colour out of Space." *Amazing Stories* 2 (September 1927): 556–567.

——— "The Shadow out of Time." *Astounding Stories* 17 (June 1936): 110–154.

Lowndes, Robert A. W. "James Blish: Profile." *Fantasy and Science Fiction* 42 (April 1972): 66–71.

Lucas, George. *Star Wars.* New York: Ballantine, 1976.

Lundwall, Sam J. *Science Fiction: What It's All About.* New York: Ace, 1971.

Lupoff, Richard A. *Barsoom: Edgar Rice Burroughs and the Martian Vision.* Baltimore: Mirage Press, 1976.

——— *Edgar Rice Burroughs: Master of Adventure.* New York: Ace, 1965.

——— "The Realities of Philip K. Dick." *Starship* 16 (Summer 1979): 29–33.

——— "Science Fiction Hawks and Doves: Whose Future Will You Buy?" *Ramparts* 10 (February 1972): 25–30.

Madle, Robert A. "Edgar Allan Poe—Ancestor." *Science Fiction Quarterly* 2 (May 1953): 71–74, 128.

Malinowski, Bronislaw. *Magic, Science, and Religion.* Garden City, N.Y.: Doubleday, 1948.

Malzberg, Barry N. *The Best of Barry N. Malzberg.* New York: Pocket Books, 1976.

——— *Beyond Apollo.* New York: Pocket Books, 1974.

——— "Robert Silverberg," *Fantasy and Science Fiction* 46 (April 1974): 67–72.

Manuel, Frank P., and Fritzie P. Manuel. *Utopian Thought in the Western World.* Cambridge: Harvard University Press, 1979.

Matheson, Richard. *I Am Legend.* Greenwich, Conn.: Fawcett, 1954.

May, John, ed. *Star Wars—The Empire Strikes Back.* Ridgefield, Conn.: Paradise Press, 1980.

McCaffrey, Anne. *The Ship Who Sang.* New York: Ballantine, 1969.

McConnell, James. "The Game of White." *Other Worlds*, no. 31 (July 1953): 6–43.

——— "Learning Theory." In *Great Science Fiction Stories by Scientists*, edited by Groff Conklin, pp. 227–240. New York: Collier, 1962.

McGhan, Barry, ed. *Science Fiction and Fantasy Pseudonyms.* Dearborn, Mich.: DeVore, 1978.

McIntyre, Vonda N. "Aztecs." In *2076: The American Tricentennial*, edited by Edward Bryant, pp. 139–194. New York: Pyramid, 1977.

——— *Dreamsnake.* New York: Dell, 1978.

Merril, Judith. *SF12.* New York: Dell, 1967.

———, ed. *England Swings SF.* New York: Ace, 1968.

Morton, Andrew Queen. *Literary Detection.* Epping, England: Bowker, 1978.

Moskowitz, Sam. *Explorers of the Infinite.* Cleveland: Meridian, 1963.

——— "How Science Fiction Got Its Name." *Fantasy and Science Fiction* 12 (February 1957): 65–77.

——— *The Immortal Storm.* Westport, Conn.: Hyperion, 1974.

—— *Seekers of Tomorrow*. Westport, Conn.: Hyperion, 1974.

—— *Strange Horizons*. New York: Scribner's, 1976.

—— "The Willy Ley Story." *Worlds of Tomorrow* 3 (May 1966): 30–42.

Myers, Ray Avery. "Into the Subconscious." *Science Wonder Stories* 1 (October 1929): 426–435, 459.

Nolan, William F. "Bradbury: Prose Poet in the Age of Space." *Fantasy and Science Fiction* 24 (May 1963): 7–22.

Noordung, Hermann. *Das Problem der Befahrung des Weltraums*. Berlin: Schmidt, 1928.

Nordhoff, Charles. *The Communistic Societies of the United States*. London: John Murray, 1875.

Noyes, John Humphrey. *History of American Socialisms*. Philadelphia: Lippincott, 1870.

Olander, Joseph D., and Martin Harry Greenberg, eds. *Arthur C. Clarke*. New York: Taplinger, 1977.

—— *Isaac Asimov*. New York: Taplinger, 1977.

—— *Robert A. Heinlein*. New York: Taplinger, 1978.

Olsen, Bob. "Wanted: A Definition for Science Fiction." *Future Science Fiction*, no. 33 (Summer 1957): 89–102.

Orwell, George. *1984*. New York: Signet, 1961.

Page, Gerald W. "The Many Worlds of Edgar Rice Burroughs." *Spaceway* 5 (May–June 1970): 42–49.

Panshin, Alexei. *Heinlein in Dimension*. Chicago: Advent, 1968.

—— "The Nature of Science Fiction." *Fantastic* 19 (August 1970): 119–122.

Parsons, Talcott. *The Social System*. Glencoe, Ill.: Free Press, 1951.

Penniman, T. K. *A Hundred Years of Anthropology*. London: Duckworth, 1965.

Peterson, Theodore. *Magazines in the Twentieth Century*. Urbana: University of Illinois Press, 1956.

Pierce, J. J. "The Devaluation of Values." *Algol*, no. 16 (December 1970): 4–11.

Platt, Charles. *Dream Makers: The Uncommon People Who Write Science Fiction*. New York: Berkley, 1980.

Pohl, Frederik. "Good-by to All That." *Destinies* 1 (February–March 1979): 46–57.

—— "A Short Term Solution." *Galaxy* 36 (April 1975): 9–17.

—— *The Way the Future Was*. New York: Ballantine, 1978.

Pohl, Frederik, and C. M. Kornbluth. "Gravy Planet." *Galaxy* 4 (June 1952): 4–61; (July 1952): 108–159; (August 1952): 104–159.

Porges, Irwin. *Edgar Rice Burroughs*. New York: Ballantine, 1976.

Porter, Andrew, ed. *The Book of Ellison*. New York: Algol Press, 1978.

Pournelle, Jerry, and Larry Niven. "Building the Mote in God's Eye." *Galaxy* 37 (January 1976): 92–113.

Rachman, Stanley. *The Effects of Psychotherapy*. Oxford: Pergamon, 1971.

Rand, Ayn. *Atlas Shrugged*. New York: Random House, 1957.

—— *The Fountainhead*. Indianapolis: Bobbs-Merrill, 1943.

—— *The Virtue of Selfishness*. New York: Signet, 1964.

Reynolds, Mack. "Speakeasy." *Fantasy and Science Fiction* 24 (January 1963): 66–126.

Rhine, J. B. *Extra-Sensory Perception*. Boston: Bruce Humphries, 1964.

Richardson, Darrell C. "A. Merritt—Master of Fantasy." *Other Worlds* 3 (October 1951): 2, 158–163.

Richardson, R. S. "The World of 61 Cygni C." *Astounding Science-Fiction* 31 (July 1943): 67–86.

Riley, Dick, ed. *Critical Encounters*. New York: Ungar, 1978.

Robinson, Spider, and Jeanne Robinson. "Stardance." *Analog* 97 (March 1977): 12–65.

Rogers, Alva. *A Requiem for Astounding*. Chicago: Advent, 1964.

Rogow, Roberta. *Trexindex*. Patterson, N.J.: April Publications, 1977.

Rokeach, Milton; Robert Homant; and Louis Penner. "A Value Analysis of the Disputed Federalist Papers." *Journal of Personality and Social Psychology* 16 (1970): 245–250.

Rose, Mark, ed. *Science Fiction*. Englewood Cliffs, N.J.: Prentice-Hall, 1976.

Rosengren, Karl Erik. *Sociological Aspects of the Literary System*. Stockholm: Natur och Kultur, 1968.

Roy, John Flint. *A Guide to Barsoom*. New York: Ballantine, 1976.

Russ, Joanna. "Books." *Fantasy and Science Fiction* 57 (November 1979): 102–108.

—— *The Female Man*. New York: Bantam, 1975.

—— "The Image of Women in Science Fiction." *Vertex* 1 (February 1974): 53–57.

Russell, Eric Frank. "I'm a Stranger Here Myself." *Other Worlds* 4 (March 1952): 32–41.

Sagan, Carl. *The Cosmic Connection*. New York: Dell, 1973.

Sargent, Lyman. "Utopia and Dystopia in Contemporary Science Fiction." *Futurist* 6 (June 1972): 93–98.

Schmeidler, Gertrude, ed. *Extrasensory Perception*. New York: Atherton, 1969.

Schweitzer, Darrell. *SF Voices*. Baltimore: T-K Graphics. 1976.

Sell, William. "Other Tracks." *Astounding Science-Fiction* 22 (October 1938): 56–69.

Shaftel, Oscar. "The Social Content of Science Fiction." *Science and Society* 17 (Spring 1953): 97–118.

Shaver, Richard S. "I Remember Lemuria!" *Amazing Stories* 19 (March 1945): 12–70.

Shaver, Richard S., and Raymond A. Palmer. "Mantong—The Language of Lemuria." *Amazing Stories* 19 (March 1945): 71, 206.

Shea, J. Vernon. "H. P. Lovecraft: The House and the Shadows." *Fantasy and Science Fiction* 30 (May 1966): 82–99.

Shelley, Mary W. *Frankenstein or the Modern Prometheus*. New York: Dutton, 1912.

Silverberg, Robert. "Diversity in Science Fiction." *Fantastic* 18 (February 1969): 4–5, 108.

—— "Harlan." *Fantasy and Science Fiction* 53 (July 1977): 63–70.

Skidmore, Joseph William. "The Romance of Posi and Nega." *Amazing Stories* 7 (September 1932): 512–523.

—— "A Saga of Posi and Nega." *Amazing Stories* 10 (May 1935): 93–114.

Smith, Edward Elmer. "Galactic Patrol." *Astounding Stories* 20 (September 1937):

8–37; (October 1937): 58–87; (November 1937): 122–151; (December 1937): 54–81; (January 1938): 115–141; (February 1938): 72–96.

────── "Gray Lensman." *Astounding Science-Fiction* 24 (October 1939): 9–54; (November 1939): 9–52; (December 1939): 45–162; (January 1940): 102–153.

Smith, Edward Elmer, and Lee Hawkins Garby. "The Skylark of Space." *Amazing Stories* 3 (August 1928): 390–417; (September 1928): 528–559; (October 1928): 610–636, 641.

Smith, Henry Nash. *Mark Twain's Fable of Progress.* New Brunswick, N.J.: Rutgers University Press, 1964.

Snow, C. P. *The Two Cultures.* London: Cambridge University Press, 1964.

Spielberg, Steven. *Close Encounters of the Third Kind.* New York: Dell, 1977.

Spinrad, Norman. "The Future of Science Fiction." In *Nebula Winners Fourteen,* edited by Frederik Pohl, pp. 111–118. New York: Bantam, 1982.

────── *The Iron Dream.* New York: Avon, 1972.

Stark, Rodney, and William Sims Bainbridge. *The Future of Religion.* Berkeley: University of California Press, 1985.

────── "Towards a Theory of Religion: Religious Commitment." *Journal for the Scientific Study of Religion* 19 (1980): 114–128.

Stark, Rodney; William Sims Bainbridge; Robert D. Crutchfield; Daniel P. Doyle; and Roger Finke. "Crime and Delinquency in the Roaring Twenties." *Journal of Research in Crime and Delinquency* 20 (1983): 4–23.

Stark, Rodney; Daniel P. Doyle; and Lori Kent. "Rediscovering Moral Communities: Church Membership and Crime." In *Understanding Crime,* edited by Travis Hirschi and Michael Gottfredson, pp. 43–52. Beverly Hills, Calif.: Sage, 1980.

Stark, Rodney; Daniel P. Doyle; and Jesse Rushing. "Beyond Durkheim: Religion and Suicide." *Journal for the Scientific Study of Religion* 22 (1983): 120–131.

Stark, Rodney; Lori Kent; and Daniel P. Doyle. "Religion and Delinquency: The Ecology of a 'Lost' Relationship." *Journal of Research in Crime and Delinquency* 19 (1982); 4–24.

Stephan, Karen H., and G. Edward Stephan. "Religion and the Survival of Utopian Communities," *Journal for the Scientific Study of Religion* 12 (1973): 89–100.

Stone, Leslie F. "Women with Wings." *Air Wonder Stories* 1 (May 1930): 984–1003.

Strauss, Erwin S. *Index to the SF Magazines, 1951–1965.* Cambridge: M.I.T. Science Fiction Society, 1966.

Sturgeon, Theodore. "Damon: An Appreciation." *Fantasy and Science Fiction* 51 (November 1976): 17–25.

────── "How to Avoid a Hole in the Head." *Marvel Science Stories* 3 (May 1951): 114–116.

Taurasi, James V. "The Story of Science Fiction's Editors." *Other Worlds,* no. 19 (June 1952): 67–78.

Taviss, Irene. "A Survey of Popular Attitudes toward Technology." *Technology and Culture* 13 (October 1972): 616–621.

Technocracy, Inc. *The Energy Certificate.* Savannah, Ohio, 1938.

────── *Technocracy: Technological Social Design.* Savannah, Ohio, 1975.

Tenn, William. "Brooklyn Project." In *The Road to Science Fiction,* edited by James Gunn, vol. 3, pp. 155–164. New York: Mentor, 1979.

Tiptree, James, Jr. *Up the Walls of the World*. New York: Ace, 1978.

Tolkien, J. R. R. *The Fellowship of the Ring*. New York: Ballantine, 1965.

—— *The Hobbit*. New York: Ballantine, 1965.

—— *The Return of the King*. New York: Ballantine, 1965.

—— *The Two Towers*. New York: Ballantine, 1965.

Tuck, Donald H. *The Encyclopedia of Science Fiction and Fantasy*. 2 vols. Chicago: Advent, 1974, 1978.

Tuttle, Lisa. "The Birds of the Moon." *Fantastic Stories* 27 (January 1979): 62–71.

—— "Mrs. T." *Amazing Science Fiction* 50 (September 1976): 66–74.

—— "Stone Circle." *Amazing Science Fiction* 49 (March 1976): 42–49.

Twain, Mark. *A Connecticut Yankee in King Arthur's Court*. New York: Harper, 1917.

U.S. Bureau of the Census. *Census of Population: 1970—Occupational Characteristics*. Washington, D.C.: Government Printing Office, 1973.

Van Dyke, Vernon. *Pride and Power: The Rationale of the Space Program*. Urbana: University of Illinois Press, 1964.

van Vogt, A. E. "Far Centaurus." *Astounding Science-Fiction* 32 (January 1944): 68–85.

—— "Slan." *Astounding Science-Fiction* 26 (September 1940): 9–40; (October 1940): 9–42; (November 1940): 119–160; (December 1940): 119–162.

—— "The World of Null-A." *Astounding Science-Fiction* 35 (August 1945): 7–46, 156–178; 36 (September 1945): 7–46, 166–178; and (October 1945): 60–98, 156–178.

Varley, John. "In the Hall of the Martian Kings." *Fantasy and Science Fiction* 52 (February 1977): 6–44.

Veblen, Thorstein. *The Engineers and the Price System*. New York: Viking, 1940.

Verne, Jules. *From the Earth to the Moon*. New York: Crowell, 1978.

—— *A Journey to the Center of the Earth*. New York: Heritage, 1967.

—— *Twenty Thousand Leagues under the Sea*. New York: Crowell, 1976.

Vinge, Joan D. *The Snow Queen*. New York: Dell, 1980.

Walker, Paul. *Speaking of Science Fiction*. Oradell, N.J.: Luna, 1978.

Waltz, George H., Jr. *Jules Verne*. New York: Holt, 1943.

Warner, Harry. *All Our Yesterdays*. Chicago: Advent, 1969.

Weinbaum, Stanley G. "A Martian Odyssey." *Wonder Stories* 6 (July 1934): 174.

Wells, H. G. *The Discovery of the Future*. New York: Huebsch, 1913.

—— *The First Men in the Moon*. New York: Berkley, 1967.

—— "Men Like Gods." In *28 Science Fiction Stories of H. G. Wells*, pp. 1–268. New York: Dover, 1952.

—— "The Time Machine." In *The Science Fiction Hall of Fame*, edited by Ben Bova, vol. IIA, pp. 452–526. New York: Avon, 1973.

—— *The War of the Worlds*. New York: Airmont, 1964.

Wertham, Frederic. *The World of Fanzines*. Carbondale: Southern Illinois University Press, 1973.

West, Anthony. *H. G. Wells: Aspects of a Life*. New York: Random House, 1984.

West, Robert H. "Science Fiction and Its Ideas." *Georgia Review* 15 (Fall 1961): 276–286.

Whitfield, Stephen, E., and Gene Roddenberry. *The Making of Star Trek*. New York: Ballantine, 1968.

Wilhelm, Kate. *Fault Lines*. New York: Pocket Books, 1978.

Williamson, Jack. "Collision Orbit." *Astounding Science-Fiction* 29 (July 1942): 80–106.

––––– *The Humanoids*. New York: Grosset and Dunlap, 1950.

––––– "The Legion of Space." *Astounding Stories* 13 (April 1934): 10–29; (May 1934): 99–118; (June 1934): 113–132; (July 1934): (August 1934): 123–140; and 14 (September 1934): 118–136.

––––– "The Legion of Time." *Astounding Science-Fiction* 21 (May 1938): 4–31; (June 1938): 33–53; (July 1938): 118–139.

––––– "Minus Sign." *Astounding Science-Fiction* 30 (November 1942): 43–79.

––––– "The Next Century of Science Fiction." *Analog* 98 (February 1978): 5–15.

––––– "Operation Gravity." *Science-Fiction Plus* 1 (October 1953): 22–28.

Wood, Susan. "Women and Science Fiction." *Algol* 16 (Winter 1978–1979): 9–18.

Wright, S. Fowler. *The Amphibians*. Chicago: Shasta (Galaxy), 1949.

––––– *The World Below*. Chicago: Shasta (Galaxy), 1949.

Wynn, Mark. "Who Are the Futurists?" *Futurist* 6 (April 1972): 73–77.

Zelazny, Roger, "He Who Shapes." *Amazing Stories* 39 (January 1965): 72–112 and (February 1965): 50–90.

Zinberg, Dorothy. "The Past Decade for Women Scientists." *Trends in Biochemical Sciences* 2 (1977): N123–N126.

INDEX